Staff Challenges

"The Best of Exchange"
Reprint Collection #13

Child Care Information Exchange
PO Box 3249 • Redmond, WA 98073-3249 • (800) 221-2864

"The Best of Exchange"

Reprint
Collection #13

This is a Best of Exchange Reprint Collection of articles originally published in *Child Care Information Exchange*. The issues in which these articles originally appeared are noted in the Table of Contents on the following pages.

Every attempt has been made to update information on authors and other contributors to these articles. We apologize for any biographical information that is not current.

Child Care Information Exchange is a bimonthly management magazine for directors and owners of early childhood programs. For more information about *Child Care Information Exchange* and other *Exchange* publications for directors and teachers, contact:

Child Care Information Exchange
PO Box 3249
Redmond, WA 98073-3249
(800) 221-2864
info@ChildCareExchange.com

ISBN 0-942702-18-2

Cover Photograph:
Bonnie Neugebauer

Staff Challenges

— Table of Contents —

Chapter 4 — Motivating and Supervising Staff

Chapter 5 — Overcoming Challenging Situations

Introduction:
The Paradoxes of Leadership

by Bonnie and Roger Neugebauer

In the past 20 years, we have had the opportunity to observe hundreds upon hundreds of leaders in action in child care centers. In addition, we have had 20 years to develop our leadership on the job as we struggled, sailed, failed, and succeeded in growing Child Care Information Exchange. From all of these experiences, we have learned a few things about the paradoxes of leadership.

Paradox #1
You need to enjoy your work, but you can't avoid the uglies.

Pop psychologists are forever advising "if you're in a job you don't like, get out of it." Easy for them to say. For many people, finding a fun job is simply not an option — there are simply not enough Ben and Jerry's taste tester jobs to go around.

However, for nearly everyone, there are parts of one's job that are enjoyable and parts that are wretched, parts that are stimulating and parts that are boring. In a perfect world, you would be able to delegate the drudge jobs and hold on to the exciting ones.

Unfortunately, this is not a perfect world. While there are many mundane tasks you, the center director, can delegate, there are certain ugly ones that you can't give away, ignore, or avoid. If you listen to the pop psychologists and only attend to the things you enjoy, you're setting your organization up for disaster.

If you don't fire a lousy teacher, her continuing presence will lower motivation of other teachers and deprive the children of the experiences they deserve. If you hate writing grant proposals, you may miss an opportunity to attract employer support for your center.

Your best bet is to get the ugly jobs out of the way right away. If you procrastinate on the uglies, even when you are working away at jobs you enjoy, this pleasure will be spoiled by the knowledge that the ugly work is still out there. So eat your cauliflower fast, then sit back and enjoy the Cherries Garcia.

Paradox #2
The more staff strive to protect you, the more they hurt you.

Many of us seem to have this need to take care of everyone. We want everyone to be happy, satisfied, productive, supported, connected. It takes a lot of time and energy to Mother Hen the world, but we do it because we need to.

So when the tables turn and staff want to take care of us, it can feel pretty good. It's certainly great to know that others are noticing when we are overburdened, that they see the magnitude of our responsibilities, that they are sensitive to the fact that a piece of information or news might *put us over the top.*

Though done with the best of intentions (of course this could also be done with less positive motivation), this protective behavior will ultimately prove harmful. There will be information missing, holes in the big picture — and this will hinder the effectiveness of your decision making. If you don't know that two staff members are not getting along, that a parent is upset about a staff comment, that the key to the storage unit is missing, that you are running out of peanut butter, things will fall apart when these specifics would inform your decision making.

Staff need to understand that you, as director, need to know everything. Their motivations for protection can be acknowledged and appreciated, while the act of protection can be firmly, continually rejected. Perhaps staff can learn to deliver the bad news with a gentle touch or a chocolate chip cookie (or would we come to fear cookies?).

Paradox #3
When you are most discouraged, you need to be most motivated.

Art Dronen, Roger's high school track coach, had only one piece of advice for all of us would-be heroes — "Ya gotta wanna." We, of course, treated this as trite nonsense. Decades later, Roger now sees that Art was a wise man.

His wisdom is best exemplified in the world of sports where typically athletes' success will in large part be determined by their determination to succeed. We all remember the Swiss female Olympic marathoner who stumbled into the Los Angeles Coliseum totally exhausted. She staggered wildly and painfully about the oval, waving off the assistance of her coaches. Finally, she stumbled across the finish line and fell unconscious into the arms of a race official. She had been training for ten years to complete an Olympic marathon, and when her body gave out in total exhaustion 400 yards from the finish line, her sheer determination kept her going until her mission was accomplished.

While center directors are seldom cheered on by a spirited crowd of 100,000, they do frequently demonstrate amazing feats of perseverance.

In fact, it is in the very nature of the director's job to be confronted, on an almost daily basis, with daunting challenges — replacing sick teachers at 6 am, dealing with an accusation of child abuse, juggling cash flow when reserves are depleted, finding a way to get children home from a field trip when the bus breaks down. Confronted with such frustrations, many directors throw in the towel — they either quit or quit caring.

The directors who succeed, and go on to manage the best programs, are those who don't cave in when the going gets tough, those who are determined, against all odds, to maintain a focus on delivering quality services. These directors have a "Ya gotta wanna" attitude that consistently carries them to the finish line.

Paradox #4
To accomplish the most serious results, you need to believe in the value of whimsy.

Never underestimate the value of humor. Why did laughter get the bad rap for indicating lack of seriousness, slacking off? Our staff meetings are great fun. When an outsider overhears the tone of our meetings, he or she will usually comment with something like: "There was so much laughing going on. How do you get anything done?"

It is the laughter that binds us together, that creates an environment and a sense of teamwork that enables people to share their joys and sorrows, as well as their frustrations and needs. People who can laugh at and with each other, trust each other.

Consider the staff meeting when we were in our usual stories with laughter mode and Roger arrived a bit late and announced: "We have a lot of work to get done today, so we'll just

chit chat for a few more minutes and then get down to it." Suddenly, no one had anything to say. We just sat around and ate our lunch and talked through the issues of the day. Laughter was minimized as was the amount of work accomplished.

A playful approach to life issues, whether personal or professional, fosters creative potential, reduces stress, and just makes living a whole lot better.

Paradox #5
The longer you work, the less you are appreciated.

You were hired as director when the center was in the red and struggling to survive. You slashed expenditures to the bone, cracked down on late payments, built up enrollment, and got the center on the right track. Then you steadied the course when a disgruntled former teacher started spreading nasty false rumors; you kept the center going through a flu epidemic; and you even kept things afloat when a glitzy new center opened across the street.

Now you've been on the job 12 years and the center is running as smooth as can be. You naturally assume that, with all your heroic accomplishments in the past, you have a vast store of good will and credibility built up. Then you have to fire a popular teacher for valid reasons, but reasons you can't share with the staff. The teachers revolt and call for your resignation.

What happened to all that credibility? Since you single-handedly saved the center time and time again, why can't they give you the benefit of the doubt now?

The problem is that organizations have short memories. Given normal turnover, many of your teachers weren't even around when you were leaping tall buildings in a single bound. And those who were around, now that times are easier, tend to forget how stressful life was in the past. As a matter of fact, the longer your center sails along smoothly, the more staff may think your job has become a slam dunk, even though it is your brilliant management that is responsible for the good times.

Don't be too harsh on staff for their fickleness. Maybe you are contributing to the problem. Isn't it possible that after all those years of major stress, now you are content to settle into a mode of management that is steadying the course? Just maybe you've become a bit stodgy — reluctant to rock the boat, to try new ventures, to listen to new ideas, to tolerate parents or staff who don't fit a certain profile.

Longevity and credibility don't go hand in hand. Don't ever assume that you have so much good will built up that you can rest on your laurels. The relevant question is: "What have you done for the center and all its players lately that earns their appreciation?"

Paradox #6
Everyone's your friend when things are going well, but your true friends stand by you in the tough times.

When a crisis rears its ugly head, it is your support system that will save you. We have been rescued on many occasions by the concern and response of our friends — and that might very well include you.

Friends are not, in this case, the people who come up with all the platitudes: "This is really good for you." "Every cloud has a silver lining." "Everything works out in the end." People who say such things provide comfort and cry with you (or drive you crazy), but they don't pull you through.

Friends in crisis are the people who really put themselves into your problem, who put their minds and hearts into understanding where you are and what options you have. They are the people who say, "Have you tried . . . ?" "Why wouldn't this work . . . ?" "If other people can do this, why can't you . . . ?" "Here's an idea that might work . . . ."

These are the people who will help you see your way out. They are the people who will expand the boundaries of your thinking, who will challenge you to use the skills you possess (which they might also remind you of). Be sure you have such friends around you. They are honest and blunt — essential and beyond value.

Chapter 1

Recruiting
and
Selecting Staff

Caregivers of Quality

by Sally Cartwright

Building toward a topnotch child care staff is anything but easy. More than love for children, more than training and experience makes a valuable caregiver. Below, named in bold type, are the essential ingredients in caregivers of quality.

Good physical health is a prerequisite for caregivers at work with young children. More difficult to assess is **emotional maturity**. It was clarified by Barbara Biber of Bank Street College of Education when she wrote that a caregiver "needs to be a person so secure within herself that she can function with principles rather than prescriptions, that she can exert authority without requiring submission, that she can work experimentally but not at random, and that she can admit mistakes without feeling humiliated" (Barbara Biber, in *Childhood Education*, March 1948).

One discerns such qualities in a caregiver neither by resumé nor interview, but by observing him at work with children. Watch the caregiver for these qualities, and watch the children as well, for their behavior reflects caregiver competence. Is there cooperative child initiative? Is there a mix of friendly humor and purpose? Most of all, are the children deeply involved in their work and play? Clear, consistent evidence of a caregiver's personal integration and inner sense of security is truly important for his success with children.

A matured and perceptive **kindness** or unconditional love, so important in good caregivers, means both heart and detachment (discussed below) in helping children to help themselves. A good caregiver knows intuitively what child at which moment requires warm and close concern. She is approachable and friendly. She listens well, gives support as needed, and shares in laughter with, not at, the children.

A good caregiver is keenly aware of emotional and physical safety for each child. His care is shown in constructing the environment for active child learning with his discerning choice of equipment, materials, and spacial arrangement within a consistent, predictable program framework. Children need the support of steady, warm approval. A good caregiver may condemn a child's words or action, but not the child himself.

A good caregiver needs courage and integrity. **Courage** means a strong, upbeat will to work through whatever odds for what one most cares about, in this case the children. A courageous caregiver goes to bat for child needs, often working closely with other staff members, parents, and/or community leaders.

Integrity means a well-knit personality along with honesty in all one does. It means what Polonius told his son: "To thine own self be true, and it must follow as the night the day, thou canst not then be false to any man" (Shakespeare).

As caregivers develop **self-awareness**, they improve each quality mentioned as well as self-evaluation. Caregivers may help each other toward self-awareness through constructive criticism with mutual trust and respect. Quiet reflection and professional counseling may help as well. Working with children will sometimes stir emotions from the caregiver's own childhood. A truly fine caregiver will have searched and brought to light salient unconscious factors in herself. She's aware of their influence when at work with children, and steers her own behavior accordingly.

Good caregivers need a **theoretical ground**, a conceptual framework in which to see children. The developmental-interaction point of view put forward by Bank Street College of Education (Betty Boegehold, Harriet Cuffaro, William Hooks, and Gordon Klopf, *Education Before Five*, Bank Street College, 1977; Barbara Biber, Ellen Shapiro, and Elaine Wickens, *Promoting Cognitive Growth from a Developmental-Interaction Point of View*, NAEYC, 1971; and Ellen Shapiro and Barbara Biber, *The Education of Young Children: A Developmental-Interaction Approach*, Teachers College Record, Vol. 74, No. 1, September 1972) is perhaps the most useful foundation and guide for helping youngsters learn at their best. The word *development* suggests a continuing, complex process of growth and learning, while *interaction* occurs internally between the child's emotional, physical, and cognitive growth, and externally between the child and his expanding physical and social environment. The accent is on *integrative* action by the children themselves. Developmental-inter-action is clearly aligned with NAEYC's developmentally appro-priate practice (Sue Bredekamp and C. Copple, *Developmentally Appropriate Practice in Early Childhood Programs*, NAEYC, 1997).

Research in the last ten years indi-cates that a caregiver's intellectual understanding of DAP is often sadly unable to implement appropriate practice with the children (Loraine Dunn and Susan Kontos, "What Have We Learned About Develop-mentally Appropriate Practice?," *Young Children*, July 1997). Hands-on workshops can be somewhat helpful in training caregivers, but protracted, daily participant experience in a child care environ-ment that supports active child learning, peer cooperation, creativity, and the keen interest shared by the children in their self-impelled work of learning together is by all odds the best training for beginning caregivers.

A good caregiver, daily responsible for child experience, should have, besides the thorough background in developmental psychology men-tioned above, the **equivalent of a college graduate's general knowl-edge**, and effective access to the media, libraries, and the internet.

Experience with elemental care of our physical environment and with young children's books is also valu-able, while a working knowledge of grass-roots democracy will support cooperative learning. It is through cooperative learning experience from age three onward that children grad-ually come to understand the bene-fits and responsibilities of democratic community, which, not incidentally, is so important to the health of our country today.

Child care experts know that, aside from their attainment of needed skills, young children do not need proficiency in traditional academic subjects. The salient point is not so much what, but *how*, they learn. And, again, how children learn best is through their own action: asking questions, finding answers, and test-ing their answers by using them in their work and play, all with adult *guidance*, not didactic instruction. Good caregivers know the value of a child's innate curiosity and deep sat-isfaction in the experiential learning process. Let no child care environ-ment dampen a child's interest and joy in learning!

Good caregivers show unfailing **warm respect for and courtesy to children** as a group and to each child as a unique and unrepeatable indi-vidual. Helping a child to make con-structive, independent choices toward self-disciplined creativity depends very much upon our gen-uine, full, and caring respect for that child and his way of working, his way of learning. Such respect cannot be accomplished without a very real knowledge of child development, as

well as the personal caregiver quali-ties of inner security, integrity, and self-awareness.

Allied to respect is a good caregiver's **trust in each child** to find his own way, in a supportive child care envi-ronment, toward personal integrity, acceptable behavior, good learning purpose, and ultimately to realize his unique potential. Genuine trust in a child depends on fundamental knowledge of child development, close observation of the individual child, and the caregiver's own inner sense of security mentioned above.

Integrity and respect invite **discre-tion**. A child's problems should remain confidential. Respect for the privacy of the child and her family is essential for their trust and confi-dence in the caregiver.

Contrary to strictly linear thinking, which western science and philoso-phy have championed for three cen-turies, intuition, a non-reasoning, often quite sudden, insight is finally gaining credence. Einstein said, "Imagination is more important than knowledge," and imagination lives with intuition. For many of us, intu-ition often sways our thinking sim-ply because it feels right and it works. A well-balanced, mature, and keenly observant caregiver *knows in her bones* how to be with a child.

Professional **detachment** allows respect, trust, and kindness (uncon-ditional love) to come through to the child. On the surface, detachment and love may seem a paradox, but precisely the opposite is true. A care-giver with inner security and mature self-awareness, a caregiver at ease and fulfilled by her own adult devel-opment, does not impose her person-ality needs onto her relations with children.

Detachment in caring allows em-pathy without projection, without naively attributing her own unconscious negative feelings to the children. Detachment gives the children psychological space. It avoids sarcasm and contempt which are crushing to a child. Detachment helps the caregiver test and use her knowledge of child development with a degree of wisdom.

Don't forget **laughter**. One sign of detachment is often delightful humor, and humor in the classroom is important. It signals enjoyment. It invites friendship. It often opens the way for cooperative learning. While shared humor lights the morning, laughing at a child's expense should be nipped at once. Affectionate laughter is an indispensable quality in good child care.

Finally, the **caregiver is a model.** Whether conscious of it or not, he models feeling, thought, and behavior for the children in his care. An inevitable part of child learning is copying; trying to think, feel, and act like persons consistently near and admired by the child. A beloved provider may demonstrate values which the children cherish all their lives. The personality of a caregiver, her instinctive kindness, her deep integrity, her lively interest in life and learning, will all affect the children. It is a sobering responsibility, an inspiring challenge.

Sally Cartwright, with an MS from Bank Street College of Education, has taught children and teachers across five decades. She has written eight books for children and much material on early childhood learning, especially as experienced in her own experimental school.

Guidelines for Effective Staff Selection

by Carl C. Staley, Jr., Edna Runnels Ranck, Joe Perreault, and Roger Neugebauer

All I have to do is talk to a person for five minutes and I know whether she will be a good teacher or not.

Everyone's heard at least one director make a boast like this. To this director, staff selection is no mystery. More often than not, however, this person is exhibiting self-deception more than self-confidence.

Selecting the right person to work with young children in a child care setting has never been an easy task. How can you be sure which candidate will be able to nurture children, challenge children to grow, establish rapport with parents, and work well with the other teachers; and who will be able to do all this for low pay in a church basement 35 hours a week for 50 weeks a year? Certainly not in a five minute conversation.

And the job just got tougher. On the one hand, sex abuse scandals have chased many good candidates out of the field of child care, and have also made directors, parents, and public officials highly conscious of the need to screen out potential abusers from working with children. On the other hand, looming staffing shortages are shrinking the pool of teaching candidates. So now directors are faced not with selecting the best candidate from a long list of highly qualified applicants but, more often than not, with finding a low-risk, acceptable choice from a handful of marginally qualified applicants.

To be effective under all these restraints, a selection process needs to be well planned and carefully executed. The following are some guidelines on how to accomplish this. At the close of the article are some additional resources to pursue for more detailed assistance in upgrading your selection process.

Planning for Success

Time invested in planning the selection process will yield valuable returns in the smooth operation of your program. The following three areas need particular attention before you screen your first resumé.

• **Clarify your objectives**

Obviously the prime objective of the selection process is to secure the best available individual for a position. However, there are two additional not-so-obvious objectives that people involved in the hiring process must appreciate:

1. *To sell the organization to the candidates.* What good does it do to select just the right candidate only to have her turn down the job because she gained a negative impression of your organization during the selection process? While you are checking out the candidates, they are checking out your organization as well. It is in the best interests of both parties to make a favorable impression. Even candidates who are turned down should leave feeling that they were treated fairly and respectfully. Sore losers can do much to damage your reputation in the community.

2. *To initiate the contractual process.* Job advertisements and job interviews should be treated as the first steps in the process of negotiating a contract. A new employee's commit-

ment to the center may be seriously undermined if the center reneges on promises made or expectations aroused during the selection process.

• **Prioritize qualifications**

Whenever a position becomes vacant, it is a good opportunity to take a close look at what qualifications are really needed for adequate performance. It may be helpful to sort out those qualifications which are *required* (by licensing, funding, or operating agencies), *essential* (to implement the goals and philosophy of your center), and *desirable* (to perform in an exceptional fashion). During the selection process, your prime attention should be devoted to assessing candidates in terms of the *essential* qualifications.

To keep your attention from being defused in too many directions, you should try to narrow your list down to four or five qualifications. If your list is too long, try putting them in priority order in terms of the impact they have on job performance. Then, in the selection process, focus on the four or five that make the biggest impact.

Once you have identified the qualifications list, you should put yourself in the role of a detective. Your job in the selection process is to methodically ferret out pieces of evidence as to whether the candidates do or don't meet these qualifications. Adopting such an attitude can prevent you from being misled by general impressions or irrelevant factors.

• **Select your evaluation tools**

In preparing to screen job candidates, you have a number of tools at your disposal. None of these tools can provide you with all the information you need to make a decision. Therefore, it is best to evaluate candidates with a combination of tools. At a minimum, you will want to screen

written applications, conduct interviews, and check references.

There are other steps you may want to consider as well. For example, most centers try to observe candidates working with children. Since the way teachers describe their teaching behavior in an interview often bears little relation to how they perform in real life, such observations can provide invaluable feedback. Some centers have gained insights into candidates' teaching styles by having them build whatever they want with blocks. Other centers have learned about candidates' teaching philosophies by having them design on paper their ideal classroom.

Many states now require centers to pursue criminal records checks on prospective employees in order to prevent sex offenders from being employed in centers. However, the center certainly should never use criminal records checks in lieu of interviews and reference checks.

Screening Applications

The review of written submissions provides an efficient means of assessing candidates' work experience and academic preparation but not much beyond that. As such, they should be used primarily to screen out candidates who do not meet the minimum job requirements.

This preliminary screening is most reliable if it can be based on information provided on application forms developed by the center. Resumés tend to be less useful sources; the way candidates present their qualifications can exclude or cover up information which reflects poorly on them. A center-designed application forces candidates to present all needed information in a uniform, understandable format.

In reviewing written submissions, look for long gaps between jobs,

lengthy descriptions of educational experiences, an overabundance of personal trivia (resumés puffed up with hobbies, scouting awards, etc.), long lists of short-term jobs, employment and training situations which run concurrently, long stretches of employment outside one's field of specialization, and evidence that one may have been fired. Findings such as these should be viewed as red flags to be investigated, not necessarily as grounds for rejection. A teacher may have been fired from a job, for example, but maybe because her boss was unstable and not because of her inadequacies.

Conducting Interviews

The interview can be very helpful in revealing the personality of candidates, their communication skills, and their knowledge of early childhood education. However, it is the most complex selection tool, and its advantage can be lost if it is not carefully planned and executed.

• **Logistics**. Be sure to allow sufficient time to interview candidates in depth at a relaxed pace. Set aside at least 45 minutes for each interview and schedule a 15 minute break between each interview. Try not to schedule more than three interviews consecutively or mental fatigue may set in.

Don't create a Spanish Inquisition setting. A candidate walking into a room with a panel of 12 interviewers can't help but become anxious. The more people a candidate is interviewed by, the harder it will be for him to relax and give a fair accounting of himself. Restricting the number of interviewers may fail to satisfy all constituencies within the organization, and it may mean that certain points of view are not adequately represented. But having too many interviewers will inhibit an open exchange. Ideally, the director and one other person should conduct the interview. One person can lead the conversation and the second can observe for body language and tone of voice.

Plan ahead for recording information. By the end of an interview, interviewers generally have already forgotten 50% of what was said. By the next day, 85% of what was said has been lost in space (Nichols). The best method for recording information is tape recording. Candidates may find this disconcerting initially; but after a few minutes, they will forget the recorder is on. The next best method is to take notes onto a specific format with spaces set aside for each qualification. In either case, interviewers should also write down their reactions immediately after the interview.

• *Questioning.* Your initial objective in the interview should be to put the candidate at ease. You can do this by finding some point of common interest on the application and commenting on it: "I see you grew up in the Midwest just like I did; do you ever think about moving back?" Then lead into the interview with some specific, easy-to-answer questions.

The pattern of questioning that has been found to be most effective for the substantive portion of the interview is to spend some time pursuing each essential qualification. Lead off with a prepared introductory question or two, and then follow up by asking specific spontaneous questions which seek clarification of issues raised in the candidate's response. Liberal use of the word *why* can move a candidate away from her cautious, programmed replies.

If, for example, the candidate states that she loves to work with kids, follow up with "Why do you find this so rewarding?" or "What activities do you most like to do with children?"

It is usually a mistake to ask trick questions or to purposely put the can-

---

Advice from Hiring Experts

In selecting a candidate, you should consider two issues only: capability — what the candidate can do — and personality — what the candidate is like. Of these two, personality is by far the more important. Over 87% of all people fail not because of capability but because of personality.
— *Kurt Einstein*

In an interview, value the good you discover in others and comment on it favorably when you do. You'll be amazed at how much more people will reveal to you.
— *David Viscott, MD*

I've read thousands of resumés in my career, and I have yet to find any significant correlation between the quality of a resumé and the likelihood that the candidate who wrote it will be a successful employee.
— *Robert Half*

The best way to find a candidate's weaknesses is to create an atmosphere so reassuring, so comfortable, that he will realize it is better to unload those secrets now than be detected later.
— *Kurt Einstein*

---

didate under stress with threatening or overly personal questions. This creates an atmosphere of mistrust and tension. Much more can be learned by straightforward, respectful questioning.

Don't do all the talking. The more you talk, the less you learn about the candidate. Keep the candidate talking by responding with phrases such as "I understand," "I see," or "That's very interesting," which encourage her to continue but don't give any clues as to whether you are reacting positively or negatively to what she is saying. Encourage honesty and openness by praising her for answering questions fully and frankly.

Close the interview by describing the organization and the position, and by expressing a willingness to answer questions about the position. Explain the process that will follow, and let the candidate know when and how he will be notified of the final decision.

Checking References

Information obtained from checking references may be the only effective way to evaluate many qualifications, such as dependability, flexibility, initiative, and communication with parents. Checking references can also serve to verify information gathered in other portions of the process.

On your center's application form, or when you call to set up interviews you should alert candidates to the fact that you intend to contact references to verify their job qualifications. Be wary of those candidates who balk at supplying any references or who supply only the names of personal (non-employer) references, as they may well have something to hide.

• **Selecting references**

You should not limit yourself to contacting references supplied by the candidate. As a matter of practice, you should always contact at least one reference not supplied by the candidate. In today's nervous climate, you may do well to routinely contact a candidate's last three employers. Contact first the head of each organization, and at the close of the interview ask for the name of someone else in that organization who may have worked directly with the candidate. Then contact this employee for an additional point of view.

Sometimes a candidate will ask that you not contact his current employer because he doesn't want his boss to know he is job hunting. This may be a legitimate request or it may be a ruse for avoiding a negative reference. You should honor this request with the proviso that if the job is offered it will be contingent upon the receipt of a favorable reference from the current employer.

The best reference of all is someone you know. This person is likely to know the type of person you are looking for and is more likely than a person who doesn't know you to give a candid appraisal. For that reason, when you are seriously considering employing someone, you should put your antenna up in the community to see if anyone on your staff or any of your parents knows this person and can provide a reference.

Another approach is to get to know officials at the local or state level who are responsible for receiving child care related complaints. Routinely run the names of persons you are about to hire past these officials to see if they have been identified in any complaints.

• **Soliciting information**
Securing candid information from references is no easy matter. Especially in today's suit-happy society, employers are not eager to offer less than favorable references. As Robert

Half laments, "A bad reference is as hard to find as a good employee."

As a general rule, the more personal your means of contact, the more candid views you are likely to receive. Letters of recommendation that candidates attach to their resumés are not likely to be of any value whatsoever. Reference letters supplied at your request will only be slightly more useful. People are highly resistant to putting any but the most guarded, neutral statements in writing. For best results, you should contact references over the telephone. Better yet, for critical positions, it may even be worthwhile to interview references in person.

• **Probing for information**

There are a number of techniques you can employ to make references more forthcoming. To begin with, when you call, you might find it less intimidating to say you are seeking verifications rather than references. Lead off with factual questions such as dates of employment, position title, and responsibilities, and then gradually move on to more subjective questions.

Ask the employer being interviewed if she would hire the candidate again. If she answers no, or if there is a noticeable hesitation in her reply, probe the response in more depth. Use silence to get the reference talking. After she has given a cursory response to one of your questions, don't respond. Give her an opportunity to get nervous about the silence. She just may attempt to fill it by elaborating upon her response.

If the interviewee is still being reticent, you may find it helpful to note that with all the attention on incidents of abuse in centers, you really need help in carefully screening candidates who will be working with children. Describe the candidate's potential position, as well as center

and state policies on child discipline and sexual abuse. Ask if the candidate, in her view, would have any difficulty complying with these procedures.

Be wary of references that are overwhelmingly positive or negative, as there may be some ulterior motive in operation. Be wary as well of major discrepancies between references and candidates' reports. In both cases, be sure to track down at least a second or third opinion.

Making the Decision

This is the stage where the process most often goes awry. All too often center representatives will knock themselves out reading resumés, conducting interviews, and checking references. Then, when they get to the point of making a decision, they make a snap judgment based on *gut feelings* alone, a decision which as often as not they live to regret.

The most common cause for errors at the decision point is the *halo effect* — letting one outstanding characteristic (positive or negative) of a candidate shape the opinion about her overall suitability. For example, in an interview one of the candidates may display a tremendous amount of personal charm and vitality which deeply impresses the interviewer. This impression may cause him to overlook the fact that the candidate had a reputation for absenteeism and irresponsibility at her previous two jobs.

To arrive at a sound decision, it is helpful to follow through on the detective approach. For each candidate, consider what pieces of evidence were uncovered in terms of each qualification. When you look at the pattern of evidence, how many of the qualifications did each candidate display? The decision comes down then to considering the weight of the evidence as opposed to subjective impressions.

Don't rush this stage of the process. You should even be willing to go back and call a candidate or two for a second interview if you have some nagging doubts. An hour or two saved at this point may cost you days later on if the candidate you select doesn't work out and you have to start all over again.

Another safeguard worthy of consideration is placing new employees on probationary status. This puts them on notice that you will be carefully monitoring their performance at the outset to make sure it conforms with expectations raised during the selection process. When you have made your decision, notify the candidate you have selected by telephone, and follow up with a letter outlining the title of the position, rate of pay, starting date, benefits, and length of the probationary period. If the candidate accepts this offer, notify all other candidates of this decision, including those who were eliminated early in the process.

References and Resources

Half, R. (1985). *Robert Half On Hiring*. New York: Crown Publishers, Inc.

Ingber, D. (September 1984). "Omigod, I've Hired a Turkey!" *Success*.

Nichols, R. (September-October, 1957). "Listening to People." *Harvard Business Review*.

"Preventing Sexual Abuse in Day Care Programs." Office of Inspector General, United States Department of Health and Human Services, Region X, January 1985.

Viscott, D., MD (1985). *Taking Care of Business*. New York: William Morrow and Company.

An Experiential Approach to Staff Selection

by Merle W. Leak

When is the last time you played with blocks? If you had been applying for a position in the day care agency I directed you would have been able to relive this bit of childhood as part of the interview process. You also would have had the opportunity to explore cartoons, design a room, write about your childhood, and tell me what you think of Sesame Street. All these activities are parts of an experiential staff selection process I designed and utilized with the Bucks County Coordinated Child Care Council in Southampton, Pennsylvania.

This selection process grew out of some real discouragement with the normal selection techniques. So often in day care we come to selection decisions which turn out not to be good ones. I believe that in the early childhood setting it is very important to achieve a real match between the person selected and the setting in which they will work. If a very controlling, structured person is elected to teach in a center with an open and creative philosophy, everybody is going to be unhappy — the director, the other teachers, and the new teacher. Unfortunately, with the selection techniques normally used in child care, we often can't learn enough to make such a match. We are not able to discover what the candidates are really like as persons.

Therefore, I set out to develop a selection process that gave people an opportunity to say something to me about themselves through other means than verbal responses to questions. I wanted a process that would show me something not only about what the candidates knew, but also something about them as persons — what they thought about children, the world, and themselves.

The process that resulted was used with great success by the Bucks County Coordinated Child Care Council. The process was used by myself and other agency personnel in screening over 500 candidates when we were setting up eight new centers and filling later vacancies in these centers. I will describe the process we used, but I don't necessarily recommend that other centers use it exactly as is. Rather, it should be viewed as an example of the types of experiential techniques that can be employed by centers to get to know candidates better in order to achieve a successful match.

The Selection Process

The selection process I developed had seven components. These components were used as the initial screening process for directors, educational supervisors, head teachers and child care workers. For a typical position there were usually 50 to 60 applications. Of these we selected about 10 to 20 to screen with the seven step process in order to recommend two or three candidates. The candidates who survived this initial screening were then interviewed by a parent board and/or a center director, and sometimes observed in the classroom, before a final decision was made.

Our hiring process was a very serious one and a very long one. Since all of us in the agency were convinced that the adults working with the children are the key to the success of a child care program, we were willing to invest the number of hours needed to find the right match. The seven step screening process described below usually required 1½ to 2 hours for each position. Some screenings lasted as long as 4 to 5 hours as we never put an outer limit on the time allotted to candidates.

Resumé Reviews. The first step in the screening process was a review of the candidates education and experience as described in their resumés in terms of the specific job requirements. We tended to give the benefit of doubt in reviewing resumés to things that went beyond normal degrees and things like that. We had a feeling that there probably would be some good people who would be lost if we only looked for degrees in early childhood education. As a result, we probably accepted an unusually large number of candidates for extensive screening — as many as 10 to 20 per position. These candidates were invited for the remainder of the screening which always took place in a center that had a complete set of Community Playthings' nursery school blocks.

Personal Interviews. When a candidate arrived at the center he or she was interviewed by one staff person for about 20 to 30 minutes. At the outset, the interviewer talked a little bit about the job and explained the process that was to follow. Then each candidate was asked seven questions. We kept the format and the questions the same for each candidate in order to have comparable responses. The seven questions looked at three things: interest in and knowledge about child development, specific relevant skills, and who the candidates were as individuals. The questions were:

• What does fantasy have to do with childhood?

• What are the three most significant books that you have read in the past twelve months?

• What does open education mean to you?

• What is your favorite story or picture book for children?

• What does the phrase "you cannot teach anyone anything" mean to you?

• What do you think of Sesame Street?

• At what age do children begin to form peer relationships?

Block Building. After the interview, the candidates were brought into the room with the complete set of blocks. They were instructed that what they were to do was to build whatever they wanted to and to take as much time as they needed. When they were finished, a picture was taken of their final product. They were told they could share their thoughts on what they had constructed or they could say nothing and that was fine. After the first time we also learned to ask the candidate to put away the blocks — otherwise the person doing the interviewing would spend the rest of his life putting away blocks.

Some candidates completed their structures in 15 to 20 minutes, whereas others plugged away for well over an hour. I particularly remember one woman who worked on something for nearly an hour, and when she added the last block to the top the entire structure collapsed. So she turned around and built an entirely different structure for 45 minutes more.

Cartoon Exploration. The balance of the process was in writing. The candidates were ushered to a quiet room, given instructions for the remaining four parts and invited to take as much time as they required. The first written portion provided candidates an opportunity to respond to five cartoons. These cartoons zeroed in on early childhood settings and were selected in order to illicit candidates' feelings about working with young children in a group setting and what their priorities were. For example, one cartoon

depicts a little girl holding a sloppy paint brush, covered from head to toe with paint, standing in the midst of paint containers and paint slopped all over the floor, exclaiming to an adult — "Art is my favorite interest center!" Responses varied from suggestions on controlling children's access and use of art materials in order to avoid messes to opinions that children's exploration of various art medium should not be inhibited in any way.

Sentence Completion. Candidates were given the opening phrase of fifteen sentences and asked to complete them in their own terms. The fifteen were traditional sentence completions such as:

"A child feels unhappy when..."

"Teachers need..."

"Children are wonderful, but..."

Autobiographical Questions. In order to get a broader picture of what the candidates were like, we asked them to respond to the following four autobiographical questions:

• What were you like as a child?

• Give a picture of your family life as a child?

• What were the meaningful relationships of your childhood?

• What kind of children interest you?

Evaluating the Results

None of the questions or tasks had right and wrong responses. However, in each instance there were certain types of responses we were looking for. Before administering the test we went through and identified the range of responses we would look for given our philosophy and attitudes. Then in evaluating the candidates' responses we liked for those that were closest to our responses. In this way we were able, in almost every hiring, to achieve a successful match between the person hired and the center they worked in.

In general, we were looking for people who were open, creative, caring, growing individuals. Therefore, we looked for people who demonstrated these characteristics in their responses. In the "art is my favorite interest area" cartoon, for example, we tended to prefer those who laid stress on encouraging children's exploration rather than on those whose prime concern was with keeping the mess under control.

As another example let's consider interview question #6 — "What do you think of Sesame Street?" From those candidates who had seen Sesame Street we tended to get three types of responses. There were many who thought Sesame Street was marvelous — the most wonderful thing that had ever happened to children in the United States. Then there were some who said it was absolutely terrible because no child should ever be encouraged to sit in front of a TV. We tended to like and look for those who gave a third, more thoughtful response. They took the time to point out some of the positive aspects of Sesame Street as well as some of the negative aspects.

The block building results were a most instructive part of our evaluation process. First as you can see varying degrees of openness and creativity in the block building of children, the same can be seen in that of adults. I believe that the block building of adults and children has very similar stages and patterns. Its openness or closeness and the nature of its creativity reflects an enormous amount about the person — who they are, their possible ways of working with young children, and their approach to something new. Candidates' structures varied

between two extremes. At the one extreme were tiny square buildings with roofs and no windows. These certainly conveyed a very closed, tight feeling without any real expression. At the other extreme were the structures which recreated whole cities or, in one instance, a beautiful flower garden. These very open creative structures were clearly what we were looking for.

In the overall evaluation of a candidate's responses, we never zeroed in on any one thing. We always looked at the total package. The candidate's responses in all seven components were considered together to form a more complete picture. What we generally found, however, is when the match was there in one or two cartoons, it was also there in the interviews and the block building. In other words, there turned out to be a high degree of consistency in what was revealed by these various techniques.

Candidates' Reactions and Responses

In the five and one-half years I used this process, I never had anyone who was reluctant to do it. Some reacted to the block building portion with amazement, but then settled down and dug right into it. Most candidates actually seemed to enjoy and, in many cases, appreciate the process. At the end one candidate said it was one of the most fascinating interviews she had ever had, that it was the first time a selection process was really being taken seriously, and the first time she felt she had a chance to show who she really was. Similar sentiments were frequently expressed by candidates.

Even though candidates willingly and often eagerly took part in the process, I was continually amazed at the range of performance levels. In the interview portion, for example, I was amazed at how few people

could ever name an appropriate children's story book. When it came to room design, extremely few candidates were able to recreate what many of us would feel were appropriate early childhood settings with interest areas, various ways of blocking off the room, etc. Most designed what looked like a typical first grade room with desks and chairs in rows and a teachers desk and an American flag up front. Those who employed more open designs often tended to build all the activity areas around the four walls and leave a great vacant space in the middle. What is even more amazing is that the candidates often created these inadequate designs while seated in the midst of a well-designed early childhood classroom.

Another point that interested me was that very often the candidates with little if any formal training out-performed those with degrees in early childhood education. Many of the first grade classroom designs were contributed by candidates with degrees in education. Likewise, candidates with extensive training were no more able than candidates with very little training to identify names of children's books or to come up with profound responses to the cartoons.

Analyzing the Process

In retrospect I can see that, for me, certain components of the process were more effective than other parts. I found the most instructive part by far was the block building. I learned more about the candidates from this than from all the other components of the process. The next most illuminating part was the personal interview, followed by the cartoon exploration, and then the room design.

I believe that I didn't really begin to tap the great potential of the sentence completions and the autobiographical questions. This is because I lacked the specific skills to reliably interpret the responses in depth. Skilled interviewers and counselors can learn a great deal about persons from these techniques. For example, I showed, anonymously, the sentence completion responses of several candidates we had hired to my independent study adviser at Bank Street College in New York City. From their sentence completions alone she was able to accurately describe a lot about these persons and how they worked with young children. In relation to the autobiographical questions, there is a growing body of research which indicates that people's experiences as children significantly affect how they, as adults, will work with young children. By analyzing a teaching candidate's childhood, a trained counselor can predict what age group of children this person can best work with.

Another conclusion I've reached is that this process could be used effectively to select any type of teacher. For our purposes we looked for candidates who demonstrated openness and creativity in the screening. An employer who was looking for a more structured controlled teacher could use the exact same techniques but look for responses that demonstrated those characteristics. These types of techniques are open and flexible enough to enable any program to attain a successful match between people and program.

This is not to say, of course, that all programs should or could adopt the techniques exactly as I have described them above. I see what I've done as something very appropriate for me in terms of my interviewing and what I was looking for. I think it is critical that each of us takes a new look at staff selection and designs a process that would be experiential which would allow people to tell us as much as possible about themselves and their abilities. My techniques are simply illustrative of what you might consider. Your own process might incorporate parts of this and it might be totally different. It should include techniques that you feel comfortable with and which enable you to best assess the skills and attitudes that are important to you. Set some time aside and let your creativity loose. A number of persons have made some great adaptations of my process. You can too!

References

Almy, M. (1975). *The Early Childhood Education at Work*. New York: McGraw Hill Book Company, Chapter 2, "The Early Childhood Educator: An Emerging Role."

Hirsch, Elizabeth S., Ed., (1974). *The Block Book*. Washington, DC: National Association for the Education of Young Children.

Rosen, J. L. (1972)."Matching Teachers with Children," *School Review*, Volume 80, Number 3, pp. 409-431.

Shapiro, E., Biber, B., & Minuchin, P. (1957). "The Cartoons Situation Test: A Semi-Structured Technique for Assessing Aspects of Personality Pertinent to the Teaching Process," Society for Projective Techniques and Rorschack Institute, Inc.

Yardley, A. (1973). *The Teacher of the Young Child*. New York: Citation Press.

Zimilies, H. (1961). "Teacher Selection and Personality Assessment," *The National Elementary Principal*, Volume 12, Number 2.

Zimilies, H., Biber, B., Rabinowitz, W., & Hay, L. (1964). "Personality Aspects for Teaching: A Predictive Study," *Genetic Psychology Monograms*, Volume 69, pp. 101-149.

Credits

The selection process described in this article was developed as my independent study leading to a Masters of Education in Supervision and Administration of Early Childhood Education at Bank Street College in New York City. Some of the techniques were adapted from matriculation materials developed by the staff at Bank Street College.

Merle W. Leak is currently senior program analyst, day care unit, with the Massachusetts Department of Social Services, and formerly executive director of the Bucks County Coordinated Child Care Council.

Selection Interviews: Avoiding the Pitfalls

by Roger Neugebauer

The interview is the most frequently used — and most frequently misused — staff selection tool in child care. Nearly all child care centers use interviews as a major part, if not the only part, of the process of evaluating the employment suitability of job candidates. Indeed, the interview can provide an employer with useful insights on the qualifications of prospective employees. However, the interview is the most complex of all selection techniques. Centers employing it can encounter any of a number of pitfalls. This article will outline the most frequently encountered pitfalls and will describe techniques for avoiding them.

Pitfall #1

Attempting to assess too much. The interview can be an effective technique for assessing some — but not all — job qualifications. While a candidate's performance in an interview may give a reliable indication of her skills in relating to adults, it sheds little light on her ability to relate to children. To rely solely on an interview to evaluate the suitability of a candidate is placing too much faith in this technique. It is put to best use when used in conjunction with a variety of other techniques such as observations and reference checks.

The interview is most effective in assessing the knowledge, attitudes, and personality of candidates. Even in these areas, however, the interview can only be effective if it is used to assess candidates in terms of a limited number of job qualifications. When interviewers are asked to assess candidates on more than a half dozen factors, they begin to suffer from information overload, and the reliability of their judgment begins to plummet (Shouksmith). Therefore, it is critical at the outset to isolate no more than six key job qualifications to be probed in interviews. It may be helpful to review the full list of qualifications for a job and to distinguish between those which are essential and those which are nice to have but not critical. Then, during the interview, concentrate attention on the "must have" and not on the "nice to have" qualifications (Jensen).

Pitfall #2

Attempting to interview too many candidates. The interviewers had just completed interviewing ten candidates for the position of director in two nights. When they met to select the best candidate, they spent most of their time not objectively weighing the qualifications of each candidate but just trying to unscramble who said what. This incident is not atypical. The more candidates interviewed, the harder it is for interviewers to retain distinct impressions of each of them.

There is, on the other hand, a real advantage in seeing as many candidates in person as possible. This lessens the likelihood of a candidate with the ideal personality for a job falling through the cracks simply because she lacks skills in putting together an impressive resume. One way to solve this dilemma is to converse with all candidates who possess the minimum job requirements in a brief (five to ten minutes) screening interview.

The purpose of this interview is to outline the nature of the job — its duties, rate of pay, hours, etc. — to the candidate and to secure from the candidate clarification about information on her resume. From this personal interchange, the interviewer should be able to eliminate from further consideration all candidates whose preparation and/or personality is clearly unsuitable, as well as those who are no longer interested in the job described. The interviewer should also be able to spot those candidates with unimpressive credentials who nonetheless appear to possess the appropriate personality and temperament for the job.

Information overload can also be minimized through judicious scheduling. To give interviewers sufficient opportunity to digest and retain information about candidates interviewed, no more than three interviews should be scheduled for one sitting. Allow 45-60 minutes for each interview, with breaks of at least ten minutes between interviews.

Pitfall #3

Failure to establish rapport. At the outset of an interview, a candidate is likely to be uptight and nervous. Until he relaxes and feels comfortable with talking frankly, he will not present a realistic impression of himself.

Certain details can be arranged to help relieve tension prior to the interview. When the candidate arrives for the interview, he should be made to feel immediately welcome either by having someone greet him or by having a notice posted indicating he is in the right place and that someone will come and get him when it is time for his interview. If there is time, the candidate might be offered a tour of the center.

The candidate should be personally escorted into the interview room and introduced to the interviewers while they are standing. If there is more than one interviewer, the candidate should be seated so that he can easily see all the interviewers, yet not feel like he is on display himself. With one interviewer, both parties should

be seated in comfortable chairs, preferably not on opposite sides of a cluttered desk. After the candidate is seated, there should be a pause which allows him to catch his breath and get his bearings.

To help the candidate *warm up*, an interviewer should get the candidate talking with some easy, non-threatening conversation or questions. This should not be small talk about the weather as this will heighten the tension as the candidate waits for the ax to fall. The interviewer could start with some point of common interest from the resumé — "I went to North Dakota State also. How did you like it there? — or with a series of specific, easy-to-answer questions. Do not rush this phase of the interview as the interchange will not be open and frank until rapport has been established. Then once you are ready to begin in earnest, brief the candidate on what the interview will be like so he knows what to expect.

Pitfall #4

Having too many interviewers. The most common pitfall in child care selection interviews is the *Spanish Inquisition* syndrome — bringing candidates before a panel of four to ten inquisitors. It is hard enough for a single interviewer to establish rapport with a candidate. When there are two or more interviewers, it becomes much more difficult, and when there are four or more, it is usually impossible. As a result, there is "a loss of sense of intimacy, a diminution of empathy, a confused interviewer, and a consequent inhibition of communication" (Lopez). In a panel interview setting, it is also much more difficult to proceed in an organized fashion, to carry out a line of questioning to completion, and to ask spontaneous follow-up questions.

There are, nonetheless, occasions when, for either political or programmatic reasons, it is necessary to have more than one interviewer. An alternative to consider in these situations is the serial interview whereby one candidate is interviewed by a number of interviewers individually in sequence. Each interviewer covers different job qualifications or aspects of the job. In the end, all interviewers meet to share their impressions and findings.

Pitfall #5

Failure to provide enough structure. Research on selection interviews has uncovered many shortcomings of informal, unstructured interviews: They are highly inconsistent and highly susceptible to distortion and bias (Pursell); the same materials are not covered for all candidates; interviewers tend to talk more than interviewees; and interviewers tend to make their decisions early in the interview (Stewart). In addition, interviewers tend to spend more time formulating their next question than listening to what the candidate is saying (Goodale).

For best results, most personnel experts recommend a well-prepared for, semi-structured interview format. Prior to the interview, the key job qualifications to be probed in the interview should be identified, and one or two open-ended introductory questions should be developed for each qualification. After the interview has progressed through the rapport-building stage, the interviewer should introduce a job qualification with one of these open-ended questions, and then follow up with specific spontaneous questions which seek clarification of issues raised in the candidate's initial response.

Pitfall #6

Being swayed by general impressions and stereotypes. Interviewers often are struck by a single aspect of a candidate's personality or background or by a single statement and allow this single factor to determine their overall assessment of the candidate. For example, the physical appearance of a candidate, especially one who is very thin, fat, short, tall, good looking, well dressed, or poorly dressed, will often color an interviewer's judgment about a candidate (Jensen). Interviewers also tend to be influenced more by unfavorable information revealed by a candidate than by favorable information; and the earlier in the interview the unfavorable information is disclosed, the greater its negative impact (Stewart).

To keep such biases and distortions from undermining the selection process, interviewers need to be encouraged to concentrate on gathering specific pieces of relevant evidence about candidates' qualifications, rather than general impressions. One way to do this is to spend some time prior to the interviews reviewing the job qualifications so that interviewers are well aware of what information to probe for. A second approach is to provide training on effective listening skills (see Nichols).

Pitfall #7

Failure to record information. By the end of an interview, interviewers generally have already forgotten 50% of what was said. By the next day, 85% has been forgotten (Nichols). Therefore, even though it may be somewhat distracting or discomforting to the candidate, it is critical to record information during the interview.

The best method is to tape record interviews. When doing this, tell candidates at the outset that the interview will be taped and for what purpose. A candidate may feel uptight with being recorded, but generally after the first few minutes everyone tends to forget about the recorder and converse normally.

The next best method is to take notes onto a format prepared in advance which provides spaces for each qualification. When taking notes, however, it is necessary to avoid telegraphing what you want to hear by stopping to write whenever the candidate says something of interest. Instead, the interviewer should make a mental note of valuable points and record these when attention shifts to another interviewer or point in the discussion. In either case, after the interviews, the interviewers should take a few minutes to record their reactions.

Pitfall #8

Asking discriminatory questions. Interviewers are barred by equal employment opportunity guidelines from asking questions that can lead to discrimination on the basis of race, religion, age, sex, marital status, arrest record, handicaps, or national origin. Questions such as the following are not legal:

• Do you live with your parents?

• Who will watch your children while you work?

• How do you get along with other women?

• Do you have any physical disabilities?

• Where were you born?

• Have you ever been arrested?

• How would you feel about working with people younger than yourself?

• Does your religion prevent you from working weekends?

This does not mean, however, that no questions can be asked about these subjects. They can be asked in reference to bona-fide occupational qualifications. For example, although a candidate cannot be asked "Are you

More Do's and Don'ts for Selection Interviews

• To encourage a candidate to be open, praise her for answering questions fully.

• To be sure you understand a candidate or to probe for more details, restate what she told you, but in an expectant tone — "You say you have had difficulty working with aggressive parents. . . ."

• Use silence to draw candidates out. People tend to be uncomfortable with silence in a conversation. When a candidate stops talking but has not supplied enough details on a point, don't rush to fill the void. Wait for the candidate to speak up.

• Don't do all the talking. The more you talk, the less you learn.

• Don't ask questions which are answered in the resumé.

• Don't telegraph what you want to hear by describing the philosophy of the center at the outset or by asking leading questions — "Do you believe in open education?"

• Don't reveal your reactions or feelings either through gestures, expressions, or remarks. This may cause the candidate to clam up or tailor her remarks to suit you.

• Don't debate issues with the candidate or seek to give advice.

• Don't ask trick questions. You cannot encourage the candidate to be open and frank if you are being devious yourself.

• Don't rely on general questions about teaching philosophies. How a candidate describes her approach in theory and how she performs in practice often bear little resemblance. Specific situational questions — "What would you do if . . ." — may be more instructive.

• Don't allow the interview to get sidetracked on an interesting but non job-related tangent.

• Don't let the candidate take control of the interview.

• Don't allow the candidate to sense your impatience.

---

a U.S. citizen?," the question "Can you, after employment, submit verification of your legal right to work in the United States?" is acceptable (Jensen). Centers which are uncertain about the legality of their selection procedures should contact their state's Equal Opportunity Commission.

Pitfall #9

Failure to sell the organization to the candidate. Interviewers can become so preoccupied with assessing the candidates that they may not be aware of the impression they are making on the candidate. It is counterproductive to select the best candidate in the batch if that candidate is so turned off by the image the organization conveyed during the selection process that she turns down the job offer.

Throughout the interview process, all candidates should be treated warmly and professionally. Appointments should be clearly made and adhered to. Candidates should be made to feel welcome when they arrive and respected when they depart. Having a well-structured interview not only yields more information about the candidates; it also shows the candidates that they are dealing with a professional organization and that the organization takes the job under consideration seriously.

Near the end of the interview, time should be set aside for describing the organization and the job to the candidate. Questions from the candidate should be welcomed at this point also. In describing the job and answering questions about it, however, care should be taken not to oversell it. If there are negative aspects of the job (low pay, a split shift, or a recent history of staff turmoil), these should be discussed with candidates. The interview should be viewed as the first step in negotiating a contract. A new employee's commitment to the center may be seriously undermined if the center can't deliver on promises made or expectations aroused in the interview.

At the close of the interview, the candidate should be told the process that will follow and when and how she will be notified of the decision. Unless a candidate clearly lacks some basic job qualification, no indication should be given at this time about whether or not the candidate is likely to get the job.

References

Goodale, J. G. (July 1981). "The Neglected Art of Interviewing." *Supervisory Management.*

Jensen, J. (May/June 1981). "How to Hire the Right Person for the Job." *The Grantsmanship Center News.*

Lopez, F. M. (1965). *Personnel Interviewing: Theory and Practice.* New York: McGraw-Hill Book Company.

Nichols, R. G. (November 1980). "Improve Your Listening Skills." *Child Care Information Exchange.*

Pursell, E. D. (November 1980). "Structured Interviewing: Avoiding Selection Problems." *Personnel Journal.*

Shouksmith, G. (1968). *Assessment Through Interviewing.* Oxford, England: Pergamon Press, Ltd.

Stewart, C. J., & Cash, W. B. (1974). *Interviewing: Principles and Practices.* Dubuque, IA: William C. Brown Company, Publishers.

Staff Selection:
Using Group Employment Interviews

by Roger Buese

It has often been said the foundation of a good program is good people. Certainly the key element in a successful child care program is the staff. Regardless of the limitations of a facility or budget, any child care program can flourish with a good staff. Therefore, hiring becomes a task with monumental consequences.

At the Berea Children's Home we have enjoyed considerable success in the hiring process by employing the group interview technique. In group interview we invite up to a dozen promising applicants to appear for an interview at the same time. Candidates are asked to answer questions directed to them individually, but also to jump in and share their reactions to other candidates' statements. At the conclusion, the candidates are evaluated by observing staff members not only in terms of the content of their answers, but also in terms of their group interaction skills.

By utilizing the method of group interviews, all applicants can be screened in an expedient manner. Rather than scheduling a dozen applicants at 12 different times and repeating your program objectives and job needs, one interview time is offered, one explanation of the program given. The time savings can easily be six hours for every 12 applicants interviewed.

More important than economy of time in hiring is the selection of the best applicants. The group method offers the prospective employer a better tool for assessment and selection. Information on the resumé or letter or application is not reviewed in the interview. Rather, questions for the group interview are designed to elicit information, knowledge of child care, personality traits, and group interaction. Some applicants can manipulate an individual interview, being compliant and giving the answers that are expected. However, a group interview not only discloses the applicants' knowledge of child care, but also how they interact with others. It provides the opportunity for insight into how a person may function within a child care staff.

This interview concept also allows for team building , especially when several job openings exist. Selecting a staff member is not like a pro football draft where coaches take *the best available player*. The best applicant

may not be suited for the child care team you have established. There needs to be a blending of talents and temperaments to get the maximum potential from staff. The person selected should meet group needs as well as specific job requirements.

Group interviews are especially effective tools to hire several staff at one time. The opening of a child care center, major expansion, or development of new programs all present opportunities for multiple hirings. The group interview offers a tool by which a team can be selected. Supervisors and subordinates can be matched for strengths and weaknesses to create the best team to reach the goals of the organization.

To further strengthen the team concept, team members can sit in and observe an interview. During evaluation of the interview, their input can be helpful in selecting new members for their team. This process increases staff participation at the most critical point in the administration of the organization.

Setting Up the Interview

The following process can be used to set the stage for group interviews.

• Place an advertisement through the local newspapers. Request letters or resumés be sent to you or a box number.

- After you have acquired your applicants' written material, set up specific times for your group interviews. An evening time may be necessary. Eight to ten is the ideal number for a group. Overbook your session with 12. You will probably have a few *no shows* or cancellations.

- Contact your applicants by telephone, tell them you are holding a group interview, and ask if they can attend. If you have many applicants, you may wish to tank order your calls based upon impressions gained from the written responses you received. If you have scheduled several groups, give your top applicants first choice for group times. These will be the people you want most want to see. Be aware of

basic interview techniques. All questions should be job oriented. Keep phone contact to a minimum. Your intent on the phone is to schedule a time, not to interview. Avoid questions which the group interview is intended to answer.

- At the group interview, take your candidates from a gathering area to a group interview room. Again, be careful not to be chatty. Stay focused on your task. In the interview room, have name tags for your applicants. Place your chairs in a circular arrangement. You need to place yourself so that you have visual contact with everyone present. Depending upon your management practices, you may wish to involve one or more of your staff as observers. Ideally, a leader and a recorder are sufficient for an effective interview process. As noted, this is an ideal opportunity to

involve staff in the selection process.

The Three Part Interview

Interviews have three components — introductions, explanations, and questions:

- Introductions consist of some form of staff introduction and introductions of applicants. One approach is to use a chalk board or newsprint and have applicants come forward and write their names. Each person is asked to explain something about their name such as its meaning, history, family stories, nicknames, or feelings. The interviewer should first give everyone an example of the exercise by using his own name.

The introduction is not designed to be a verbal resume. Rather it offers

---

Group Interview Questions

What would you do if . . .

- A parent brings a child over a three week period with bruises on her shins and upper arms. The child is particularly fussy at arrival and departure.

- A six month old child is not sitting up and the parent expresses concern in as much as his two year old sat up at four months.

- A child begins to cough violently, and you are the only one in the classroom.

- A parent is upset because her child screams and clings at drop off time.

- A 14 month old child bites and hits the other children and adults frequently during the day. Her parents claim this does not occur at home.

- Two four year olds are in your bathroom area *playing doctor*.

- A two year old in your class is wearing shoes several sizes too small, and has been for weeks.

- You are the director and you notice that the part time staff person is consistently a half hour late in the afternoon, but signs herself in on time.

- A parent asks you to spank her child when he misbehaves.

- The mother of a three year old insists that her child be taught letters and numbers.

an opportunity for a person to identify herself to the group in a non-threatening way while giving you a sense of some personality traits and social skills. Whatever process you choose should be consistent throughout your interviews and should observe all equal employment opportunity guidelines.

The best applicant may not be suited for the child care team you have established. There needs to be a blending of talents and temperaments to get the maximum potential from staff.

- Next explain your center's program philosophy and give information about the specific job opening(s). Job descriptions may be read and the table of organization may be explained. This orientation gives recorders time to make notes about the applicant's introductory remarks while information about the program is being given. The entire interview lasts about one hour. The introduction and explanations take approximately 15 minutes.

- Questions usually fill the remainder of the hour. This process involves the interviewer asking applicants a series of *what would you do* situational questions. A suggested strategy is to have the group sitting in a circle and number the group in your mind left to right. Start number one with the first question. Then ask number two to give a response to the same question. Number three gets a new question and number four gets to offer the second response.

In the second round, even numbers are the original questions and odd numbers give the second response. The process concludes with questions being offered for responses from any member of the group. This *grab bag* approach quickly divides the assertive from the passive candidates. The responses, along with the group interactions, provide more information than can be acquired in an individual interview. The box on page 32 poses some questions which have proved effective in past interviews.

Applicants are given an opportunity at the end of this question period to ask their own questions. This is an opportunity to hear who has listened and thought about the job. Applicants are told, if they have not asked already, that they will be contacted regarding any possible future interviews.

Evaluating the Interview

After the interview, the staff involved evaluate and rate the applicants. A numerical system can be used; but a simple rating system of low, medium, and high may be sufficient to determine which applicants you will want to see again.

Specific correct answers are only part of the evaluation. Personality traits such as compassion, honesty, and sense of humor may be more important. Remember, it is easier to acquire correct knowledge than to change personality. Decide what personality traits are important and what level of knowledge about child care or supervision is necessary. Use a uniform evaluation system for all your candidates.

Regardless of the limitations of the facility or budget, any child care program can flourish with a good staff.

During the interview, a designated recorder has filled out individual evaluation forms. These forms help recall specific incidents and responses during the evaluation.

Staff share their impressions of the applicants and decide who will be offered an individual interview. This decision can be made on an objective point system basis or on a subjective level — "I would want my child to spend time with this person." Those selected are invited to an individual interview by a phone call during the following days.

Interview Expectations

The interviewing team, facilitator, and observers have certain expectations as they approach the interview. The team has to decide what personality traits are most valued and what characteristics they desire in an employee. Different roles may dictate different attributes. You may desire an assertive head teacher but more compliant or more passive team members. Those interviewed are not told what personality traits you seek. They are simply given program background information, job description, instructions, and questions. The result is probably a more candid and genuine response from the candidate.

The Facilitator's Role

The group facilitator needs to be consistent. The goal is to let the group respond to the questions and interact. The facilitator should develop a format for the interview and follow that pattern for all interviews. Too much interaction by the facilitator can take the responsibility for responses away from the group members. If annoying or problem behaviors arise (withdrawal, *show boating*, verbal domination), let the group handle them. Don't attempt to draw out the withdrawn or squelch the squawker. Expect the group to take responsibility for its individual and collective behavior.

Allow your candidates to monitor and comment on their own interactions. If you give good instructions and ask appropriate questions, then the applicants' task is clearly to give their best responses and earn consideration for the job that is offered. The consistent facilitator can compare group and individuals knowing that the presentations were nearly identical.

Feedback and Summary

"A group interview! I've never been interviewed in a group." "You mean we come as a group, and then you interview us individually?" "Group interview? That certainly sounds different." These are typical responses to initial contacts. However, after the interview there is usually a feeling of excitement. Candidates feel positive about the program (good public relations even if they are not hired) and have secretly selected their own favorites.

Staff who went through the process give good feedback (as expected, they were hired). Many candidates not chosen responded by letter indicating their positive feelings about the process. Staff really enjoy participating in later group interviews as observers. They appreciate being part of the selection process and being able to say, "I'd like to work with her." This process builds a sense of ownership with your staff.

The group interview process offers many advantages to traditional methods of staff selection. It is especially effective and cost efficient for a child care setting where you want a volume of applications for staff positions, including secretarial. This method also offers a unique opportunity for staff participation. This form should provide you with the best applicants through a practical approach to staff selection.

Roger Buese, M.A., M.Div., is director of the Family Life Center at the Berea Children's Home in Berea, Ohio.

Observing Teaching Candidates in Action

by Roger Neugebauer

"We found that everyone loves children in the abstract, but will they love them eight hours a day in the classroom?" Thus Nancy Alexander explained the reason her center in Shreveport, Louisiana, instituted a policy of observing all teaching candidates before they were hired. At first, when teachers were selected strictly on the basis of their performance, she found that there often was a wide variance between how individuals described their child caring skills and how they actually performed in action. By observing likely candidates working in a center, Nancy Alexander was able to much more reliably assess them. As a result, she nearly eliminated hiring mistakes.

This experience is not unique. Most child care centers and nursery schools now include observations as an integral part of their selection procedures. To provide readers with ideas on how to conduct an effective observation, *Child Care Information Exchange* surveyed eight child care organizations which have experienced positive results with this staff selection technique. The results of this survey are summarized below.

Before the Observation

An observation can provide a reasonably reliable forecast of a candidate's likely performance if it is properly prepared for. This preparation should center around the identification of what you hope to learn about candidates in the observations.

You probably can generate a long list of qualifications you would like to find in your ideal teaching candidate. Some of these, such as *level of training*, can be reliably measured by a resumé review; and others, such as *knowledge of child development*, can be assessed well in interviews. Many others, especially those relating to personality traits and teaching style, can only be assessed by observing the candidates in action. Identify about a half dozen of these qualifications or traits that are most critical to the accomplishment of your center's curriculum goals. Don't attempt to assess too many or your attention will be dispersed in too many directions to effectively measure anything.

For each trait, identify some specific indicators to look for during the

observation. For example, if an important qualification is *positive interaction skills*, helpful indicators of this might be *maintains eye contact at the child's level* and *listens patiently to children*. At the end of this article are listed 29 such indicators that the surveyed directors found to yield insightful data on the candidates.

Thoroughly discuss the list of qualifications and their indicators in a staff meeting. Make sure that anyone who will participate in observations understands what to look for. Make any revisions that come out of this discussion for improving or clarifying the list. Then print it up in a checklist format to hand to observers before each observation to be sure the traits and indicators are attended to.

With this degree of preparation, observation can be a more reliable staff selection technique than the interview. It would be desirable to be able to observe all candidates who meet the center's minimum training and experience standards. This might enable you to identify candidates who don't have impressive formal qualifications and who do not express themselves skillfully in the interview but who, nevertheless, are naturally gifted in interacting with children. Unfortunately, observations are time consuming and a bit disruptive to the flow of classroom activities. Therefore, most centers tend to use observations sparingly — only observing the top two to five candidates from the interviews. If this is the approach your center must take, follow your hunches from time to time. Include among those to be observed candidates who didn't fare well through the interview stage but who you have a gut feeling may do well in practice.

Bea Ganson, a director in Abilene, Texas, is able to get a maximum use of observations by requiring all candidates to serve as paid substitutes before they can be hired. Thus she can observe many candidates over a period of time before making selection decisions.

During the Observation

One teaching candidate, upon inquiring at a center about a job, was immediately assigned for his *observation* to care for 15 children in the nap room by himself. Many of the children could not be comforted by this *stranger*, and most of the others took the opportunity to test him. The result was chaos. The candidate had a miserable experience and never considered returning to that center, and the center didn't get the foggiest picture of what the candidate was like as a teacher.

For the best results, the center should schedule observations carefully. Centers have found that observations should last at least two to four hours to get a reliable picture of a candidate. Shorter periods do not allow candidates enough time to get acclimated.

Time of day is also critical. Nancy Alexander schedules interviews during a free play period rather than a group activity time so that candidates are more likely to get involved with the children rather than sitting

back and observing an activity. Peg Persinger, a director in Eugene, Oregon, tends to assign candidates to the most challenging groups to really test their skills. Most directors also assign candidates to work with teachers they would actually be working with if they were hired, so that the current teachers can assess whether this is someone they would be comfortable with.

In any event, try to have all candidates for a single position be observed by the same staff people. Barbara Day, a director in Edmonton, Alberta, recommends scheduling all observations for a single position in the same week so that the memories of the first candidates won't fade by the time the last ones are observed.

For the candidate to present a true picture of herself, she needs to be as relaxed and comfortable as possible. For the candidate to be interested in working for the center, she needs to have as pleasant an experience as possible. Both these requirements call for the director to take specific steps to put the candidate at ease about the observation and to ease her into it gently. Start by telling all candidates from the beginning that they may be expected to participate in an observation. When scheduling interviews, tell them exactly what will be expected of them, how long the observation will last, and what the class is like that they will be in.

On the day of the observation, the director should escort the candidate into the room and introduce her to the teaching staff and the children. At this point, Barbara Day leaves the candidate, and the supervisor (or head teacher) leads the candidate on a brief tour of the room.

The candidate's involvement in the activity of the room should be allowed to expand gradually. Most centers allow for a 30 minute *warm-up* period in which no official obser-

vations are made. Candidates under observation at the North Pocono Preschool in North Pocono, Pennsylvania, are encouraged by director Gail Laskowski to start their four hour observation by observing what is going on for a while, then working with the teachers for a while, and finally working on their own when they feel comfortable doing so.

Many centers ask the candidates to plan and present a specific 20-40 minute activity for the children. Karen Miller, Evergreen, Colorado, has found that if some of the less experienced candidates are not given such a specific task, they tend to sit around, giving no hint of their potential. Staff should go out of their way to cooperate with the candidates in providing materials and assistance for the activities. Give the candidates every opportunity to do their best.

During the observation, it is best not to heighten their sense of being followed by all eyes. The director should not pull up a chair and formally observe the whole period. Gail Laskowski simply makes a point of being in the area with a purpose often during this period. The teachers should also go on about their business and not take notes or talk about the candidate in her presence.

On the other hand, the staff should not ignore the candidate but should be alert to her performance. While observers should take note of a candidate's general demeanor, they should most keenly observe how he handles specific incidents. The data they should be trying to collect is not general impressions but as many small pieces of evidence as possible — especially pieces of evidence relating to the indicators identified beforehand.

After the Observation

There should be a definite closure to the observation. The director should return to the room to retrieve the candidate, or the head teacher should thank her and ask her to report back to the director. At this point, Barbara Day invites the candidate to share her reactions. These reactions can be very revealing. The candidate's impressions of specific incidents can disclose a great deal about her knowledge and philosophy. For example, the candidate may talk about the *misbehavior* of a certain *troublemaker* when in reality this child's behavior was well within normal bounds. This may be a clue to you that either this candidate is not tuned in to child development, or else that she may have a more restrictive approach than you prefer. If the candidate shares only general reactions, it may be useful to prod her memory with open-ended statements about specific incidents.

After the candidate leaves, all those who observed her should take the first opportunity to record their reactions. Gail Laskowski has all observers rate the candidate on a selection criteria matrix and then include some narrative comments. Then, as soon as possible, while the experience is still fresh in everyone's minds, the observers should meet together to share their assessments. The director should steer this discussion away from generalities. One way to do this is to read through the list of traits and their indicators. For each indicator, ask observers to describe specific incidents where this indicator was demonstrated in a negative or positive way. If the indicator relates to the candidate's success in integrating children into the group, the observers would describe a candidate's various attempts to do so and the outcome of the attempts. By reviewing as much specific evidence as possible, the observers will eventually have a reasonably solid basis for deciding whether or not to hire the candidate.

Observations can add a strong element of reliability to staff selection decisions. However, this technique does not guarantee that all mistakes will be avoided. Charlene Richardson, director of the Child Development Center in San Diego, places new employees on a three month probationary status. During this period, she carefully monitors their performance using the same procedures as in the selection observation. Such pre- and post-hiring observations do require considerable effort on the part of staff members; but in the long run, they assure a more consistent program for the children.

What to Look For

The directors surveyed for this article identified the following performance indicators as ones they have used with the best results. Overall, the indicators that were cited most frequently related to the way the candidates relate to the children. As Nancy Alexander explained, "We want to see if they treat them as sweet cutesies or as thinking human beings." In this vein, the most popular indicators were tone of voice, eye contact, body language, and listening skills.

Physical Appearance and Personal Attitude

- Does she use positive body language?

- Is her tone of voice appropriate?

- What are her facial expressions as she interacts with children? Is she animated, angry, or "bored to tears"?

- Does she maintain eye contact at the child's level?

- Does she dress appropriately, "as if she expects to sit on the floor and have tempera paint spilled over her?"

- Does she convey an overall sense of enthusiasm?

- Is she having fun or is she tense and resentful?

Interaction Skills

- How does she react when children approach her?

- How does she answer children's questions?

- Does she listen carefully and patiently to what children tell her? How does she signal interest in their communications?

- Does she appear comfortable talking to children?

- Does she serve as a good language model?

- How does she help integrate children into the group?

Direction and Control

- Does she maintain control? How?

- How does she show tolerance for child-like demands, impatience, mood swings, self-assertion, negativism, exuberance, angry feelings, tears, and testing behavior? How does she guide children at such times toward adequate coping and socially acceptable behavior?

- Does she allow children to resolve their own conflicts?

- How much are children allowed to diverge from her directions?

- If a child has lost control, can the candidate accept the child's feelings and help him regain control? Does she retaliate or offer alternatives? Does she tear the child down or build him up?

- Does the candidate use a positive approach — "Blocks are for building." — or are her directives negative — "Don't throw that block."

Teaching Skills

- Is she actively engaged or merely babysitting?

- If she brings in an activity, is it appropriate for the age group?

- Is she able to follow a schedule while still remaining flexible?

- Is she able to adjust to unforeseen incidents?

- How well does she hold the interest of the children?

- How well does she arouse children's curiosity?

- Does she move around the room to help children and show interest in what they are doing?

- Does she provide an appropriate balance of unstructured and structured activities?

- Does she demonstrate a willingness to learn herself? Is she open to new ideas? Does she ask questions about particular activities and materials?

- Does she work comfortably with other staff in the room?

Recruiting Male Volunteers to Build Staff Diversity

by Bruce Cunningham

*"I'd love to have a man on my staff,
but where do you find them?"*

*"The children love it when a father visits our center.
How can we get more men to volunteer?"*

These are the most common statements directors make about men, or rather the lack of male staff, in early childhood settings. It is true that there are relatively few well-qualified men who can assume teaching positions in early childhood classrooms — particularly when compared to the number of similarly qualified women. Only about 3% of staff working directly with young children are men — an estimate based on the National Association for the Education of Young Children (NAEYC) membership. This number is considerably lower than the 6% doing the same kind of work in the early 1970s (Robinson, 1981). Yet there are ways a program for young children can hire and retain men. While all the strategies for doing this will not be appropriate for all types of programs, there are compelling reasons for every program to recruit and retain male staff.

The Case for Men

Common sense tells us that children need to spend time in the company of both men and women to form healthy, realistic images of adults. Young children particularly need to see men and women getting along together, communicating and sharing tasks. Unfortunately, many young children have little exposure to men in their lives at home (Horne, 1996) and even less in their child care arrangements. In the absence of men, boys and girls will form their images of men from what they see on television, videos, movies, and computer games. These images rarely depict men as being nurturing and frequently show men to be violent (Levin, 1994).

The point is that young boys will grow up to be men and young girls will grow up to interact with men. Children need positive interactions with men in a variety of roles and settings during early childhood to establish a strong foundation for healthy development later in life.

What we know about diversity also tells us that recruiting more men will make early childhood education a stronger profession. Clearly, whenever the membership of a profession is strongly homogeneous, that profession has a more limited perspective and fewer resources than if it includes members of different groups. There is also an unhealthy dynamic when the membership of a profession does not reflect the make up of the population it serves.

And, finally, research shows that men often have a different style of interacting with children (Lamb, Pleck, & Levine, 1985). This includes a more physical style of play, encouraging more independence and a tendency to vary routines rather than to repeat them in the same ways over time. This same research shows the children clearly benefit from this style of interaction — by scoring higher on a variety of tests of intellectual ability and cognitive skills, having a more positive sense of self-competence and sex role development, and having more success in school (Horne, 1996).

Making a Statement of Policy

Because these ideas are compelling, it is important to put them into policy. Most programs are supported by documentation such as policy manuals, philosophy statements, mission statements, parent hand-books, or other documents for outlining program beliefs and guide-lines. Most programs also have a process for writing or adding infor-mation to these documents. The key parts of such a policy that speaks to the importance of male staff can include such statements as:

- The presence of men is essential to the lives of young children — particularly in light of the chang-ing dynamics of families and the influence from media images of men.

- Men can be highly competent caregivers.

- Men bring needed diversity to a program and the field of early childhood education.

- Parents and staff must accept men as caregivers who perform all caregiving tasks with all age groups of children.

- Men will be actively sought to fill caregiver positions.

- When a man and a woman of equal qualifications apply for a position, the man will be chosen so as to add diversity to a staff that has been predominantly female.

While these kinds of statements may be viewed as being merely token or symbolic steps, making them is a vital starting point. When these ideas are written into a policy, they can be used to support goals and actions that make recruiting men a strategic priority.

Starting with Volunteers

Using volunteers is one way to bring men into the lives of children, given the shortage of well-qualified male applicants. Before recruiting male volunteers, it is important to con-

Getting Out the Word

A variety of other strategies can be used to attract men. These include:

- Post flyers for vacant positions around the community in places where men will see them. Places to find men include health clubs, sporting events, video stores, auto supply stores, the weight room of a local college, and men's restrooms at early childhood conferences.

- Organize a table or booth at a high school or college job fair. Consider collaborating on this task with other programs and also be sure to staff the booth or table with a man to draw the attention of other men.

- Encourage men currently in the profession to visit and speak to child development and other related classes in high schools and colleges. If you teach a course or have the opportunity to speak to a class, encourage the students to invite their male friends to sit in on a few class sessions. Invite these young men to volunteer.

sider how to sell men on the idea of volunteering. The question to think through is one of *What would a man get out of volunteering?* or, if you are contacting an institution, *How would a high school or college benefit from hav-ing a male student volunteer with young children?*

The answer will depend upon who you are targeting as a volunteer; but if the men are students, they will gain valuable experience working with children — experience that will enhance their training, parenting skills, personal growth, and future employability. This is particularly true because few other men will have had experience working with young children. In short, early child-hood settings have something valu-able to offer men, so it is important not to be shy about asking men to volunteer.

High schools, colleges, and universi-ties — public and private — are good sources of male volunteers. If you are calling a school district main office, ask for someone who is in charge of service learning. This is a program in which students fulfill requirements

toward graduation through work experiences. If you are calling a college or university, start with a placement office that handles intern-ships and practicum experiences. Be sure to ask about courses in edu-cation, psychology, sociology, home economics, family life, and physical education. These types of programs often have practicum experience requirements.

At any type of educational institu-tion, you will eventually be referred to an instructor. When talking to an instructor, offer your program as a career exploration, practicum, or student teaching placement site. If you feel confident to do so, offer to speak to students in classes about the importance of men being involved in the lives of young children.

Other sources of volunteers include retired seniors' programs, seminaries, and scouting organizations.

Growing Male Staff

It is important to think through the ways in which male volunteers can be involved. An early childhood classroom is a confusing place to anyone who has not spent time there. An invitation to just jump right into the activities is not particularly helpful advice. Consequently, many men, even if they have been given an orientation to the activities and expectations of the program, may be initially more comfortable interacting with children in ways they are familiar with — such as on a playground or at a woodworking table. However, it is important not to limit men to these activities.

A sound strategy is to offer men a choice of ways to be involved, such as in saying, "You can settle down in the book area and read stories to the children for a while or you can help children use the tools at the woodworking center." Male volunteers will appreciate this guidance and the availability of options. As male volunteers become more comfortable in the classroom, staff can offer suggestions on ways to expand their roles with children.

Many men working in early childhood settings entered the field in nontraditional ways rather than making it an initial career choice for which they undertook education and training. It is often the case that a man starts as a volunteer, a part-time worker, or a support person such as a bus driver, maintenance worker, or food service worker. These men enjoy their interactions with young children so much that they begin or continue their education. These men can grow into valued staff when offered encouragement and support.

References

Horne, W. (1996). *Father facts II: Revised edition.* The National Fatherhood Initiative.

Lamb, M., Pleck, J., & Levine, J. (1985). The role of the father in child development: The effects of increased paternal involvement. In B. Lahey & A. Kazdin (Eds.), *Advances in clinical child psychology,* (Vol. 8, pp. 229-266). New York: Plenum.

Levin, D. (1994). *Teaching young children in violent times: Building a peaceable classroom.* Cambridge, MA: Educators for Social Responsibility.

Robinson, B. (1981). Changing views of male early childhood teachers. *Young Children,* 36, 27-31.

Acknowledgments

Several individuals contributed to this article by previewing earlier drafts and offering additional ideas and feedback. They are: Bryan Nelson, Wendy Roedell, Bruce Sheppard, Gregory Uba, and Steve Weber.

Bruce Cunningham has worked in early childhood settings as an assistant, a teacher, a director, and an educator. He is currently an education coordinator with the Early Childhood Education and Assistance Program (ECEAP) through the Puget Sound Educational Service District in Seattle, Washington.

Hiring and Retaining Male Staff

by Bruce Cunningham

"We advertise for teachers all the time but no men ever apply."

*"We have one male teacher but
I'm afraid he'll leave our program."*

Directors who make these comments acknowledge the challenges in hiring and retaining male staff. While there are relatively small numbers of well-qualified men who can teach young children, there are also effective ways of recruiting them.

Hiring men requires a change in recruitment strategies, and retaining men requires a change in workplace practices. Yet an intentional approach to recruiting and supporting male staff can be successful — and the results can make your program more diverse and responsive to the needs of young children.

Advertising for Men

Due to the cost of classified advertisements, most programs keep the wording to a minimum, speaking only to the most important or required qualifications of education and experience. When additional descriptive words are used, it is to acknowledge something about the nature of the work — such as using the word *energetic*, which speaks to the physically demanding nature of the work in the most cheery way possible.

Occasionally, other descriptors are used, and these most commonly include *nurturing, caring, affectionate,* and *gentle*. These are important characteristics, and most programs have many staff who exemplify them. However, if you are interested in attracting men and diversifying the characteristics of your staff, consider using words that are more attractive to men. These words include *physically active, outdoors, fun,* and *socially important work*. Many men think in terms of this last phrase to rationalize the low wages they receive.

Advertising directly for male staff with the words *Men wanted* is unacceptable to most newspapers. Yet it is an acceptable practice to add a line to the advertisement that says *Men encouraged to apply*. The reason for this is that the standard for child care positions is women and this line draws the attention of the advertisement to a target audience of men without excluding women.

Such a line is similar to other frequently seen phrases such as *Equal opportunity employer, Committed to workplace diversity,* and, particularly in higher education, *Women and minorities encouraged to apply*. However, in this case, the intent is not one of affirmative action — to provide employment opportunity to members of a group who have previously been excluded. Instead, the intent is to provide children with the presence of men. The additional cost of this phrase will likely be the cost of adding one more line to the classified advertisement — the price of which will vary from newspaper to newspaper.

Most classified advertisements are placed under the categories of *day care, child care, preschool, teachers,* or *education*. These are appropriate places for the position but are not the first places many men tend to look. An alternative strategy is to place advertisements in categories that men will be more likely to see. These categories include *activities coordinator, recreational supervisor, playground supervisor, computer applications with children,* or *general labor*. The idea is that an entry level position of teacher aide or teacher assistant in many programs has important but very general qualifications.

Advertising the position in a way that will bring it to the attention of men is a first step in getting men to apply for the position. This idea need not be deceptive when the advertisement also includes more detailed information that is also given to potential applicants making phone inquiries and to those actually applying.

Another strategy for placing advertisements is to seek out alternative publications in the community. Many larger cities, for example, have a men's organization that distributes a newsletter with articles about men's issues, events, gatherings, support groups, and other services of interest to men. While the circulation of these publications will be small and not approach the circulation of a daily newspaper, the readership will be almost entirely male.

Asking the Right Questions

In a job interview, it is important to ask questions that elicit information about the qualifications of the applicant. Yet, when a man is interviewed, particularly by a panel of women, he may be reluctant to admit a lack of experience or he may not recognize relevant experiences that apply to the position. The women who are interviewing the man may subconsciously believe that a man is not entirely capable of working with young children and may not ask enough probing questions.

In this situation, general questions such as *Tell me about yourself* will not reveal the most important kinds of information. More specific questions that lead applicants to speak about relevant experiences are needed, and these include:

Have you worked around young children or youth before? Have you been involved . . .

- *in sports as a coach or referee?*

Getting Out the Word

A variety of other strategies can be used to attract men. These include:

- Encourage your staff to recruit applicants for vacant positions. This word-of-mouth advertising can be effective when linked to cash incentives. Typically such incentives include a cash reward to the employee at the time the person he/she referred signs a contract. Another reward (sometimes split between the two employees) may be made when the new employee, in this case a man, completes a probationary period.

- Establish a resumé bank of potential male applicants. Invite currently employed men and men in teacher training programs to submit resumés and then inform them as positions become vacant.

- *in swimming lessons or as a lifeguard?*

- *as a playground supervisor or recreational supervisor?*

- *in a church youth group?*

- *as a counselor at a summer camp or an outdoor school?*

- *with a scouting group?*

- *in babysitting younger siblings or neighborhood children?*

When the man answers yes to one of these questions, it is important to follow up with more probing questions to find out how the involvement in these activities applies to the position. Such questions include:

What kinds of things did you do? Did you . . .

- *plan activities?*

- *teach a skill?*

- *supervise children? how many? what ages? for how long at a time?*

- *enforce rules? discipline children? break up a fight?*

- *keep written records? attendance? scores? an activity log?*

- *care for equipment? what kind of equipment?*

- *meet parents? explain activities to parents?*

Retaining Men

Once men are hired, it is important to retain them. Many men who are the only man on a staff of women experience feelings of isolation (Nelson & Sheppard, 1992). Yet men will stay in an environment they feel is equitable, safe, values men, and supports them in personal and professional growth.

If you have a man on staff, make sure the assignment of tasks to men and women is equitable. For example, are male staff able to work with all age groups of children rather than just the older groups of children? Do male staff have the opportunity to work with different groups of children or is the man placed with the children most in need of guidance in the assumption that he will provide the guidance that is needed? Are men automatically scheduled to spend more time on the playground than female staff? Men may enjoy spending more time out of doors but often resent being automatically expected to do so.

Think about other job-related tasks such as taking out the garbage, lifting heavy objects, and changing light bulbs in high places. Of course, men will do these things but will certainly resent always being expected to do so.

Consider whether men are allowed the same freedom in their individual teaching style as are women. Many male teachers develop a style that includes activities that are more physically active, louder, messier, and involve more humor, joking, and silliness. This style is appropriate under the broad umbrella of developmentally appropriate practices and can be a valuable addition to the styles of other teachers in a program.

Men will continue to work in an environment in which they feel safe and protected. Many men feel they are but one false accusation away from having to leave a satisfying career working with young children. It is important to have policies that protect men — and all staff —such as those specifying that no staff person is left alone with a child.

Men also feel protected when they receive support from their supervisors. This is particularly important when parents raise questions about the appropriateness of a man doing certain tasks such as diapering infants and toddlers. A supervisor can use such an opportunity to educate the parents by referring to the policy that speaks to the importance of men as competent caregivers. This kind of support affirms the status of a man as a valued member of the staff who can and will perform all tasks required by the profession.

Valuing Men

Male staff are inclined to stay in a work environment that values men. Images of men — such as fathers with children — on posters, bulletin boards, and other wall decorations reflect this importance. Magazines in a staff lounge, a parent lounge, and a lobby area should reflect the interests of men as well as women. Work uniforms can be modified or adapted to emphasize that men are staff members, too. Social activities among staff can include talk and activities that are also of interest to men. A good way to examine the workplace environment is to spend some time answering the question *What would our program look like if half the staff were men?*

Another way of examining the overall environment is to consider the degree to which it is *father friendly* (McBride & Rane, 1996). A key idea here is the amount of father involvement your program has generated. For example, *Do as many fathers come to parent activities as mothers?* The attitudes and practices that support the involvement of fathers are the same kinds of things that will retain male staff (Levine, Murphy, & Wilson, 1993).

It is also important that men see the topic of men intentionally included in staff training activities. For example, when diversity is addressed — in any of its many forms of parent involvement, staff working relationships, and multicultural/anti-bias curriculum — make sure the topic of men is included in the discussion. Address and challenge the common assumptions that all evils in our society are the fault of men. Explore the significant contributions men make to child development; debunk the many stereotypes of men as being uncaring or inherently untalented to care for young children.

Examine how our society does not always favor men in that the vast majority of the homeless, alcoholics, substance abusers, and victims of violent crime are men — and that men have a shorter life expectancy than women. In sexual harassment training sessions, make sure that the discussion and the examples given do not always assume that the harasser is a man and the victim is a woman.

Men will want to stay in an environment where they have opportunities for personal and professional growth. Men who are just beginning in the field will appreciate flexibility in their work schedule and tuition support to continue their education. Men who have been in the field for some time will appreciate opportunities, encouragement, and freedom to undertake interesting projects, such as working with different age groups of children to develop new teaching skills, planning innovative curriculum activities or materials, becoming more involved with parent-involvement activities — perhaps in the form of a father and child event or ongoing series of father and child activity nights.

Male staff also feel less isolated when they have the opportunity to interact with other men in the field. The presence of more than one man on a staff and the presence of fathers and male volunteers has a snowball effect which makes the environment increasingly friendly towards men. Consider sponsoring a group of male teachers who wish to meet on a regular basis by providing space for a meeting, or supporting the publicity of such a group through a mailing, or providing a continental breakfast or refreshments for such a meeting.

Finally, it is important to support worthy wage and cost, quality, and affordability initiatives. One of the reasons many men give for not entering or for leaving this field is the low wages. Men, and all staff, need to know that this is an issue that is being addressed.

References

Levine, J., Murphy, D., & Wilson, S. (1993). *Getting men involved: Strategies for early childhood programs.* New York: Scholastic Inc.

McBride, B., & Rane, T. (1996). *Father/male involvement in early child-hood programs.* ERIC/EECE Digest, EDO-PS-96-10.

Nelson, B., & Sheppard, B. (1992). *Men in child care and early education.* Stillwater, MN: nu ink press.

Acknowledgments

Several individuals contributed to this article by previewing earlier drafts and offering additional ideas and feedback. They are: Bryan Nelson, Wendy Roedell, Bruce Sheppard, Gregory Uba, and Steve Weber.

Bruce Cunningham has worked in early childhood settings as an assistant, a teacher, a director, and an educator. He is currently an education coordinator with the Early Childhood Education and Assistance Program (ECEAP) through the Puget Sound Educational Service District in Seattle, Washington.

Chapter 2

Developing Policies and Procedures

An Ounce of Prevention:
How to Write an Employee Handbook

by Joe Perreault and Roger Neugebauer

Hopefully your employee handbook will be the best written document you never use.

In an ideal world, you and your employees will work in perfect harmony, with communication flowing back and forth unhindered and work being performed in an exemplary fashion. In this dream world, your employee handbook will gather dust on the shelf.

In the real world, however, even the best-intentioned director is going to encounter frustration, anger, and disappointment in working with others. You may fail to clearly explain all center rules and procedures to a new employee, or exhibit poor judgment in denying a raise to an old employee. Teachers may arrive late, take shortcuts with health procedures, or make inappropriate remarks to parents.

In the real world, you and your staff periodically will need to refer to an employee handbook to resolve disputes and miscommunications. A well-conceived employee handbook helps soften these bumps and grinds by (1) spelling out what types of behavior are encouraged and discouraged and (2) informing employees about their rights and benefits.

In this article, we will provide some pointers on overall organizational issues such as content, the development process, design, and writing style of an employee handbook.

Cover the Waterfront

An employee handbook should be more than just a listing of rules and rewards. It should serve as a one-stop source of answers to any questions that might arise regarding one's employment. The sample table of contents included in this article demonstrates the range of issues that some centers include in an employee handbook.

In reviewing dozens of personnel documents developed by child care centers, we noted that their most common weakness content-wise was a failure to provide employees with a sense of the history and mission of the organization. At a minimum, an employee handbook should open with a statement of the goals or philosophy of the organization. Such introductory comments provide an important framework for all the rules and procedures that follow.

Manuals that provided the broadest array of information even pulled together descriptions of center routines — procedures for health and safety, problem solving, field trips, emergencies, abuse reporting, grievances, telephone answering, and center visits. Having all such procedures located in one place makes it easier to find than if they are scattered about on various memos and bulletin boards.

Reach Out for Ideas

No matter who makes the final decisions on personnel policies and procedures — whether it be an owner, a board of directors, or a center director — these decisions will be improved if ideas from a variety of perspectives are scrutinized during the development process.

Obviously, employees affected by these decisions can offer valuable insights. Their opinions on the fairness of policies and procedures should be considered before decisions are made. In addition, their opinions on whether the writing is comprehensible are important. If procedures are described poorly, they will not be followed. The fact that a procedure makes sense to the person writing it up is not a measure of how well it will be understood by those who have to carry it out.

It is also useful to do some brainstorming about what needs to be included in an employee handbook. You might ask every member of the organization (teachers, substitutes, cooks, secretaries, and janitors) to write down five "what if" questions that the handbook should answer. For example, people might ask, "What happens if I have sick leave left at the end of the year?" or "What happens if a snowstorm hits in the middle of the day?" or "What happens if a newspaper reporter calls for an interview?"

It may also be stimulating to take a look at the personnel manuals of other child care centers. This might give you some alternatives to consider on thorny policy questions, as well as some ideas on content and design. However, you should avoid borrowing policies word for word from other manuals without modify-

ing them to fit your unique circumstances.

You should also have a lawyer review your handbook before it is printed. He will need to check whether your policies and procedures are in compliance with applicable laws. He might also provide useful advice on whether what you propose is too vague or cumbersome, and whether you are leaving yourself enough flexibility.

Finally, you should have someone who knows your organization very well review your handbook to see if it consistently reflects the style and values of your organization. If your management style is firm and authoritative, your employee handbook shouldn't sound like it was written by Abbey Hoffman.

Likewise, if you run a freewheeling, do-your-own-thing operation, your handbook shouldn't read like the Marine Corps' drill sergeants' rule book. The dissonance between what you say in writing and what you do in real life will confuse and frustrate employees.

Make It User Friendly

Research by the American Management Association found that the major criticisms of employee handbooks by users are problems in finding information, and in understanding what is said. The way a handbook is organized and written will in large measure determine if it helps or hinders the supervisory process. Here are some suggestions for ensuring that the messages you want to convey in a handbook are communicated:

- Start with a detailed table of contents. An employee with a question on reimbursement for travel expenses shouldn't have to wade through the sections on benefits, attendance, and compensation in

order to find an answer. She should be able to find out where to look in the table of contents.

- Number pages consecutively throughout. In other words, don't start numbering over with each section (A1, A2, A3 . . . B1, B2, B3 . . . C1, C2, C3, etc.). This type of numbering makes it easy for editors who need to insert frequent updates, but it is user hostile. How can you turn quickly to page E23?

- If your handbook is more than 20 pages long, consider using some device to visually differentiate major sections. Print each chapter on differently colored paper or use chapter dividers with plastic tabs. Find the book *A Sign of Relief* (New York: Bantam Books, 1984) and see the devices it uses to help make its first-aid information quickly accessible.

- Make it easy on the eyes. Have your final product printed on a letter-quality printer. Choose an easy-to-read type font. Leave plenty of white space on every page. If your resources are limited, spend your money on high quality printing rather than on fancy paper or deluxe binders.

- Don't make it cumbersome to read. The personnel documents we reviewed were printed in all shapes, sizes, and formats. Of all of these, two set-ups seemed to work best. Letter-sized sheets, three-hole punched, to go in a three-ring binder were our first choice. In this format, the pages lie flat — you don't have to hold the pages down to keep from losing your place; updated pages can be easily replaced; and you can insert other center documents in the same binder for convenience.

Our second choice was letter-sized sheets stapled together in the upper left-hand corner. This format worked

Typical Contents of an Employee Handbook

I. **Introduction**
    A. Table of contents
    B. How to use this handbook
    C. How the handbook is updated

II. **Welcome to Hippity Hop Child Care Center**
    A. History of Hippity Hop Child Care Center
    B. Philosophy of Hippity Hop Child Care Center
    C. Goals and mission statement of Hippity Hop Child Care Center
    D. Organizational structure of Hippity Hop Child Care Center

III. **Terms of Employment**
    A. Categories of employment (i.e., permanent full time, permanent part time, temporary part time, probationary, substitute, etc.)
    B. Job descriptions
    C. Hiring (posting vacancies, screening procedures, hiring of relatives, physical exams and other pre-employment requirements, and non-discrimination statement)
    D. Compensation (salary plan, timekeeping, pay periods, pay days, overtime)
    E. Supervision and evaluation
    F. Discipline and termination
    G. Voluntary resignation
    H. Grievance procedures

IV. **Expectations of Employees**
    A. Attendance (hours, absenteeism, lateness, inclement weather days)
    B. Staff development (participation in meetings, planning, and training)
    C. Interactions with children (guidelines for interactions with, and discipline of, children)
    D. Interactions with adults (guidelines for written, in person, or telephone communication with parents, staff, board members, visitors, media representatives, vendors, and public officials)
    E. Problem solving procedures
    F. Health and safety procedures
    G. Field trip procedures
    H. Emergency procedures
    I. Reporting requirements (injuries and accidents, suspicion of abuse, safety concerns)
    J. Other requirements (outside employment, dress, eating, smoking, telephoning, leaving premises)

V. **Benefits for Employees**
    A. Time off (holidays, vacations, personal leave, sick leave, jury duty, parenting leave, disability leave, leave without pay)
    B. Bonuses and awards
    C. Insurance (health, life, dental, Social Security, workers' compensation, unemployment, etc.)
    D. Other benefits (breaks, meals, uniforms, travel reimbursement, tuition assistance, reductions in child care fees, retirement plans, etc.)

well for shorter documents because pages can easily be turned. If you choose this format, it works best to print only on one side of the page.

- Use consistent formatting for all center documents — parent handbooks, operations manuals, curriculum guides, business plans. All your documents will be easier to access if the same formatting, style, and organizational logic is followed. This also lends a more professional tone to your efforts, and gives them more credibility.

- Write like you talk. Just because you are writing a manual doesn't mean you have to lapse into unintelligible bureaucratize. After you write a paragraph, read it out loud. If it sounds stilted and clumsy as you talk it, that's how it's going to come across to someone reading it.

- Make it lively. Inject zest into your writing by leading off with a punch, attending to the cadence of your sentences, and sticking to active, colorful words.

- Make the organization abundantly clear. Use headlines and subheads as a road map for the reader to guide him to the exact information he wants as directly as possible.

- Don't sound like a nag. No one enjoys being beat over the head with page after page of rules and restrictions. Set a positive tone by opening with an upbeat summary of the strengths and goals of your organization. Stress the positive environment you are striving to establish for parents, staff, and children. Wherever possible, state your policies and procedures in terms of the positive behaviors to be emulated, rather than the negative behaviors to be avoided.

Create a Living Document

Writing an employee handbook is hard work, plenty of hard work. You don't want to go to all this trouble if the handbook is going to fall into disuse in six months. Make sure your work stands the test of time by making it easy to update. Here are some suggestions:

- The best way to extend the life of any manual is to develop and store it on a computer. That way, when sections require revision, all you have to do is bring up the portions in question on your computer, make the necessary changes, and print out the new version of the page, chapter, or section.

- Whenever you make a change to the handbook, replace at least an entire page. Don't circulate attachments or appendices intended to supersede sections that remain in the manual. Such updates are messy and confusing.

- Enter the effective date on the bottom of every page in your handbook. This minimizes confusion as to which is the current information.

- Do not include in the body of your handbook information that changes frequently or which is explained in detail elsewhere. Package your handbook in a binder with front and back pockets.

A Final Caution

An employee handbook is not the cure-all for employee headaches. Having policies and procedures spelled out clearly in writing doesn't guarantee that they will be carried out.

Look upon the handbook as one means of communicating the policies, procedures, and priorities of the center to employees. To ensure that all staff are performing appropriately, you need to supplement written guidance with an active orientation, ongoing staff development, and responsible supervision and monitoring.

A well-written employee handbook is an important cornerstone of an effective supervisory process. It sets sights, clarifies expectations, and establishes ground rules. Hopefully, all other components of the supervisory process will work so well that this handbook will seldom be used.

Developing Your Employee Handbook: Leave Policies

by Joe Perreault and Roger Neugebauer

In developing your center's employee handbook, you are continually striving to reconcile the personal needs of employees with the day-to-day realities of operating your center. No section of your handbook better exemplifies this balancing act than the policies regarding time away from work.

All workers need opportunities to restore their physical and emotional health and to deal with personal and civic responsibilities. At the same time, in order to provide a quality service, a child care program needs to maintain a high level of continuity in its staffing. The center's leave policies should, therefore, seek to fulfill employees' need for time off in a way that maintains a consistent staffing pattern.

Finding the right balance is not easy. Since no two centers share exactly the same mix of resources, goals, educational philosophies, and management styles, there is no ideal set of leave policies that will work in every center. In fact, in reviewing employee handbooks from over 50 child care organizations in preparing this article, we found over 50 unique versions of leave policies.

In this article, we will outline for you the many choices that you will need to make — the questions you will need to answer — in molding leave policies to meet the needs of your center. In addition, we will share examples of the varied policies that centers have adopted. (Note: Centers whose leave policies are cited are listed at the end of this article. We have not credited excerpts specifically since, taken out of context, they may not fairly reflect a center's overall posture.)

Vacation Leave

How much vacation time should be offered? Centers typically grant full-time employees between five and ten days of vacation time per year, with the average closer to ten days. The number of days granted increases as employees accrue years of service, usually at the rate of one additional day per year.

Should part-time and temporary employees be granted vacations? Some centers grant vacation time only to full-time employees. However, as it is becoming harder to recruit qualified staff, more centers are offering such benefits to help attract solid part-time staff. Often vacation time for part-time staff is granted in proportion to hours worked. For example, a teacher working half time would be granted one half the vacation time of full-time teachers.

When can vacation time be taken? For new teachers, there is often a probationary period during which vacation time cannot be taken. Typically this waiting period is 90 days but extends as long as six months in some centers. In most centers, new teachers still accrue vacation credit during this period.

Most centers require that time taken off for vacations be approved in advance, and some even restrict the times during which these vacations can be taken. Some examples:

Vacations shall be planned for the mutual convenience of the staff and the center. In deciding preferences for vacation time, the primary consideration will be the necessary coverage of the center's services. Otherwise, position and seniority of service, as well as mutual agreement among staff, will be considered. Requests for vacation should be made at least one month in advance in writing. These requests will be granted on a first requested, first received basis. No more than two employees in each group may take a vacation at any one time. Employees are encouraged to spread their vacations throughout the year and cooperate in planning their vacations so that everyone may use the periods best suited to their needs.

Vacation must be taken at Christmas time or between June 1 and August 15.

Can vacation time be used in advance or, conversely, not used and carried over from year to year? Most centers require that vacation time must be earned before it is used and that it must be used in the same year that it is earned. Some centers allow time to be carried over, and some even provide that employees can be paid for unused leave upon termination. Frequently, directors have authority to grant exceptions in unusual circumstances. Some examples:

Vacation leave is to be utilized on a yearly basis based upon anniversary of employment. Leave not utilized by anniversary date must be forfeited.

Unused vacation leave may be carried over to the following year to a five day maximum. Accumulated vacation pay, up to a limit of two weeks, may be paid upon termination of satisfactory service if notice is received two weeks in advance.

How will vacation time be calculated? To avoid confusion and disputes, the method of calculating how much leave an employee has earned should be spelled out clearly. It is recommended that this method be as simple as possible. (These points apply equally to all forms of leave.) For example, some centers grant one half day of leave at the end of each pay period. Others credit the employee with one or two days of leave at the end of every full month of service completed by the employee.

Sick Leave

How much time off for sickness should be offered? Centers typically offer full-time employees from seven to twelve days of sick leave per year. Some offer sick leave to part-time employees on a prorated basis. One center offers sick leave to all employees ". . . at the rate of one hour earned for every 21 hours worked."

For what purposes can sick leave be used? Most centers restrict the use of sick leave to instances where the employee is physically unable to perform. Other centers allow it to be used more flexibly. Some examples:

Sick leave may be approved for personal illness or injury, for an employee who is required to take care of an illness in one's immediate family, or for an employee who has been exposed to a contagious disease which might endanger fellow employees or children.

Sick leave may be used for illness of the employee, illness of a minor child residing in the employee's home, for a doctor's appointment which cannot be scheduled during off hours, in the event of a death or serious illness in the immediate family, and for absence due to pregnancy.

How will the appropriate use of sick leave be verified? Many centers insert language and procedures into employee handbooks to protect against the abuse of sick leave. Many require an employee to notify one's supervisor in advance of using sick leave and to provide a doctor's verification of illness for extended periods of leave. Some examples:

An employee who will be absent shall notify the director before scheduled starting time on the first day of illness (or the night before if possible) and each successive day. Request for sick leave for a medical, dental, or optical examination shall be submitted to the director as far in advance as possible.

Approval of sick leave is not automatic. An employee requesting sick leave must notify his/her supervisor of the nature and expected duration of the illness or injury. Employees must keep their supervisor informed about their condition and the probable date of their return to work. Employees who do not keep their supervisor so informed are subject to disciplinary action or termination.

Any employee missing work for health, mental, or emotional reasons can be required by the supervisor to supply a doctor's statement confirming the condition and/or the recovery. The supervisor, not the doctor, has the responsibility and authority to determine if an employee is sufficiently recovered to return to work and if the doctor's written confirmation is sufficient to justify sick leave being authorized.

Any unapproved sick leave taken on the day preceding or following a center holiday shall result in no pay for the holiday itself.

It must be expressly understood that excessive time out for sickness hurts the quality of our program and, therefore, cannot be permitted. If, in the director's judgment, an employee's absences are excessive, counseling, probation, and/or termination with cause will result.

Can sick leave be used in advance or, conversely, not used and carried over from year to year? Most centers provide the director with the authority to grant sick leave in advance when circumstances merit. In addition, most centers allow employees to accumulate sick leave and carry it over from year to year (this practice is more common than allowing employees to carry over annual leave). The amount of sick leave that can be accumulated ranges from 20 to 132 days, with most falling in the 30 to 50 day range. About half the centers surveyed pay staff members for unused sick leave upon termination.

Personal Leave

In recent years, there has been a movement toward personal leave. This is a catch-all leave category that employees can use for personal reasons that don't fit into any other leave categories. Some centers grant vacation leave, sick leave, and personal leave; other centers grant vacation leave and personal leave; and some centers have gone so far as to consolidate all leave into one overall personal leave category designed to cover the entire range of an employee's needs for time off.

Proponents of personal leave argue that it sets up a more professional relationship with employees. They are no longer required to play the *calling in sick* game, or dip into precious vacation leave, when what they really need to do is care for a sick family member, entertain visiting relatives, meet with their lawyer, or take a day away from work to restore their emotional energy.

Opponents, on the other hand, argue that loosening leave policies in this way encourages employees to take more days off. These fears tend to be misplaced. Personnel studies have consistently shown that the amount of time off that employees take is much more dependent upon their satisfaction with their work environment than it is upon the strictness of the leave policies. In other words, employees who are unhappy with their jobs will take as much time off as they can, and employees who are highly motivated will take little time off.

Leave Without Pay

Under what circumstances will an employee be granted leave without pay? There are two general categories for leave without pay — voluntary and involuntary. Voluntary leave without pay applies when an employee needs to take time off for an extended period and does not have enough vacation or sick leave to cover this time. In this category, centers typically include leave for serious illness, pregnancy, education, or other urgent personal reasons.

Involuntary leave without pay is charged when an employee is absent from work without authorization (for example, if an employee failed to show up for work and didn't call in ahead of time as required by center policies) or when the director determines that the employee is unable to carry out his/her responsibilities (for example, if an employee was ill or injured).

What restrictions apply? Many centers restrict leave without pay to full-time employees who have been with the center for a minimum period of time. This time period ranges from six months to two years. Centers usually require that the employee request such leave 30 to 180 days in advance in order for the center to find a replacement. Some centers place a limit of anywhere from three months to two years on the length of a leave of absence.

What benefits does an employee retain while on leave without pay? In most cases, employees on leave without pay status do not accrue annual leave or sick leave, nor do they earn credit toward length of service salary increments. Some centers specifically state that an authorized leave without pay will not constitute a break in service in determining continuing eligibility for seniority and the retirement plan.

Some centers maintain the employee's medical insurance coverage up to three to six months, while others require that the employee bear the full cost of premiums in order to maintain coverage while on leave. An employee placed on leave without pay due to a job-related disability may be eligible for compensation under the Workers' Compensation Act.

Is the employee guaranteed a job upon return? Centers tend to be guarded in the language they use in this area:

If during your leave of absence it becomes necessary to fill your position, we will make every effort to return you to a similar position at a similar hourly rate. However, we cannot guarantee that a position will be available.

Other Forms of Leave

Jury duty. Centers allow employees time off with pay when they are summoned to serve on a jury. A typical policy reads:

Employees called for jury duty will be paid the difference between their regular base salary and the amount received as compensation for jury duty. A copy of the summons must be presented to your supervisor as soon as it is received. The center reserves the right to request an exemption from jury duty for an employee. No leave is charged for jury duty.

Military leave. Federal law requires that employers provide employees leave for certain forms of military service. One center's policy:

Employees who present official orders requiring attendance for a period of active military duty will be entitled to military leave with full pay, less that paid for military service, for a period not to exceed two weeks.

Bereavement leave. Most centers grant employees up to three days of leave with pay to attend the funeral of an employee's or spouse's immediate family member (spouse, children, sister, brother, parent, grandparent).

A Final Caution

The purpose of this article was to outline the range of choices you should address when developing your center's leave policies. Since labor laws vary in all states and localities, this was not intended to provide legal advice. Before adopting your policies, you should have your lawyer review them in terms of applicable local, state, and federal labor laws. While centers have a great deal of latitude in the policies they develop, in certain areas — such as maternity leave, disability, jury duty, and military leave — legal restrictions will apply.

Sources of Examples

Central Learning and Day Care Center, Memphis, TN; Child Care Center, Evanston, IL; Child Inc., Austin, TX; Children's World Learning Centers, Golden, CO; Day Nursery Association, Indianapolis, IN; Episcopal Child Day Care Centers, Jacksonville, FL; Handicapped Children's Association, Johnson City, NY; Ithaca Child Care Center, Ithaca, NY; Jane Addams Day Care Center, Toms River, NJ; Janet Rich Day Care Center, Rochester, NY; Mercy Child Development Center, Des Moines, IA; Mercyhurst Child Care Center, Erie, PA; Moffett Road Baptist Child Development Center, Mobile, AL; Neighborhood Centers Association, Houston, TX; Nursery Foundation, St. Louis, MO; Ohio State University Child Care Center, Columbus, OH; Playcare Child Care Centers, Rochester, NY; Presbyterian Child Development Center, Wellsboro, PA; Rainbow Chimes, Huntington, NY; Reston Children's Center, Reston, VA; Summit Child Care Center, Summit, NJ; The Learning Center, Jackson, WY; and United Day Care Services, Greensboro, NC.

Developing Your Employee Handbook: Job Descriptions

by Joe Perreault and Roger Neugebauer

A job description is a simple but complete description of the duties involved in the performance of a particular job. If used properly, a job description can be an effective tool in the supervision of the individual employee. An employee handbook is useful because it covers a wide range of topics the employee needs to know, but a job description zeros in on the one job the employee is most interested in — his own.

The job description tells the employee what is expected and to some degree offers guidance on how to perform the job. It can be used to orient a new worker or in the ongoing supervision of an employee. Because the job description is a clear statement of duties, the employer can also use it to hold the employee accountable for performing the job satisfactorily.

A job description contributes to effective center management in other ways, too:

- Before filling a staff vacancy, it is important for people involved in the hiring process to read the job description to be certain that potential candidates meet all the qualifications the job calls for.

- The job description is used to determine the dollar worth of the job. That is, information about education, experience, and the nature of the work contained in the job description are the basis for deciding the salary of anyone hired to work in the job.

- Some directors review job descriptions as part of a process to develop a yearly training plan for staff.

- Job descriptions can be used to document compliance with state or federal personnel laws.

- Finally, the total set of job descriptions in the center helps clarify roles. A complete list of jobs is a composite of all the major duties at the center, and it ensures that all duties are assigned and helps eliminate overlapping job responsibilities.

Getting Started

The simplest way to write a job description is to collect job descriptions from other child care centers similar in size and organizational sponsorship to your own. Job descriptions vary from center to center in terms of how much information or how detailed a description of duties is included. Some centers use the employee handbook or a center policy manual to describe job expectations that are common to all employees and do not need to include this information in each separate job description. In other cases, the job description is the only document being used by the center to convey a written message about job expectations so each job description is lengthy.

Another factor influencing the content of job descriptions is the age and organizational maturity of the center. Brand new centers typically have short job descriptions. Usually a new director has little time to write job descriptions and needs just enough information to determine which candidates qualify for each vacancy. A new center usually describes each job in general terms because there is a need for staff to be flexible while the new center gets off the ground.

In a more established center, job descriptions tend to be more specific about expectations and duties. In these settings, the director is more likely to be using the job description as a supervisory tool. Staff may even have requested more detailed job descriptions because clear job descriptions represent a clear and orderly process of assigning duties and evaluating jobs. Assuming that your center has or is willing to develop an employee handbook, the authors believe a well written job description should be from one to three pages in length. It should be fairly detailed, although it is not possible or desirable to identify every single duty that the job entails.

What to Include in the Job Description

All job descriptions have certain basic elements:

Job title. The job title is simply the name your center chooses to give to a certain job or class of job. Most organizations try to develop job titles that are simple and descriptive of the nature of the job. That is why a director of a child care center is called a *director*. It is simple and to the point.

Deciding on the job titles in a child care center is relatively easy. There are some points to consider, however.

Each job title in the center should be sufficiently different from every other job title so the average person can tell the difference. For example, most centers think that the employee in each classroom who has primary responsibility in that classroom has a more responsible job than any other employee(s) who works in that same classroom. Thus the person who has overall responsibility is usually

called the *teacher, lead teacher,* or *head teacher,* while anyone else in that room is called an *assistant teacher, teacher's aide,* or *aide.*

A job title should convey a positive image about the job. Some people think the title *custodian* is a more positive title than *janitor*. Some people think that the title *food service worker* is a more positive title than *cook*. Sometimes the discussion of what title to use seems frivolous. Actually, the debate is almost always based on a sincere attempt to tell an employee his job is important and contributes to the professionalization of the child care industry. Be prepared for a little healthy debate on job titles.

Job summary. A job summary is a brief description highlighting the general characteristics of the job. It is usually three to eight sentences in length. It indicates clearly what the employee must do and includes sufficient information to identify the major function and activities of the job. When announcing a job opening, the job summary is often quoted to job applicants or printed in newspaper advertisements.

The job summary usually contains a statement defining who is the immediate supervisor of the employee. For example, the job summary of the cook might say "the cook reports directly to the director," or the teacher aide summary might say "the teacher aide will be supervised by the head teacher." Acknowledging the supervisory line of authority helps the employee know who to go to with a question or how to get clarification about a specific job expectation.

Description of duties. The description of duties is a more detailed statement of what is necessary to perform the job. It lists all major tasks, particularly tasks for which the employer intends to hold the employee accountable. Sometimes

the description deliberately identifies job duties that may not be pleasant as a way of forewarning the employee that this is a required duty. Sometimes tasks which are performed infrequently but which are important are included.

Job requirements. This portion of the job description identifies any qualifications a person must meet in order to be hired for the job. Some qualifications may be determined by the child care licensing standards in your state. Be sure to write every one of these qualifications into the job requirement section. Most qualifications, however, will be determined by you, based on your knowledge of what education, experience, and personal qualities are required to do the job well.

It is important to have education and experience requirements on most jobs, but it is wise to avoid writing requirements in such a way that the position is hard to fill. To avoid this dilemma, job descriptions often specify several different combinations of education experience that could meet the job requirements.

"But it's not in my job description."

Sooner or later an employee is going to make this statement as a way of implicitly or explicitly refusing to perform a task you have asked her to do. Even if the duty is not specifically mentioned in the job description, don't despair. Unless your job descriptions are negotiated as part of a collective bargaining agreement with a union, they need not be absolutely inclusive. It is generally recognized that a job description identifies a range of duties that is normal for that particular job but does not cover every single duty that will be required. The duties listed are illustrative rather than exhaustive. Many job descriptions include a

Sample Job Description

Head Teacher

The head teacher is responsible for the supervision and management of a classroom in accord with the goals and curriculum plan of the Hippity Hop Child Care Center. The principal duties of the head teacher include: develop action plans, carry out activities on a daily basis and evaluate the effectiveness of child development activities, supervise staff assigned to assist in the classroom, ensure the safety and physical well-being of the children, maintain regular communication with parents, and contribute to the effective operation of the overall child care center program. The head teacher reports to the child care center director.

Description of Duties

- Plan and conduct an effective child development program to meet the physical, social, emotional, and intellectual needs of each child. This should be done based on the goals and general curriculum plan of the Hippity Hop Child Care Center.

- Ensure that child care routines are carried out in a manner that is prompt, hygienic, and consistent with the good child development principles. This includes routines related to diapering, potty training, hand washing, tooth brushing, eating, napping, and transitioning between activities.

- Ensure the safety of children through constant supervision, effective arrangement of space, proper maintenance of equipment, and regular practice of fire drills and other emergency procedures.

- Operate the classroom in compliance with all child care licensing standards, paying particular attention to ensure that standards prohibiting corporal punishment are obeyed.

- Provide supervision to all staff assigned to the classroom and include staff in planning and child development assignments.

- Create a pleasant, inviting classroom atmosphere in which children feel comfortable and secure.

- Provide positive guidance to help children develop the ability to be self-disciplined.

- Provide experiences which promote individual self-expression in conversation, imaginative play, and creativity.

- Provide a variety of language stimulation activities.

- Provide experience involving thinking skills such as generalizing, classifying, sorting, and problem solving.

- Provide a variety of opportunities to help children develop and understand appropriate relationships with others.

- Ensure that parents receive adequate information about their child's experiences at the center through daily contacts and regularly scheduled parent conferences.

- Maintain written records designed to evaluate each individual child as well as the class as a whole.

- Contribute to the operation of the center by participating in staff meetings and sharing information gained through attendance at workshops and professional reading.

- Work as a member of a team to ensure continuity of curriculum and a high standard of quality in all classrooms in the center.

Job Requirements

Education and Experience

A college degree in child development or early childhood education and at least one year of experience teaching in a part-day or full-day program for preschool children; or

A college degree in an appropriate human service or education field (e.g., psychology, special education, music, social work) including some courses in child development, and at least two years teaching in a part-day or full-day program for preschool children; or

An associate degree in child development or early childhood education and at least two years experience teaching in a part-day or full-day program for preschool children; or

A child development associate credential and at least three years experience teaching in a part-day or full-day program for preschool children.

Personal Qualities

Must be physically able to perform the job of a teacher of young children. Must have a warm, supportive attitude toward children. Must be reliable. Must be flexible in receiving assignments or adapting to changes in the program. Must be willing to accept supervision in order to improve work performance.

---

general statement "and other duties as required" as a way of putting the employee on notice that certain other duties will be required. Whether you add this statement or not, you do have the right to expect an employee to perform duties not specifically stated in the job description.

Furthermore, a child care center is a living organism where conditions change from time to time; and job duties will, of necessity, change, too. An employee who says "It's not in my job description" may be raising a reasonable question about new responsibilities that have been added, making it hard to fulfill all the responsibilities of the job. It may be time to reassess duties and rewrite job descriptions.

On the other hand, "It's not in my job description" may, in fact, be a refusal to perform a duty. If that is the case, a discussion of the language of the job description probably will not help the situation. It is time to step away from the written tools of supervision and use your very best interpersonal skills to find out what really is the problem and how you can work with the employee to change his attitude and motivation.

Summary

A job description conveys to the employee the importance of the job to the overall success of the center. A job description is a brief statement usually one to three pages long. It cannot convey as much information as an employee handbook, but it is the one written document that speaks directly to an employee about her particular job. For this reason, a well written job description can contribute to effective employee motivation, and it is an important tool in the supervision process.

Developing the Employee Handbook: Grievance Procedure

by Joe Perreault and Roger Neugebauer

At the heart of every grievance are fundamental questions about the rights and responsibilities of employment.

Usually when a group approaches an employer with a complaint, they are unhappy with a center-wide decision or with a broad question of the employer's attitude to employees.

Hippity Hop Child Care Center used to be such a nice place to work. But lately things haven't been going so well. Several employees seem to be unhappy. As it turns out, they have different complaints:

Mary took two days off to attend a funeral. When she returned, the director told Mary that the days off would be without pay. There is no funeral leave policy at the center; vacation leave must be requested two weeks in advance. Mary thinks the policy is unfair since she had earned several vacation days.

Anne, an aide at the center, has a new lead teacher who has been critical of her work. Recently, the lead teacher told Anne that they will no longer meet together to plan. From now on, the lead teacher will plan and conduct all teaching activities. Anne will be responsible for clean up after activities and supervision of the children during meals, naptime, and bathroom breaks. Anne has always

been treated as an equal by other lead teachers and resents this new definition of duties.

Lynne, Karen, and Jackie are teachers in the toddler group. They are feeling a growing resentment toward the teachers in the preschool group. From their perspective, the preschool room is consistently given more supplies and equipment than the toddler room.

Why a Grievance Procedure Is Necessary

Hippity Hop may sound like a director's nightmare. But keep in mind, it's a nightmare for the employees, too. At the heart of every grievance are fundamental questions about the rights and responsibilities of employment:

- Does an employee have a right to question the decision or actions of the employer?

- Are there some decisions an employee is automatically entitled to question and others that an employee can question only if the employer grants permission?

- If a grievance is of a very serious nature, should an employee be given an opportunity to communicate directly with the owner or board of directors rather than through the normal chain of command?

- If an employee has a right to express a grievance, how can the employee be given a "fair" hearing and protected from being punished for exercising that "right"?

Most employers recognize there are times when an employee's grievance needs to be heard. It may be that a decision affects the employee negatively and the employer is not aware of the full implication of the decision. It may be that an individual supervisor is acting contrary to the intention of the organization. Yet, how does an employer acknowledge these potential failings of the organization and give the employee a chance to petition for a change? The employer must make an enlightened decision, one that spells out the rights of an employee to air a grievance and which set limits on the kinds of grievances and the extent to which a grievance will be heard. These issues should be clearly spelled out in the center personnel policies in a section entitled "Grievance Procedure."

What Is a Grievance Procedure?

A grievance procedure is simply a written statement informing employees that they have a right to express complaints and a right to expect the employer to review and respond to the complaint. The grievance procedure is generally designed to address two basic issues:

1. Interpretation of personnel policy. No matter how clear the personnel policies, there are always judgment call situations, as well as new situations which do not seem to fit the written policies. Because these possibilities exist, the grievance procedure usually allows an employee to seek interpretation or review of personnel policies when necessary. In some grievance procedures, the language is more open-ended, allowing the employee to question other kinds of center decisions which have a clear relationship to the employee's specific job.

2. Employee-supervisor conflict. Incidents of sharp disagreement between an individual employee and the immediate supervisor occur in child care as in all work settings. A grievance procedure accepts that reality and explains how an employee can appeal a decision or action of the supervisor to a level of supervision higher in the organization. If there is no clear way to express a grievance, there is a danger that a weak supervisor becomes a petty dictator and the director or owner will not be aware of the problem.

Acknowledging the employee's right to file a grievance also implies an

---

The Supervisory Process

Employees at the Hippity Hop Center can expect consistent, direct, and constructive information from their supervisor about their work. Supervisors are responsible for helping staff develop the skills and abilities necessary to function successfully in their positions.

After completing the probationary period, employees are assumed to possess the basic skills and qualities necessary for their position. The goal of supervision for these employees is to assure that these skills and qualities are reflected in day-to-day activities, to promote personal and professional growth, and to insure that the center's policies and program philosophy are effectively carried out.

The basic elements in the supervisory process include:

- A clear statement of what is expected through job descriptions and written center policies.

- An opportunity to participate in establishing individual goals.

- A regular mechanism for reviewing information about job performance, including regular meetings with the supervisor or an annual written employee evaluation.

---

employee responsibility. The employee should use every means possible to resolve the conflict directly with the supervisor before resorting to the center's grievance mechanism. In some personnel policies, the employer includes a description of the purpose and process of supervision as a way of emphasizing how disagreements should be resolved routinely.

For a sample grievance procedure and statement of supervisory policy, see "College Avenue School Grievance Procedure" (page 63) and "The Supervisory Process" (above).

What Should Be Included?

The grievance procedure is basically the description of a process: It should state who can initiate a grievance. Most centers allow any employee to initiate a grievance, although some centers limit this right to full time

employees (as opposed to part time or probationary employees). Some centers allow the employee to file the grievance verbally but most require a written statement before the grievance can be formally reviewed. Describing who should receive the grievance is important, especially in larger child care organizations. Should it be the educational coordinator, director, owner, board of directors, or who?

The next issue is how the complaint will be reviewed. Usually a hearing is held within a specified number of days. The employee is allowed to present the grievance fully. In supervisory disputes, the supervisor is also present and is given equal opportunity to explain the situation. Some grievance procedures stipulate that only the employee is allowed to be present at the hearing, while others allow the employee to have witnesses (for the purpose of presenting information) or an advisor present. In some policies, the employee is responsible for proposing a "remedy." That is, the employee must describe the change or action which needs to occur in order for the grievance to be resolved.

The procedure should also assure prompt employer action by stating when a decision on the grievance will be made. Usually the hearing is held within one or two weeks after the grievance is filed, and a final decision about the grievance is made as soon after the hearing as possible.

Finally, the grievance procedure may offer a means of appeal. For example, in some centers the director is expected to make a determination on all grievance issues. If the employee is not satisfied with the director's decision, the employee may then appeal to the board of directors (or owner).

Handling a Group Grievance

If a grievance is filed, it will most likely arise from the interpretation of personnel policy or a supervisory dispute. But what about the example of Hippity Hop where a group of teachers have a grievance? Hopefully, these circumstances will never occur at your center, but you do need to think about how to handle such a grievance.

Usually when a group approaches an employer with a complaint, they are unhappy with a center-wide decision or with a broad question of the employer's attitude to employees. There are lots of possible examples. The issue could be salaries, staff scheduling, a decision to open or close a particular classroom or program, or favoritism of one group of staff over another by the director.

Often when grievance procedures are established, the owner or board does not envision using them to cover a

College Avenue School Grievance Procedure

Initiation of Grievance

- Any permanent employee or group of employees (group may include probationary employees).

- Any parent or group of parents with a child or children presently enrolled in the school.

- Any employee or group of employees of College Avenue Baptist Church.

The complaint must be submitted in written form and signed by all complainants. It must be specific and with documentation of complaint or grievance and with a list of steps already taken to solve the problem.

To Whom Complaint is Addressed

- The initial grievance must be presented to the director in writing. A reasonable time for solution of a grievance must be agreed upon by the director and complainants. A third and neutral party may be called upon to negotiate this time line.

- If no resolution is forthcoming, the grievance may be taken to:
  — the Minister of Education of College Avenue Baptist Church and/or
  — the Children's Committee of the Christian Education Council of College Avenue Baptist Church.

Either of these parties must respond in writing to the complainants within one working week with an outline of their planned course of action. This may include follow-up study, conference with director, or a specific action.

Follow Up

- The written grievance must be responded to with a written proposal for solution and within a period of 15 working days.

- All staff involved in this procedure are guaranteed no undue retaliatory action.

Grievances That Apply to This Procedure

The following are complaints that are valid grievances:

- Breach of licensing regulations.

- Detriment of health and safety of children and/or staff.

- Breach of fair labor standards.

Reprinted from Staff Handbook of the College Avenue School in San Diego, California — Kathryn Prickett, director.

group situation. Although the inter-personal dynamics of a group grievance are complex, the principles for handling the grievance are similar to any other individual grievance and can be used to give the group a fair and objective hearing.

Some centers address the issue of group grievances in personnel policies, although not necessarily directly. These centers include statements which talk about communication, decisionmaking, or even conflict resolution. For example, they might describe the purpose of staff meetings, how often staff meetings are held, and what role staff is expected to play. They might also discuss how staff are involved in making certain kinds of program decisions related to curriculum, equipment, or other decisions affecting daily work or the long term success of the center. These statements show staff that they will be listened to. They describe the appropriate time and place to raise questions or state disagreements. The more these mechanisms are provided, the less likely that the center will be caught by surprise some day with a group grievance.

Improving Employee Benefits: Doing the Right Thing

by Joe Perreault

Employees believe that if they commit a significant part of their life to reaching the goals of their employer, the resources of the employer should be used to meet their individual goals.

Summarizing studies from around the country, the Institute for Women's Policy Research in a report entitled High Skill and Low Pay: The Economics of Child Care Work stated that "only one-third to one-half of child care workers have any kind of employer-provided health care coverage . . . [and] retirement pensions and life insurance are received by perhaps one-fourth of child care employees."

Do you remember **Car 54 Where Are You**? It was a TV comedy several years back about two likable but inept policemen. The theme song describes crises happening all over the Bronx and finally the police dispatcher calls out, "Car 54 where are you?" You would like to believe the heroes can solve the myriad problems described, but you suspect they will only make matters worse.

As a director, you may feel the same way about employee benefits. Where do I begin? What benefits should I offer? Why add health benefits when other employers are trying to cut back on the cost of health benefits? Why spend compensation dollars on benefits at all? Wouldn't employees prefer higher wages rather than wider benefit coverage?

There are no easy answers for the director/hero who wants to improve employee benefits. However, there are reasons to understand your staff's benefit needs and work toward improving the benefits you offer. This article presents an overview of why benefits are needed in child care and describes dilemmas in improving your benefit package. Two additional articles are planned on health insurance and other benefits for small employers.

Developing Your Philosophy about Employee Benefits

As a child care employer, you may be offering almost no benefits or a relatively generous benefit package. The difference between these extremes is not just a matter of what you can afford. It stems from your belief about the nature of the employer-employee relationship and how you hope to maintain the employee's long term commitment to your center. In making benefit decisions, it is useful to define what your philosophy toward employees is.

You may also be confronted with situations where your *self-interest* conflicts with the employee's *self-interest*. For instance, as an owner or director, you may feel you cannot *afford* to spend any more on benefits while employees feel they cannot *afford* to work for you unless wages and benefits are improved. This is clearly a case where employer and employees are far apart. However, keep in mind that employee benefits are a commonly accepted part of American work life because the needs of employer and employees often complement or coincide with each other. In deciding what benefits to offer, remember to analyze how the benefit helps *you* as well as the employee.

Benefits from an Employer Perspective

There are a number of reasons why employers offer benefits:

Federal requirements and tax incentives. Certain benefits including Social Security, unemployment insurance, and worker's compensation are required by federal and state law. These benefits are often referred to as *mandatory* benefits. Mandatory benefits furnish a basic floor of protection to employees. Social Security is most often thought of as a retirement program but it also provides protection to employees who become permanently disabled. In the event of an employee's death, Social Security also provides survivor's benefits to the employee's children until they reach 18.

Unemployment insurance furnishes temporary benefits to an employee who is laid off through no fault of the employee. Worker's compensation pays medical bills and provides income to an employee who is injured on the job.

The government encourages the provision of additional *voluntary* benefits by offering exemption or deferral from taxes. For example, employer sponsored health insurance contributions are tax deductible to the employer.

Pension contributions and some savings plans are tax deductible business expenses for the employer. They are tax deferred income for the employee since pension income is taxed only after it is distributed.

Productivity and quality of work. Leave time — including paid sick, holiday, and vacation leave — is viewed as having the positive effect of relieving stress and improving productivity and work quality. Time away from work helps employees return refreshed and enthused. Using sick leave in the early stages of an illness helps employees return to work sooner.

Recruitment and retention. In an atmosphere where the pool of women interested in working in child care is shrinking, centers may offer benefits as a way to attract and retain workers. Many centers offer free or reduced price child care to their own employees with the intention of recruiting women with young children to work for them. In some cases, centers offer a more generous package of benefits to certain employees. The center is willing to go to extra expense to retain *key* employees whose job skill or contribution is vital to the continued success of the organization.

It's the right thing to do. Most child care employers have a conscience. They work side by side with their employees, sharing successes and failures. They know when the center benefited from the hard work, loyalty, and commitment of individual workers and the entire work force. They know who suggested new and promising ideas leading to the growth of the center. They take an interest in the personal well being of employees. In these centers, it is quite natural for the employer to use benefit coverage as a means of sharing the success of the center with employees.

Benefits from an Employee Perspective

In one sense, the employee perspective is a mirror image of the employer perspective. However, employees have their own slant on benefit issues which should be understood.

Recognition of employee needs. Employees have basic human needs which exist whether the employer chooses to acknowledge them or not. For the sake of employees' sense of dignity and fair play, it is best for the employer to recognize and play a role meeting these needs. Mandatory benefits are primarily designed to ensure workers' personal security against crises associated with work.

However, non-work related crises are equally important to employees and can be protected through health, life, savings, retirement, and other programs.

Pays for or shares the cost. One clear employee expectation is that employers pay for or share the cost of benefit programs. Employees believe that if they commit a significant part of their life to reaching the goals of their employer, the resources of the employer should be used to meet their individual goals. In some cases, individuals only have access to certain benefits through their employer.

Administrative support. The range of alternatives available in the field of health, life, and retirement insurance is complex. Often employees want help in selecting the program or programs which are most desirable. They are willing to share some of this decision with an employer who is able to study the options and receive professional advice before selecting a limited number of choices to present to employees. Furthermore, most employees recognize the convenience involved in having the employer assist in completing forms, processing claims, and deducting the employee's share of costs directly from their pay checks.

A deferred form of compensation. Employer and employee attitudes toward benefits are constantly evolving. When benefits were first introduced, they were considered employer gifts in recognition of long and faithful service. The *employer gratuity* theory meant there was no obligation to provide benefits.

Later on, a *human depreciation* theory arose. Since the employee's value as a worker depreciated over his or her work life, employers were thought to have a moral obligation to provide for their employees when they were too old or ill to continue in the labor force.

More recently, a *deferred employee wages* theory is being advanced. Under this theory, an employee is viewed as having a choice between immediate wage increases versus benefits, particularly pension related benefits. If the employee chooses benefits, the benefits are looked at as a form of deferred wages. This approach is gaining greater understanding and acceptance by employees who have an increasingly sophisticated understanding of their personal financial situation.

Availability of Benefits in Child Care

In recent years, a number of statewide or city-wide salary surveys have been conducted which include questions about benefits. A recent issue of *Child Care Employees News* reports on 19 separate salary surveys performed in 1989, and additional studies have already been completed this year. The information coming in is not positive, although there is some evidence that progress is being made.

Among states surveyed, health insurance is most available to child care workers in Hawaii, where 90% of teachers have coverage. It is least available in Colorado, where only 15% of teachers reported having employer provided health insurance. Reports from other states include Rhode Island (50%), North Carolina (approximately 50%), and Illinois (16%). Among cities, child care workers in San Diego fared best with 41% receiving health coverage, while only 7% of workers in Houston are covered.

Fewer workers are covered by retirement plans. Rhode Island performed best in this category with 50% of workers covered. Other states where data is available are Hawaii (30%), Illinois (24%), North Carolina (24%), and Colorado (11%). Some of the city surveys offer bleak news. Only 9% of center teachers in a northern Virginia

area survey are covered by a retirement plan and only 2% of teachers in Houston are covered.

Summarizing studies from around the country, the Institute for Women's Policy Research in a report entitled *High Skill and Low Pay: The Economics of Child Care Work* stated that "only one-third to one-half of child care workers have any kind of employer-provided health care coverage . . . [and] retirement pensions and life insurance are received by perhaps one-fourth of child care employees."

Before placing blame on child care employers, it should be understood that lack of employees' benefits is a problem facing most small employers in this country. A 1985 study by the National Federation of Independent Business indicates that only 65% of employers with 100 or fewer employees offer health coverage to their workers. According to the Employee Benefit Research Institute, "In businesses with 25 employees or less, only one in seven workers is covered by a company-sponsored pension plan, only 23% working in firms with less than 100 employees have pension coverage."

Child care employers should not necessarily accept the norm of what other small employers offer. However, this information sheds light on the difficulty child care faces in attempting to improve benefit programs. Child care employers should also recognize what employers with 100 or more employees do. A 1986 Department of Labor study of such employers determined that 95% of full time employees received health insurance, 96% participated in employer sponsored life insurance, and 89% were covered by pension plans.

Obstacles to Improving Benefits for Workers

Benefit programs are expensive. Yet, despite the high cost, centers cannot

ignore the need to improve and expand the benefits they offer. In a few states (Connecticut, Massachusetts, and New York), state funds have been appropriated to help centers improve their salary and benefit programs. It is possible that additional states will follow suit or that new federal funds will produce increased revenue for centers which could be used to improve benefits. Even without state or federal help, centers are realizing that improved benefits are a budget priority. They are studying benefit options and learning about the complexities of designing benefit programs. In the course of doing so, a number of common obstacles have been identified:

Lack of group buying opportunities. Most benefit programs are marketed and priced on the assumption that the employer has a large group of employees. But the child care industry has many small employers. When a single center with 10 to 20 employees approaches a health insurance carrier, the carrier may not be interested in selling to the child care center or may have to price the policy so high it is prohibitive. Some employee benefit companies specialize in serving small employers but, even then, the policies are expensive because the employee group is small.

There are ways to achieve the advantage of group buying, and examples of these approaches exist in the child care field. A number of church operated centers secure coverage for their employees through policies purchased by the headquarters of the denomination. Similarly, some centers operated by United Way agencies secure benefits through a program open to all United Way organizations in a given community. Other agencies may have access to benefit packages through national organizations such as NAEYC.

A number of for-profit centers have explored offering benefit programs through their state associations. This approach is difficult but would be an important justification for association membership.

Another route to group buying power is unionization. In a number of industries, the employer pays for the benefits through a union administered policy covering union members in a number of work settings. This is a common practice in the construction industry. The subject of unionization is often controversial; but remember, in this respect, a union could be your ally.

Diverse work forces means diverse needs. Even though you have a relatively small number of employees, chances are these employees have relatively diverse needs. You probably have some unmarried employees, some single parents who are the principal support of the family, and some married employees with both spouses contributing significantly to family income. It is hard to find a benefit that is of equal importance to these three groups. A benefit provider, on the other hand, may want you to buy coverage for all your employees. In that case, you may be paying for benefits for some employees who don't want or need them.

To accommodate these growing differences in employee lifestyles, employee benefit companies have developed the concept of a *cafeteria* benefit program. In this kind of policy, employees can select from a number of options so that the benefits they receive are tailored to their individual needs. The subject of cafeteria benefits will be explored further in a future article.

Salary versus benefits. If you had additional money to spend on employee compensation, should you raise salaries or expand the employee benefit program? If you left this decision entirely up to employees, what would they say? It is quite possible that employees would ask for salary increases, and you may want to honor their wishes. But the issue is more complex than that.

Studies in a number of work settings indicate that young workers are relatively disinterested in the kind of benefits which protect their health or insure their economic security. If you make such benefits available, they may not appreciate your effort. In general, they prefer an increase in salary to an increase in employee benefits.

In contrast, mature workers are conscious of their need for physical and economic security. Sooner or later these workers wonder whether they should continue working for you since you are not able to protect them through various benefit programs. Thus an employer without adequate employee benefits is likely to lose a high percentage of the employees with the most training and most experience. These are the people who function in positions of supervision and leadership. In that respect, it is in the best interest of your child care center to furnish benefits to these workers.

Searching for Solutions

As the foregoing discussion demonstrates, the provision of employee benefits is a complex challenge for all child care employers. In coming issues of *Exchange*, I will offer specific suggestions on the implementation of health and retirement benefits.

If your organization has experienced some success in providing such benefits, I would be eager to include your insights in these articles. Please call *Exchange* at (425) 883-9394 if you would be willing to share your experiences with me and *Child Care Information Exchange's* 26,000 readers.

Joe Perreault is assistant director of Save the Children Child Care Support Center in Atlanta, Georgia.

Improving Employee Benefits: Health Care

by Joe Perreault

Do you have $2,600 to spare? That's what the average American will pay for health care in 1991. A family of four — the so-called typical family — will pay over $10,000 for health care this year. All that money you would like to spend on housing, clothes, food, or maybe even a new car will go for doctors, dentists, medicine, and hospital bills.

Some employees are lucky. Their employer helps pay the cost of health services through an employer sponsored health benefit. Employer sponsored health benefits cover about 75% of American workers and pay for about 35% of all health care in the United States. Many others are not so lucky. Between 31 and 37 million Americans have no health insurance. Either they can't afford health insurance or they can't find an insurance policy at any price because of previous health problems.

Why Are Child Care Employers Involved?

As a child care employer, you have a stake in helping employees maintain good health and secure health services at an affordable price. One strong justification for addressing this issue relates to employee productivity. A healthy employee is on the job and able to reach his or her full potential. An employee who is sick is absent from work and reduces the productivity of the whole center. An employee who can't afford health care puts off seeking treatment for an illness until he or she is severely ill, resulting in a longer period of recuperation and a longer absence from work.

Ironically, child care may be what caused the employee to become ill in the first place. Child care workers are exposed to numerous colds and infectious diseases brought into the center by the children they serve. Even in centers with good disease prevention practices, it is common for new employees to experience a number of illnesses in their first year or more of employment. Back injuries are another common occupational injury in our field. Thus, as a child care employer, you have some responsibility to secure and pay for the treatment employees need.

Until recently, the primary justification for a child care employer providing health insurance was productivity. However, the new bottom line may become recruitment and retention.

It is increasingly difficult to find people willing to work in child care. To address the problem, centers are struggling to make salaries competitive with the other employment options available to the would-be employee. The availability of health insurance may be another critical factor in a successful recruitment and retention plan.

Over the last five years, the cost of health care in the United States has risen 42% faster than the cost of food, housing, or transportation. If this trend continues, employees are going to become increasingly aware that a *good job* means not only a good salary but also a place where their health care needs are being taken care of. You simply may not be able to compete for good workers without offering some form of health insurance program.

What Are the Options?

This article is written primarily for a child care center that does not offer health benefits. According to some studies, two-thirds of all centers do not offer health benefits to their employees. The article may also serve as a useful review for a center which does offer some form of health benefit. A number of alternatives available to an employer are described, including health insurance, health maintenance organizations, and preferred provider organizations.

Factors in selecting the right health benefit for your employees are considered. There are even suggestions of no cost and low cost ways to help your employees with their health care needs.

Health insurance.
The most widely known and used form of health benefit is health insurance. Health insurance is offered by commercial insurance companies, by Blue Cross/Blue Shield organizations, and as a part of the federal Medicare program. Some employers even self-fund and self-administer their health insurance program.

A *basic* health insurance plan covers health care services associated with hospitalization, including outpatient hospital charges, physician care in the hospital, and surgical procedures. Some outpatient services may also be covered, such as emergency treatment as a result of an accident. A health insurance plan that is described as *supplemental* or *comprehensive* covers additional medical services, such as outpatient hospital care, outpatient prescription drugs, and outpatient mental health care.

Basic plans typically limit the amount to be paid for any given employee. Supplemental or comprehensive plans have much higher limits and therefore meet the need for coverage in case of a catastrophic illness.

Health insurance generally excludes services that are not considered medically necessary, including most dental, visual, and hearing care. As a result, separate policies have been developed to cover these needs, or they can be added to a basic plan at an additional cost. Also, health insurance doesn't cover such routine areas as check-ups and immunizations.

Health insurance almost always has a *deductible* requirement. A deductible is a specified amount of initial medical costs that each employee must pay before any expenses are

"I believe that benefits will eventually be a more important employment draw than salaries, simply because ever-increasing taxes and insurance premiums translate ultimately into reduced take-home pay or net income."

— Margaret R. Brewer, the Lincroft Center for Children Lincroft, New Jersey

reimbursed by the plan. This often runs $150 to $250 for an individual, $500 to $1,000 for a family. As the cost of health care has risen, many employers have chosen higher levels of deductibles.

An even more substantial way to share the cost of health care between the employee, the employer, and the insurance company is the concept of *co-payment*. Under a co-payment arrangement, the employee pays a portion of a recognized medical expense and the insurance plan pays the remaining portion. The employee commonly pays 20% and the plan pays 80%.

Health maintenance organizations.
Health maintenance organizations (HMOs) are organizations of doctors and other health care professionals who provide a range of medical services for a fixed dollar amount. The services usually include routine and preventative care, as well as medical, surgical, and hospital care.

Because HMOs accept the risk of providing health care at a cost that does not exceed the fixed fee, they have an economic incentive for monitoring the employee's use of health care services and for keeping costs down.

HMOs also have an incentive to provide care early before illnesses become more serious. Many HMOs encourage adults to get annual physical exams and provide routine check-ups for children. Some HMOs have only full time staff, while others contract with physician groups who serve both HMO patients and patients in their general practice. In either case, a drawback to HMOs is that employees do not get to choose from among all doctors in the community but are limited to the doctors practicing in the HMO. Many employees find this restriction unacceptable.

Preferred provider organizations.
A preferred provider organization (PPO) is a variation of a health insurance plan in which certain health care providers furnish health services at a predetermined fee per service.

Employees covered by a PPO are free to choose any physician or hospital they wish but are given financial incentives to use the services of *preferred* providers. For example, employees who use a preferred doctor might have no deductible and a co-payment of only $5 or $10 an office visit, plus extra services, such as well baby care.

Employees who use a non-participating doctor might be subject to a $100 or $200 deductible, 20% co-payment, and no extra coverage. PPOs contend they reduce costs by selecting cost efficient providers and by applying utilization review techniques.

Selecting the Best Plan

There are many different companies that sell health insurance, and in some communities there is more than one HMO or PPO to choose from. The following factors will help you determine which plan is most suitable for your child care center and for your employees. These factors relate primarily to the selection of health insurance but may apply to a decision about an HMO or PPO also.

Level of Health Care:

• What level of health care do you want to help employees achieve?

Eligibility:

• Are part time employees allowed to participate? Some policies limit participation to employees working 25 hours a week or more.

• Do all employees need to participate (100% participation)? If not, what percent must agree to participate?

• Can the insurance provider exclude an employee who has a pre-existing health problem? Some companies exclude employees entirely who have certain health problems. Others impose a waiting

"Our one year wait (before a new employee is eligible for health insurance) is a long wait for health coverage. I would prefer to begin immediately but in an area of limited resources I prefer to spend the money on "more proven" employees. It's good for retention but difficult on recruitment."

— Robert B. Siegel, Mary Crane Nursery School
Chicago, Illinois

period before an employee is allowed to enroll in the plan.

In some cases, the insurance provider charges higher premiums based on the kinds of pre-existing health problems of employees. On the other hand, some health insurance programs offer a period of *open enrollment* when the plan is first established. During the open enrollment period, the employee may join the program, usually without taking a physical exam or furnishing their previous medical history.

• Can employees continue participation after they leave employment? A federal law referred to as COBRA guarantees that a former employee can continue health insurance for up to 18 months. The former employee must pay the entire amount of the premium including the employer's share.

COBRA applies to employers with 20 or more employees. Some states place similar requirements on employers with fewer than 20 employees. In addition, some policies include a *conversion* provision allowing the former employee to buy a health insurance policy at an individual rate.

Services Covered:

Differences in services covered between basic and supplemental or comprehensive plans are discussed throughout the article. In addition:

• Does the plan cover maternity care, including prenatal check-up, labor and delivery, and post-partum care?

• Are you required to get a second opinion before undergoing certain surgical procedures?

• Are you required to get approval from the insurance plan before entering a hospital (other than an emergency hospitalization)?

• If the plan includes a PPO option, what are the consequences if the employee does not use a preferred provider?

Payment Limits:

• What is the deductible requirement per individual? Per family?

• Is there a co-payment requirement and, if so, what is it?

• How does the insurance carrier define *customary* or *reasonable* fees? Each company sets its reimbursement level based on customary physicians' charges for services in a given area. But one company might reimburse on the charge that represents the 90th percentile while another reimburses only at the 75th percentile.

"Only through my persistence did we get a PPO. The deductible on our health insurance plan is $250, so no one could afford to use it. Now, with the option of the PPO plan, our regular doctors' visits are $10."

— Judy Morris, First Presbyterian Children's Center
San Antonio, Texas

- Is there a lifetime maximum limit to the policy? The lower the limit, the less likely the policy can cover the full cost of a catastrophic illness.

Cost and Renewability:

- Is there an employer participation requirement? Some insurance companies won't sell a plan unless the employer agrees to pay at least part of the cost.

- What is the history of rate increases for the policy? That is, how much has the policy increased during each of the last five years? Also be aware that some companies charge a low rate during the first year in order to get your business and then charge a much higher rate after that.

- Does the employer have the unconditional right to renew the policy? Does the employer have the right to renew but with conditions?

Are There Any Other Alternatives?

Health insurance, HMO, and PPO options all assume that an employer is willing to pay all or a substantial portion of the premium, thus making health care available and affordable to employees. But if you could afford to furnish a health benefit to your employees, I probably wouldn't need to be writing this article in the first place. Representatives of the various plans would be contacting you regularly to solicit your business. You would still have difficult choices to make, but you could make them.

But what about a child care employer who realizes that employees need access to health care but who just can't find money (or much money) in the budget to furnish this benefit? There are a couple of actions you might consider.

Salary reduction plan. An employer can assist employees meet health care needs with little or no expense to the employer by permitting employees to enter a *salary reduction agreement* under which the employer withholds a specified amount from the employee's pay throughout the year and applies the amount to health care expenses. If designed according to Internal Revenue Service requirements, the amounts withheld are not included in the

"We have experienced an annual crisis for the last few years related to our coverage. A 60% increase last year doomed our long term participation in Blue Cross/Blue Shield, but our alternative has been filled with other kinds of grief. We are on shifting sands and feeling that we are all but out of control."
— Carl Staley, United Day Care Services
Greensboro, North Carolina

taxable income of the employee and are not subject to withholding, social security, or unemployment insurance taxes.

The plan must be designed in accordance with IRS Code Section 125. The employer is prohibited from designing a plan that favors the owners or a few highly paid employees, but it is permissible to exclude some employees from participating, such as part time employees and employees under age 21.

At least spend a little. Even if you can't pay the annual premium for health insurance or one of the alternatives, you might consider paying something toward the cost of an

employee's individual policy or paying some of the employee's actual medical expenses.

For example, you could contribute $200 a year to each employee who purchases an individual policy or make a commitment to pay a certain amount of an employee's medical expenses. Employees would have to prove they have medical expenses in order to be reimbursed from the fund. You might include a provision that employees who have a benefit through a spouse are ineligible. That would most likely target your money to lower paid and single parent employees.

If this idea sounds interesting, check it out with a CPA or benefits specialist. It is possible that this contribution is not a deductible business expense or that, in order to make it deductible, you have to administer the benefit in a manner determined by the IRS. It might also be taxable income to the employee.

Options for individual employees. An employee can, of course, purchase health insurance or enroll in an HMO or PPO program as an individual. You might want to provide employees with information about available plans and help them make an informed decision about which to select. The August 1990 issue of *Consumer Reports* analyzes about 50 different plans and rates which is best according to several factors. I suggest you get a copy of the article and share it with your staff.

An employee may also be eligible to buy health insurance because he or she is a member of an association such as the National Association for the Education of Young Children, the Southern Association on Children Under Six, the American Association of Early Childhood Educators, or through a state affiliate of the National Child Care Association. All of these associations and many others offer some form of health insurance as a basic membership benefit.

In theory, the cost of an individual policy purchased through an association should be less than if the employee purchased similar coverage by dealing directly with the insurance carrier. Savings should occur because of the combined negotiating power of the association and other factors. However, you should encourage the employee to compare prices. Some associations' policies are more expensive than others. Some individual policies may be less expensive than a policy purchased through an association.

Possible Medicaid eligibility.

According to staff at the National Center for Clinical Infant Programs, there are some circumstances where lower paid employees or their children under age seven may be eligible for Medicaid. Congress revised the Medicaid program in 1989 so that pregnant women and children under seven are eligible for Medicaid if they meet low income eligibility requirements. The income guideline is 133% of the federal poverty level. For a family of four, that would be

approximately $1,408 per month. Under Medicaid, the child is entitled to a range of preventative services including a comprehensive health screening program. The child will also receive medical treatment or remediation of any health condition as long as it was detected during the screening.

Community-wide efforts.

There are a couple of examples of community-wide efforts to help child care employees gain access to health insurance at an affordable rate. In Rochester, New York, the Western New York Child Care Council works with Blue Cross/Blue Shield to offer a health insurance program called ValuMed. ValuMed offers health insurance coverage "to persons with low income who do not have coverage paid by an employer and do not receive Medicaid or Medicare." Child care workers are eligible to participate if they earn less than 200% of the current federal poverty guidelines and if their employer does not offer any other form of health insurance.

The policy has some deductible and co-payment features; but in addition to hospital inpatient/outpatient services and surgical cost, it also covers maternity care and some well child care costs. The rates are reasonable compared to other policies. Currently, coverage is $39 a month for a single person and $70 a month for a family.

The Western New York Child Care Council plays a role in administering the program which is one of the factors keeping costs down. The Council distributes information about the plan and handles the initial application process and eligibility determination. The Council is also available to answer questions about the program.

Many employers feel overwhelmed by the escalating health benefit premiums of the last few years and by the difficulty of containing the crisis. Child care directors may be tempted to stand on the sideline and wait until things settle down. But child care directors need to show courage and foresight.

Employers have traditionally played a key role in designing appropriate health benefits, sharing in the cost of these benefits, and influencing state and federal policies that affect the health care and health insurance system. Too many child care workers are excluded from adequate health care. You must take on the problem at your individual center level and also join collective efforts of child care associations and business groups.

Joe Perreault is assistant director of Save the Children Child Care Support Center in Atlanta, Georgia.

Chapter 3

Orienting
and
Training Staff

Understanding Adults As Learners

by Nancy P. Alexander

As center directors deal with staff turnover and retention, they often find they must wear another hat — that of trainer. Directors are increasingly spending more of their busy days providing guidance and support to staff who are learning new skills and methods of working with children.

No one expects to learn to play tennis by simply reading a manual. No one expects to be a satisfactory tennis player by having someone tell them how. Regardless of how much one reads about tennis or how much someone is told, no one can be a proficient player without hands-on experience. Learning to play tennis requires heading out to the courts with a racket and ball, practicing with an experienced player, and getting feedback. Otherwise, one will not master the skills necessary to learn to play the game.

We readily recognize the necessity of actual experience in children's learning and in adults learning motor skills. But do we always recognize the value of the hands-on learning that is necessary for child care centers to run smoothly? Or do we rely too much on *reading and telling*?

How do we ensure that the staff in our programs benefit from the training we offer? What are the best conditions for adult learning to occur? Some general principles that must be recognized for effective learning are as follows:

Adults can learn new skills. Few healthy people at any age are incapable of learning new skills. The tremendous surge in adult education, lifelong learning programs, and second careers at retirement attest to the ability to learn at all ages.

The individual must be motivated to learn. This motivation usually must be related to the person's perceived needs. Learners must see the value in changing present behavior, learning new skills, or increasing their knowledge. They must have a clear picture of the importance of what is required and see a benefit to themselves.

Learning is an active process, not a passive one. It takes action and involvement by the individual to master new skills. We easily recognize this fact in our work with children but may forget that adults also need active involvement — and may need much repetition.

The learner benefits from guidance. Trial and error will work in some situations, but it is an extremely time-consuming process. Trial and error may be detrimental to children. Guidance and feedback are essential ingredients for training. The learner must have informational data on "What is expected of me?" and "How am I doing?"

Appropriate materials and activities for sequential learning must be provided. Just as we would not expect children to run before they walk, we cannot expect adults to bypass the developmental steps in their own learning. They may need small steps of learning, with each building on and expanding their existing knowledge base.

Time must be provided to practice, to internalize new ideas or ways of responding, and to build confidence. Too often directors are under pressure to fill a vacancy or to quickly "tell them what is needed." However, learning requires time for assimilation, testing ideas and methods, reflection, and building confidence in implementing new ways of working.

Learning methods should be varied for individual learning styles. Just as with children, some staff will benefit most from visual activities, some

How do we meet the specific learning needs of adults? Here are some suggestions:

- **Give adults much control over their learning.** Adults want to select what and when they will learn. The more they can be involved in the planning and preparation, the more they will be motivated to participate fully.

- **Allow time for interactions with other staff.** Adults almost always rate training very high when they are allowed interactions with each other. This is especially true in heterogeneous groups. Adults often comment that they become aware that their problems are not unique, and that it is helpful to learn about other programs. They learn from each other, and they are more perceptive in understanding their role. Adults need to engage in reflection and dialogue about their experiences. Adult learners should have numerous opportunities to converse with their peers, making use of their own life experiences.

- **Provide times for reflection.** Writing is a valuable technique for reflection for adults. Providing time for adults to record their ideas, experiences, and reactions is very beneficial. Writing also helps to reinforce concepts to be learned.

- **Allow time for training to "take."** Adult learners need time to internalize, digest, and reflect. Allowing time for staff to try out new ideas and then come together to reflect on their experiences is an effective technique to break training into manageable steps.

- **Provide guidance and regular feedback.** Using a partner or a team approach to share information and ideas allows for reaction, clarification, and feedback. There is some evidence that adults learn best from someone who is more advanced than they are but not so far advanced that learners feel intimidated.

- **Allow for various learning styles.** Present information in a variety of ways. Allow for visual, auditory, and kinesthetic learners, and those who need a combination of approaches.

from auditory, some kinesthetic, and many will need to use several sensory modalities. Variety in training techniques also can offset boredom, keeping motivation high.

The learner must secure satisfaction from the learning. This is the old story of "you can lead a horse to water, but. . . ." The learner must see the effort as worthwhile. The "what's in it for me?" question must be addressed to the satisfaction of the learner. If training is not seen by the learner as useful, relevant, and feasible, it will surely fail.

The learner needs reinforcement. Most adult learners need fairly immediate reinforcement. Few can wait for months for behavior to be recognized and rewarded. When rewards such as raises are long range, immediate recognition and appreciation become more important.

Standards of performance should be set in conjunction with the learner.

While learning is individual, and staff will advance at differing paces, most learners like to have benchmarks by which to judge their progress. Adults want control over their training and to know they have a voice that is heard. Setting short-term as well as long-term goals will help learners to see goals as achievable.

There are levels of learning and they take different times and methods. Learning to conduct an art project is different from learning how to plan. The type of learning desired will affect the methods, level of involvement, and techniques that work best. Learning to close the classroom at the end of the day may require a few supervised experiences and a checklist; learning to follow the steps for proper diaper changing will likely require more practice.

When we look at the issue of adult learning and training techniques, we see many similarities in how adults learn as compared to what we know about children's learning. However, these basic differences stand out:

- Adults, by virtue of their life responsibilities, have more barriers to overcome to fully participate in the learning experience. They may have difficulty in focusing on learning new skills if preoccupied with outside demands. They may approach learning with psychological barriers such as past negative experiences.

- Conversely, adults have many experiences upon which to build, and these experiences can be a foundation for their learning. Adults greatly benefit from reflection, sharing, and communicating their ideas and insights with others.

- Adults need to see the relevance of the material to their immediate needs since time limitations and commitments apart from work may make it difficult to make learning a priority. Adults tend to view learning as a means to an end, not as an end in itself.

The similarity of adults as learners to children as learners is captured by Elizabeth Jones when she wrote, "Adult learners, like children, need to play . . . taking initiative, making choices, acting and interacting. Much learning should be playful and exploratory, and people in that stage of learning don't need challenges, they need shared enthusiasm." (Jones, 1986, p. 14).

References

Dean, G. J. (1994). *Designing instruction for adult learners*. Malabar, FL: Drieger Publishing Company.

Jones, E. (Ed.) (1993). *Growing teachers: Partnerships in staff development*. Washington, DC: National Association for the Education of Young Children.

Jones, E. (1986). *Teaching adults: An active learning approach*. Washington DC: National Association for the Education of Young Children.

McKeachie, W. J. (1994). *Teaching tips: Strategies, research, and theory for college and university teachers*. Lexington, MA: D. C. Heath and Company.

Nancy P. Alexander is executive director of Northwestern State University Child and Family Network in Shreveport, Louisiana. Her photographs and articles appear in many publications.

Orienting Staff Right From the Beginning

by Marlene Weinstein and Joe Allen

Orientation is a beginning. Through the orientation process, you begin to mesh the skills and information an employee brings to the job with your ideas about meeting the organization's needs. Orientation provides the information necessary to get started in the right direction so that the newcomer can assume full and competent responsibility for the job as soon as possible.

Orientation enables a new employee to develop an understanding of her relationship to the other employees and to the mission of the organization. It is the process by which the new employee gets her bearings and discovers her place in the overall organizational environment.

An employee's first days on the job present the director with unique challenges, as well as singular opportunities. Those first days are often anxious ones for employees, as they feel like strangers in their new surroundings. One task of orientation, therefore, should be to make the new employee feel welcome, to make him feel at ease. But during those first days, the new employee is also most eager to learn and to do well. Never again will he be so receptive to information you give him about the organization and his role in it. Therefore, an orientation program should capitalize on this zeal. It should instill in him a commitment to the goals of the organization and start him off right with proper work habits.

Common Evaluation Pitfalls (and Some Common Sense Solutions)

Pitfall #1

Hit or miss orientation. The new teacher arrived at the center and was ushered into the director's office where she waited patiently for ten minutes while the director finished his phone call. The director took the teacher on a tour of the center, stopping off along the way to deliver a message to one teacher and discuss a scheduling problem with a second one. Then back to the office where the director rambled on for another hour about the center and its personnel policies amidst numerous phone interruptions.

For all too many teachers, this is the extent of their orientation. A haphazard tour and introduction. The information this conveys about the center and the teacher's role in it is sketchy. The image this conveys of the center is one of disorganization. The message this conveys to the new teacher is that her value to the center is not very high.

Solution: For every position, whether it be the bus driver or the head teacher, the center should develop a specific orientation plan. This plan need not be an elaborate one, but it should spell out what points are going to be covered, by whom, and when. This way, important information will not be left out and, coming in an organized format, it will be much easier for the new employee to digest. Specific periods of time should be set aside for the orientation so that the person doing the presenting can devote full attention to the process. Time should be taken at the outset to preview the goals of the orientation and at the end to evaluate whether, in the mind of the new employee, these goals were met.

Pitfall #2

Hidden agendas. Often, supervisors see orientation as a chance to make a pitch for their own special interests, to improve on some aspect of the job done by a predecessor, to develop some kind of particular supervisor/supervisee relationship. Or they may be so eager to make the new employee feel excited about the center that they will gloss over serious problems or paint an overly rosy picture.

Newcomers, too, may have the idea that orientation is the time to make an impression, to make sure people are glad they hired her. Both perspectives are understandable and to a certain extent unavoidable. However, if either party gets preoccupied with these hidden agendas, this may cause important pieces of information about roles and relationships to be distorted or misconstrued.

Solution: Orientation should be an honest, informative experience for all participants. At some point in the first day, it should be pointed out to newcomers that it is natural to feel on the spot at the outset. They should be assured that no one will hold them to high performance standards until they have had the opportunity to get their bearings.

At the same time, the person, or persons, doing the orientation should be forthcoming about center shortcomings and problems, particularly about those that will impact upon the new employee's job. For example, if the teacher a newcomer is replacing was fired against the wishes of the parents, she should be told about this so she doesn't misconstrue any lingering hostility of the parents as being directed toward her.

Pitfall #3

Information overload. In her first three days on the job, the new teacher was introduced to all the children, all the parents, and all the staff members. She was asked to read the personnel policy manual, the parent manual, and the center's curriculum plan. In addition, the director lectured her for one hour a day on the history and philosophy of the center. Unfortunately, the teacher reached her saturation point by noon of the first day, and the last two days she simply struggled to act as if she cared. The bottom line is that the newcomer was bored silly, very little information was effectively communicated, and everyone's time was wasted.

Solution: To avoid information overload, orientation should be given in small doses spread out over several days or weeks. It is most effective to give the new employee an opportunity to spend some time on the job as soon as possible, before her enthusiasm ebbs, and to alternate periods of orientation with periods of work. This provides a change of pace between learning and doing; it provides an opportunity to see in action guidelines, policies, and procedures mentioned in the orientation; and it gives the newcomer a chance to ask questions about problems she encounters on the job.

Useful Orientation Techniques

There are a number of techniques which can be employed to increase the effectiveness of an orientation. Different people learn in different ways, so it is important to use a range of approaches for communicating information. This also makes the orientation a lot more interesting. The following are some techniques which have been used with success by child care centers:

Pre-arrival orientation. Even though orientation officially begins on the first day of work, you can effectively use the time between offering a job and having the newcomer start. Begin by making the telephone call in which the job is officially offered a warm, welcoming one. Then send a letter confirming the particulars of the job once it has been accepted. Include starting date and time, work schedule, salary and salary contingencies, and job requirements (for example, a satisfactory health assessment, a driver's license, or completion of certain course work).

Before the new recruit arrives, you may also want to send her information about the program and the job. While you should avoid overwhelming a newcomer, it is often before the first day that there is the most time and interest in reading program philosophy, policies, and history.

The warm welcome. On the first day, be certain the newcomer feels expected and welcomed. Someone should be there to greet him, and there should be a sense that things are ready for his arrival. Some centers put a welcome sign on the front door so the newcomer feels welcomed and staff and parents are also aware of him.

The introduction. Shortly after the newcomer arrives, the director should welcome her and explain how the orientation will proceed. She should be given a written outline of the evaluation schedule so she knows what to expect.

The facility tour. Staff should know the facility in which they work, including any areas which are off limits. Consider distribution of a floor plan if the facility is especially large. Be certain to take at least a brief tour through every room.

In addition to the basic room-by-room tour, also take a more detailed tour to learn the little things that enable a person to function at that site. A written list of the information covered in the detailed tour should be developed. Such a list can be made by carefully observing everything in the facility (include offices, closets, file drawers, keys) and identifying everything an employee has a reason to know about. Chances are they should know just about everything you will see. With a list organized by room, it can be a handy reference for the employee. Include information like where spare keys are kept, how to find the plumber's name and number in a hurry, where the emergency contact information is located, where personnel files are kept and what is in them, where the coffee is kept and who pays for it, etc.

Group orientation. When more than one new staff person is beginning at the same time, a group orientation is worthwhile — even if all participants have different positions. It is not only a more efficient use of time but it affords participants an opportunity to get to know other colleagues and feel less on their own. Moreover, each person's questions and comments enrich the experience for all. It allows for reinforcement of information through discussion which otherwise could not happen.

Modeling. This technique will occur with or without specific planning. While words and handouts are valuable, actions are the means through which the newcomer will really learn about the program and the people in it. Think about what you do and how well it meshes with the information being given. It is reasonable to identify ideals (e.g., what you hope will be observed), but when you know the observed activities and information are different (e.g., staff are not complying with the hand washing rules when you observe), it must be acknowledged and discussed. Otherwise, the newcomer will not only know that the ideal is not met but will know not to trust your information.

Rotating presenters. Instead of having the director or head teacher responsible for the entire orientation, it helps to pull in other staff members to share their perspectives. This provides a welcome change of pace for the newcomer and also gives them a chance to meet, in a more than cursory fashion, other staff members.

Observation and participation. As noted above, actual participation in the life of the center is one of the most effective techniques for learning information during orientation. Any orientation plan should include ample opportunities for both observing and participating. Keep in mind that to participate one does not have to be in charge of a group of children, cook a meal, or drive the bus. There are lots of little ways to participate. Actually using the sign-in, opening the file drawer to locate an item, using the telephone, or attending a meeting are all ways to get right in and do things. Where participation is not feasible, consider discussing topics while the information can be observed.

Follow the rule *see one, do one, teach one* for effective learning. Plan obser-

vations followed by participation, followed by some chance for newcomers to tell you what they experienced.

Apprenticeship. When a new teacher begins to work, having her work closely with a skilled teacher can facilitate learning about the job. This apprenticeship experience should cover the full range of activity a person will be doing on the job. It works best when specific tasks are planned in advance (e.g., new cook will spend one hour with departing cook preparing snack and will walk through all steps). The supervisor and co-worker would do well to discuss these plans and their respective roles for the apprenticeship in advance.

In addition, provision for continual feedback should be planned during the apprenticeship period. *How am I doing?* is what every newcomer wants to know. (In fact, all employees want to know the same thing.) Take time to let them know how they are doing. Reinforce the efforts and behavior you find effective and identify areas where there is difficulty.

Written materials are perhaps the least effective means of primary orientation, but they are extremely effective support for other techniques. Try to have each component of the orientation backed up with written materials. For example, after the new staff member has been introduced to all the other staff members, she should be provided with a list of all their names and positions so she won't have to be embarrassed about forgetting a name.

It is helpful to provide a notebook or folder for all of the material given. Encourage note taking on the handouts and reinforce their value by actively referring to specific information on them.

Be sure written materials are really readable. Use subheadings, visually break up long prose pieces, and consider outlines, charts, pictures. Other written materials can be readings in books. If you find certain published materials to be right on target about some point, it is appropriate to require certain readings (and discuss them). They can be recommended, too, but then be certain your real expectation is only that they *may* be read.

One good way to individualize an orientation is to identify readings which address a newcomer's personal interests or concerns. You might also ask them what books they have found helpful or interesting in the past to better inform you about their knowledge base and interests.

Audiovisual aides. To cover information about child development or nutrition, consider using a film. A slide show covering important aspects of the day at your center or a videotape of the room in which a newcomer will be working can both be very effective. You might use a photo album depicting important parts of the program or a tape-recorded commentary for photographs or slides. Or you can use a tape recorder for a self-guiding tour of the facility.

Special experiences. If you have the luxury of several days for orientation, try to provide some special experiences which may not be part of the daily routine of the job but which can be part of the job at times. It may be a chance to observe other agencies, attend a relevant workshop, meet with parents, review children's records in depth, observe other rooms at the center, or develop materials for the job.

Review. Whenever possible, build on information covered earlier and refer back to the agency's philosophy to give it more tangible meaning. Such

review is a good technique for reinforcement and helps identify what in the mass of information being shared is really important. It also gives specific definition to some of the clichés we all tend to use differently. Throughout the entire orientation period, be sure to include specific opportunities for feedback, follow up, and continued information sharing. In particular, be certain to schedule a time to review the first several weeks' experience on the job with the newcomer.

Content of the Orientation

Content for the orientation should be the information one needs to function in the organization in general, and in one's particular job from day to day. One good way to begin thinking about content for the orientation is to ask current staff members what they found helpful and/or problematic in their own orientation and what they think is important to include for others.

Generally, the following topics should be covered at some point in the orientation:

Goals and philosophy. Whether or not the interview process provides employees with information about the center's purpose and philosophy, written materials about both should be given as soon as possible after the job is offered. Frequent reference should be made to the philosophy during the orientation, and specific time to discuss it should be planned.

History, funding, and politics. A review of these topics will generally highlight the constraints on the program and provide a context for many of the policies. While the discussion need not be lengthy, employees should know how and why the program is as it is, and how their job is affected by the information given. Which money pays for what and the relative security of the job (program-

matically and financially) should be made clear. There will always be future issues about salaries, purchasing policies, and other items revolving around money. A sound foundation of information about the program's funding will provide the best hope for handling those questions effectively.

With regard to politics, identify the people, programs, and political forces significant to your program. Employees should know how to keep abreast of political developments, how to participate in the political activity affecting the agency, and what constraints are placed on their own political activity.

Community. Identify the community in which the agency is located and the relationship between the two. Who are community leaders? Any community foes? Where are the resources in the community? What about places to eat, shop, or take care of other errands on breaks? Consider giving a map of the neighborhood or even taking a tour if community information is especially significant for the job.

Personnel policies. Hopefully your personnel policies are in writing and are clearly written. Hand these out and then review, in depth, the employee's benefits and exactly how they are earned/accrued, as well as those parts which have been especially important or troublesome in the past. New staff should sign and return a document indicating receipt of personnel policies.

Program policies. Although the details of every policy and regulation affecting the program cannot realistically be discussed during orientation, be certain copies of the policies are given, highlighted, and reviewed for questions (the newcomer should be expected to read them). Sensitive issues, such as confidentiality and child abuse reporting, should be singled out for discussion. Also, given current concerns about sexual abuse, there should be a frank discussion of agency procedures designed to protect children from being sexually abused and teachers from being wrongfully accused.

Health and safety procedures. To emphasize the center's concern for maintaining a healthy and safe environment for children and adults, time should be set aside to review these procedures in detail.

For all policies and procedures, be sure to discuss underlying principles. Knowing the reasons underlying certain rules enables employees ultimately to function more independently and more effectively, and to do the job in a manner supportive of agency philosophy even in unexpected circumstances. In addition, seize every opportunity to turn a real experience into a chance to illustrate what a policy means or how it works.

The facility. Fully acclimating the newcomer with the center is an integral part of any orientation. As indicated above, the center tour should include all parts of the center and not just the room where the employee will be working.

The staff. In addition to being introduced to other staff members and being given a list of their names, the newcomer should be given a clear picture of the center's organizational structure. She should know the people who are in each position and a little bit about the job they do. For staff with whom the newcomer will be working closely, some time to meet with them directly should be allotted if possible.

Communication procedures. Generally, you should plan to discuss (with written back up) telephones, staff mailboxes, and parent mailboxes as major communication sources. In addition, remember to discuss bulletin boards, meeting schedules and content (and how agendas are established), conferences, and things that are handled via informal discussion.

To be complete, any orientation should relate the informal as well as the formal communication procedures. Must one always have an appointment to see the director, or is a knock on the door sufficient? Can you give work directly to the secretary, or does it go to someone else first? What about discussing ideas with the cook or making a request of the custodian? How is a complaint made? How do I keep people informed of my contacts with parents, or does it matter?

Caregiver routines. When a newcomer is not a caregiver, it is important to provide an opportunity to observe and discuss child care routines and philosophy. That person should know how her job is affected by the routines of the child care program and she should be conversant with the primary activity of the program.

The job description. The content of the specific job a person is hired to do should also be covered. Be sure to clarify what performance expectations go with the job, how performance will be evaluated, and how training and support will be provided.

Employees must know their *rights* as well as their *responsibilities* for each aspect of their job. Be certain to identify both.

Hopefully these suggestions will help you in developing an orientation plan. An effective orientation sets the stage for a successful working relationship between a new employee and the ongoing staff. While ongoing training and evaluation are needed to keep this momentum going, orienting staff right from the start can make a big difference.

Nurturing Green Staff from Day One

Ideas from directors

"Of all the obstacles I've faced on the job — and there have been many — the task of converting green staff into successful caregivers is the toughest."

The center director who made this statement is not alone. Developing green staff — new employees with little or no training or experience in early childhood education — is a challenge for most center directors today. To come up with some solutions to this problem, we conducted a brainstorming session at a conference on staff development that Exchange sponsored in Philadelphia. The seven directors listed at the end of this article shared the following ideas on how to nurture green staff.

Day One

The green employee's first day on the job is a bellwether event. She comes to your center excited about her new job. At no point in her career will she be more motivated to succeed.

Kindle this enthusiasm. Welcome her wholeheartedly. Let her know you are happy to have her on board. You may even want to put up a sign welcoming her and introducing her to the parents. Introduce her to all staff members. Present her with her own official t-shirt or coffee mug with your center's logo.

Don't extinguish the flame by making him sit down in the staff lounge and read the center's policy manuals. Share with him the soul of your organization, not its 17 year history. Brief him on the center's key goals. Point out how your center is unique from the others in the area. Then get him into the classroom as an observer. A green employee will also approach this first day with high anxiety. Being inexperienced, she may not know what to expect or how to behave. Put her at ease by assuring that everyone on staff is committed to helping her succeed.

Give him a list of all the staff members with their positions. Fill him in about the key logistical details — such as who to report to when he arrives, when breaks are, where he can take them, where the bathrooms are, how lunches are handled, and where supplies are located. Conclude by previewing how the orientation will proceed over the coming weeks.

Some directors have found it effective to insure that a new employee has a positive teaching experience her first day. Find a skill or interest she has that she can put to immediate use. Maybe she likes to sing and can lead the children in a song at the end of the day. Or maybe she enjoys a hobby such as origami and can share this with a few children at some point.

Your goal for the first day is to make the new staff member excited about becoming an integral part of your organization and eager to come in day two and start growing on the job.

Week One

The balance of the first week should proceed at a comfortable pace. Don't try to force feed a green employee in his first days on the job with everything he'll ever need to know about teaching at your center. View this as the time to communicate the center's most important policies and to work out an initial orientation plan.

One important piece of business to take care of quickly is reviewing the center's risk management policies. Present to the employee, both verbally and in writing, key points such as . . .

- how discipline is carried out;

- how toileting is handled;

- how children are comforted;

- what forms of contact are encouraged;

- what forms of contact are discouraged;

- what to do when accidents occur; and

- how to release children at the end of the day.

Key personnel policies should also be reviewed during the first week. A new employee will want to know about pay days, benefits, vacation days, sick leave, and pay hikes. You will want to make sure he understands about the importance of punctuality, the details of his job description, and the chain of command.

During the first week you will want to get to know a new employee better so that you can better orient her. Find out what her experiences have been in early childhood education, what level of understanding (or misunderstanding) she possesses regarding children's development, and what her attitudes are about parents leaving their children in the care of others.

You will also want to get some sense of his learning style. Does he learn best by reading, by seeing, or by doing?

Having learned this, it is time to assign a mentor. Select a senior staff

member, taking into account the new employee's knowledge, attitudes, and learning style. The mentor-neophyte relationship will be a key determinant of the success of the orientation. So take the time to find a good fit.

Ideally, the first week should include more time where the green employee is observing than teaching. The budgetary implications of carrying an employee as an observer may be difficult for most centers to bear. However, the positive dividends of breaking a green teacher in slowly will pay off down the line in employee retention and performance.

One last message you will want a new employee to receive early on is that it's OK to have fun on the job. Working with young children should be a joyful experience. You want your teachers to laugh and play with the children, as well as to enjoy each others company.

Month One

For an experienced, well-trained teacher, a brief orientation on the center's goals and procedures should suffice. Within a week she should be able to operate independently with moderate support. However, for a green teacher-in-training the orientation must become a long range training program.

Ideally, a center will have an organized curriculum for new staff members. This may be nothing more than a checklist of skills and understandings to be mastered. Or, it may consist of an organized set of training materials, either home-grown or purchased pre-packaged off the shelf, to be studied in sequence by new employees.

An employee should be permitted to proceed through the curriculum at her own pace. Skills that one person can master in a week may take

months for another person. As long as the trainee is putting forth a serious effort to improve, there should be no pressure to meet outside timetables.

In planning the training, the following suggestions may be helpful in working with green staff:

- If your center can afford it, a trainee will benefit greatly from a daily consultation with his mentor. It is helpful for a bond of professional friendship to develop in this relationship. In addition, the trainee's sense of security is enhanced if she knows she will have an opportunity every day to receive feedback and ask questions.

- In addition to having a mentor supporting the new staff member, other members of the teaching team should be encouraged to provide feedback and support. This increases the amount of feedback received and provides a variety of perspectives.

- Keeping in mind that people have different styles of learning, your training plan should encompass a wide variety of experiences. In addition to materials to be read, the training could also include directed observations where the trainee is asked to observe for specific practices or behaviors, visits to other centers, attendance at local or state workshops, and conversations with experienced teachers.

- Video training has much to offer green staff. For years many of the video training materials for early childhood were either insipid or boring. Now you can purchase training videos that are educational as well as entertaining. In addition, many centers are now developing their own video training libraries. To help orient new teachers into the practices and philosophies of the center, a director may videotape some of her best teachers conducting classroom activities, conversations with children, and meetings with parents.

- Since green staff will have little experience in the classroom, the new ideas you are sharing with him may be hard to relate to. One way to drive the message home is to relate the points you are striving to make to the new staff member's own childhood. Talk about her experiences as a child and use this as a springboard to talking about his performance as a teacher.

- To gain the support and understanding of parents, some centers have green employees wear *Teacher in Training* buttons during the orientation period.

During the first month there should be several points at which the director meets with the new staff member to appraise her performance to date. To facilitate this, the director should take many opportunities to observe the new staff person at work during her first weeks.

Unless the trainee is displaying a serious lack of effort or engaging repeatedly in practices she was cautioned against, these sessions should take on a supportive tone. The director should give feedback to the new teacher on positive behaviors she has observed and those that she has yet to observe (not on what she is doing right and what she is doing wrong). The director should ask how she can assist the new staff person in her training, and review where the training is headed in coming weeks.

Year One

A green employee's entire first year should be viewed as a period of

intense training. After the first months the employee's mentor and immediate supervisor will take over the day-to-day supervision and support. However, the director should observe periodic checkpoints to see if the new employee is continuing to progress.

If the new staff member is doing really poorly with little evidence of improvement, the director should act quickly. The employee should be clearly put on notice that her performance is falling below the standards of the center and given a short time frame in which to turn the situation around.

In hiring untrained, inexperienced teachers, you are apt to make more mistakes than when you hire a teacher with a track record you can assess. Don't confound your error by dragging your feet in correcting your mistake.

On the other hand, if it is clear that the new employee has what it takes to succeed, try to find outside training opportunities to supplement in-house training efforts. Encourage the new employee to attend early childhood courses and workshops by paying all or part of the costs.

Throughout the first year a new employee's progress should be observed and celebrated. One early celebration could be the point at which she can take off her *Teacher in Training* button. Make a big deal of little rituals such as this to demonstrate that the center truly cares about the new employee's success. At her anniversary point the new employee should be recognized in a staff meeting for having successfully completed her first year at the center.

The ideas shared in this article require a great deal of effort by the director and teachers. However, if as a result this green employee is nurtured into a solid team member, this investment will be well worth it.

Contributors

The following attendees at our May 1991 conference, "Color Your Staff Extraordinary: How to Develop Competent and Creative Teachers," in Philadelphia provided the ideas for this article:

Peggy Fulp, owner/director, Trin-Dale Children's Center, Trinity, North Carolina.

Wanda Kreutzfeltz, owner/director, Children's Learning Center, Yardley, Pennsylvania.

Barbara Kurtz, executive director, Early Childhood Options of University Circle, Cleveland, Ohio.

Gail Laskowski, director, North Pocono Preschool, Moscow, Pennsylvania.

Lois Mitten, owner/director, Children's Discovery Center, Toledo, Ohio.

Karen Strimple, director, St. Columba's Nursery School, Washington, DC.

GaleWiik, co-owner/director, Breezy Point Day School, Langhorne, Pennsylvania.

Observing From a Different Point of View

by Mary Beth Lakin

In a course I teach — "The Art of Observation" — two students compared their notes on an environment they had just observed. Patricia, a director of 20 child care sites, noted the condition of each piece of equipment, the safety of the playground, and the level of cleanliness and order. Ana, a teacher trained in early childhood education who is now working with children with special needs, talked about the quality of play for the child in that environment: "If I were a child, I'd go directly to the climbing structure. It looks exciting." Patricia replied: "I never thought about looking at the environment in that way. I am usually concerned about the children's health and safety. Ana's observation gave me a different perspective."

We do observe from different perspectives. Roles, education, and our own childhoods foster these differences. As a director, Patricia needs to be concerned with the overall health and safety of the environment. Ana, the person who spends direct contact time with the children in her classroom, needs to think about health and safety issues as well as the quality of play that the environment offers. The discussion helped Ana and Patricia expand their thinking about what to look for when observing.

Patricia has been a supervisor of a child care program in a Mexican-American community for 20 years.

She has never worked in the classroom. She spends time interviewing families when they enter the program and knows their lives and concerns well. "Grads" come back to visit her when they are 20 years old. Her focus is on the well being of the families and the success of the children. Concern for safety is one way in which she shows her commitment to the families.

But Patricia also wants to know more about children, how they develop and play, what kinds of environments are the ones in which the children will flourish. Because of this strong interest, Patricia takes the perspective of a classmate and examines the environment in a different manner: "If I were a child, how would I move about in this environment?" "What would I run toward?" "What would I avoid?" "What about Dorothy, a three year old in our program?" "What would she do here?" "What is it like to be a child in this environment?"

Colette, a teacher who has worked several years with toddlers and preschoolers, gains another point of view from Patricia: children often come from home environments that are different from the school's. Patricia observes how children and families enter the school setting and uses those observations to help shape an environment that is inviting and comfortable — an environment composed of familiar language, routines, materials, and explanation about the unfamiliar. Colette remarks that it seems overwhelming to meet the needs of all children from such diverse settings.

From this point, they discuss all the things that could be observed: interactions among family members and children; language, gestures, facial expressions that comfort the child or direct her attention; management of conflict; discipline; roles of family members; and use of authority. Learning to observe and "read" the communication in a family helps the teacher to understand a child's approach to an environment, materials, peers, and adults.

Ana, Patricia, and Colette have been sharing their different perspectives; their experiences in the college classroom suggest that there is no right answer or best way of observing. In daily practice, it is more difficult for the director to avoid one role as an observer. The following discussion presents various approaches to observing teachers in the early childhood classroom.

Collaboration: Sharing Observations

Sharing perspectives is a good strategy for directors and teachers to develop. "What did you see today?" could be a beginning question for a discussion between teachers and directors. Discussion of how we use observation and what we tend to focus on gives all the staff a fuller picture of the environment within which they work and the children and families they serve.

We can also begin to understand how who we are — roles, education, background — influences what we look for, see, and infer. A collaborative effort to observe the environment is an easy place for the director and teacher to start.

As collaborators, they might focus on what they find appealing, distracting, effective, and difficult about the environment. How do the children use it? What is used? What is not used or avoided? What do children keep coming back for? The environment can be an exciting area for collaboration, as it is one way in which directors can support teachers' good ideas. Having conversations about the environment can help the teacher and director understand each other's perspectives.

Start with knowing your perspective. Directors and teachers come to a setting with feelings and ideas based on temperament, ethnicity, culture, gender, class, family, education, and teaching experiences. Gonzalez-Mena (1993) remarks on the different reactions of adults observing and commenting on the amount of stimuli in an environment:

What one person feels is the optimum amount of sights, sounds, and movement, that is, sensory input, another feels bombards the children, and the third feels is boring. To some extent, this variation in sensory needs relates to individual preference and style, but also it connects to culture. Some cultures wish to promote calm, placid styles of interaction and temperament, so they prefer less stimulating environments. They worry that the babies will get overstimulated in the exciting play and intense interactions if they aren't toned down. Some cultures value activity; others value stillness.

The director does have a perspective when she enters the classroom; she usually has ideas about good teaching, good curriculum, and good environments. A director can become aware of how her perspective, based on training, personality, education, and cultural background, influences what she looks for in the classroom, what she sees in the classroom, and how she interprets what she sees. Some of the techniques we ask teachers to use when observing children may be useful to us as directors observing teachers. Almy and Genishi (1979) say that it is important that teachers come to terms with the feelings that children arouse in them. Directors can also focus on how a teaching style, communication style, or curriculum activity may elicit strong feelings, negative or positive. We can't ignore the fact that our feelings affect what we see and hear and how we interpret. An Anglo director with a soft manner was offended by an African-American's

loud, scolding voice; it just wasn't good child development, she thought. But by observing the loving interactions in the classroom, the director decided she did not need to worry about the teacher's tone of voice.

A useful observational technique (Sue Stadler, teacher, Boise, Idaho) for teachers observing children offers some interesting possibilities for directors observing teachers. The observer can play the following roles:

• Scientist — observe and collect physical data

• Garbage collector — sort out the garbage (feelings) from the physical data

• Advocate — put yourself in the "observed's shoes." Why did she react that way?

• Artist — consider creative change, particularly actions that support the development and interests of the observed

The Roles We Play

Our jobs seem to prescribe particular roles to play, certain pressures for accountability. It's difficult to put oneself in another's place, to be sympathetic to the daily pressures of the other. The director and teacher have similar and different issues concerning children's development, curriculum planning and implementation, and the environment. As a teacher, I often thought about my director, "She doesn't know (or remember) what it's like to be with children every day." As a director, I often thought, "Can't she (the teacher) see that this isn't good for children?"

Both teacher and director play participant observer roles, the teacher in the child's life and the director in the teacher's life. Observations often reflect evaluation and the desire for change. Many times, directors ask teachers to step back and be more objective in the observations and interpretations they make about children. Directors may see themselves as "objective outsiders" who can give teachers a different point of view. A different point of view does not guarantee more objectivity. Besides, objectivity for the participant observer — teacher observing child, director observing teacher — may be hard to reach, and not a meaningful goal to strive for. Cohen et al. (1983) note: "It is far better for a child to have a warmly interested teacher who has kept no records than a meticulous observer with no warmth!"

What's a Director to Do?

In trying to encourage a fuller and more accurate picture of a child, a director sometimes asks a teacher to consider other possibilities for a child's behaviors. What possibilities can directors consider when observing teachers? A teacher's developmental stage? A teacher's interests and skills? A teacher's fear of looking foolish? A transition period with a new group of children? A teacher's need for challenge or additional resources? Posing such questions and observing for answers can provide a fuller and more accurate picture of a teacher. Thus, a director's responses to a teacher's classroom behaviors may indicate a growing knowledge of that teacher's interests, strengths, and needs. With such knowledge, a director is more likely to add the roles of "advocate" and "artist" in her relationship with a teacher.

A director might shift her focus. Carter (1993) suggests that directors "catch teachers being good." As a trainer observing teachers in their classrooms, she found that, over a six year period, her focus shifted from

the teacher's behavior to the children's play. She suggests that the following principles she developed as a trainer will work for directors:

• They enter classrooms with a focus on children rather than teachers.

• They model an interest in children's play and initiate discussions of it as it's happening.

• They "broadcast" their observations throughout the center (using notes, sketches, photos, and audio and videotapes).

• They observe for and point out environmental factors that support play.

• They observe for and point out teacher behaviors that encourage sustained play by children — catching teachers "being good."

Carter's suggestions could foster a collaborative effort by the teacher and director concentrating on how the play of the children develops.

Presenting Teachers With Choices

As a step towards building a more collaborative effort, the director could ask the teacher, "What would you like me to look for?" What questions can the director and teacher raise together? The following can begin some interesting conversations about a child's social interactions:

• How does the child enter into play with others?

• What are the roles the child is taking on: leader, follower, other?

• How does the child make use of others' ideas?

• How does the child offer ideas to other children? What are the responses?

• Does the child seem to have special friends? How can you tell?

• What is the size of the group in which the child is playing? Does the child play with same sex or opposite sex, same ethnicity, different ethnicity?

• What play materials is the child using? How is she using them?

• How does the child handle a conflict with another child?

• How long does the play interaction last? What happens next?

The teacher and director can share what they observed, using each other's ideas for a fuller picture of the child. Often we look at one picture as being the more accurate, but two views may give us more of the dimensions. The conversation can focus on each participant's getting all the details of what the other observed and why. The teacher and director can also talk about what emotions the observation may have evoked and how those emotions affected their interpretations and desire to intervene. What word are they using to describe the actions they observed? Bossiness or leadership? Persistence or stubbornness? Sadness or manipulation?

There Are Obstacles

Teachers being observed sense our feelings if we're critical; however, they may be anxious about observation anyway. Many times they have experienced it as evaluation. Often teachers observe children carefully when "something is wrong." Directors do the same. But observation can be used simply as a way to see what is going on and describe it. We can put events in a context, with a setting and a beginning, middle, and end. This helps us to understand children better — and teachers, too. We need to concentrate on the "whats" first, then the "whys," being tentative about our analysis, understanding our contexts and the teacher's.

To reveal our own reactions to what we have observed about a child takes a certain amount of courage on the part of the director, but can encourage the teacher to reflect on her own feelings. Teachers and directors may be more secure with the role of director as "fixer upper" rather than collaborator.

When experimenting with collaborative observations, the director, in a position of authority, must be careful that, even unintentionally, her comments do not manipulate or control the teacher. A teacher may see comments as directives — "This is what the director wants, so I'll go along." The point is missed if the director's view is always the correct one. The teacher can learn from the director's modeling that everyone has expectations and biases that influence observation. To become aware of those expectations and biases is a worthy challenge.

Observing takes time that directors feel they don't have. It's a similar predicament to the one teachers struggle with in trying to observe each child in their classrooms. A realistic goal for the director may be to try for a ten minute observation in one classroom and a five minute conversation with the teacher per week.

Building Director/Teacher Relationships

As Ana and Patricia shared their perspectives on environment in the college classroom, so can directors and teachers. To make successful collaboration more likely, the partici-pants can try to look at different per-spectives as offering exciting or valu-able pieces of information. Difference of opinion does not mean that some-one is wrong, nor is it necessarily a basis for a negative conflict. Martha Foote, a teacher in a New York City private school, describes sharing observations with an intern teacher:

Aside from the written records I keep, I constantly discuss the children's be-haviors and daily incidents with the intern teacher in my classroom. At our weekly meetings as well as during snatched moments of work time, we share observations, make inferences, and discuss the emerging patterns we have been forming. It can sometimes put a strain on our working relationship if we see an incident or development differently, but I think that more often than not, our differing perspectives help us to see our students more richly. Instead of holding one overriding inter-pretation, I have another adult's observa-tions and ideas to help me gain a deeper picture of my students. I hope the same holds true for the intern's view of the children. (Genishi, 1992)

Jones (1993) notes that "observation of children is a solid, shared focus for building relationships with teachers." Directors also may find mutual inter-ests with teachers in the areas of environment and curriculum. As relationships develop, directors may also be willing to share their reflec-tions and questions, which encour-ages teachers to begin to observe themselves and think about what they do. A director can start by being aware of her own perspective when entering a classroom, observing for an understanding of the teacher's rationale. From this base, a director and teacher can talk about what they would like to look at together. The sharing of perspectives about the environment, a child, or an activity nurtures a budding collaborative effort between teacher and director, in which a common task becomes the focus for increased trust, respect, and mutual pleasure.

References

Almy, Milly, and Celia Genishi. *Ways of Studying Children* (Revised Edition). New York: Teachers College Press, 1979.

Carter, Margie. "Catching Teachers 'Being Good': Using Observations to Communicate." *Growing Teachers: Partnerships in Staff Development.* Washington, DC: NAEYC, 1993.

Cohen, Dorothy H., and Virginia Stern (with Nancy Balaban). *Observing and Recording the Behavior of Young Children* (Third Edition). New York: Teachers College Press, 1983.

Genishi, Celia. *Ways of Assessing Children and Curriculum: Stories of Early Childhood Practice.* New York: Teachers College Press, 1992.

Gonzalez-Mena, Janet. *Multicultural Issues in Child Care.* Mountain View, CA: Mayfield Publishing Company, 1993.

Jones, Elizabeth (editor). *Growing Teachers: Partnerships in Staff Develop-ment.* Washington, DC: NAEYC, 1993.

Mary Beth Lakin has been in the field of early childhood education for over 20 years. She is currently a professor at Pacific Oaks College in Pasadena, California.

Helping Teachers Improve Their Responses to Children

by Carol Keyes

Some directors find it hard to go into the classroom and confer with teachers about improvements that may be necessary. Other directors find it difficult to be supportive as they try to help staff grow. Still others have the difficulty in helping students and volunteers improve their interactions with children. Do you share any of these problems?

I have been doing systematic observation in the classroom and training child care personnel with a category system that seems to help with some of these problems. There are six categories that are easy to keep in your head and provide a common language for teachers, students, paraprofessionals, and directors. They help raise adults' awareness to how they are responding to children.

This category system was created by Dr. Sydney Schwartz, at Queens College in New York, where professionals were seeking a nonjudgmental way to supervise their students and teachers that would allow them to be comfortable when being observed or discussing the results of visits, rather than making them feel tense or intimidated. They come up with the six categories that I later refined and expanded as part of my doctoral work. I first used the category system to observe and describe classroom interaction in campus child care centers. Later I did work-shops and teacher training to help paraprofessionals, professionals, students, and parents improve their responses to children.

Description of the Category System

The focus of this category system is interactive behavior — the child's initiation and the adult's response. It is the adult's response to the child's behavior that is coded as instructional or management. Within these two modes, the behaviors are further identified as stops, changes, sustains, or extends. These are the only six terms: instructional mode, management mode, stop, change, sustain, and extend. (With beginning teachers and paraprofessionals, I often start with just four terms — stop, change, sustain, extend). The unit observed is the *teacher's behavior*, the teacher's response to a child or children. The teacher produces a *new behavior* by responding to a new child or children, changing a topic, asking a question. Each new behavior is a behavior to be coded. The behaviors are interpreted within the context of an activity. An *activity* consists of a set of behaviors that cluster around a purpose, e.g. playing dominoes or moving from inside to outside. One procedure for collecting data is to take five minute samples of teacher behavior over a period of time and summarize it (see Table 1 — Sample Summary Form). The summary represents a description of the teacher's response to children.

Let me define the behaviors now. The **instructional mode** includes behaviors within the context of early childhood curriculum which is broadly defined to include that content that promotes physical, social, cognitive, language, and affective development. The **management mode** includes behaviors related to program management routines including how activities begin and end, social behavior related to taking turns, cooperation, and fair play, where it is reactive rather than planned. Within the instructional and management mode, the teacher's behavior is further categorized as:

- **Stop.** The adult halts or limits a child's action verbally or non verbally.

- **Change.** The adult redirects the child through verbal means, directions, or materials to a new activity or behavior.

- **Sustain.** The adult may make a neutral comment, a brief response, or participate without influence.

- **Extend.** The adult extends or expands a child's activity through such modes as giving information, challenging, adding new materials.

The System in Action

When I was refining and testing the system, and using it in my own child care center with students and parents, I began by describing what I felt were our goals and objectives in terms of the center and in terms of our responses to children. Our goal was to have the most sustaining and extending responses and the least amount of stopping and changing responses. I suggested to the staff and parents that each time they stopped or changed the behavior of a child, they should reflect on what was happening to see if there was another way to design our system that would allow a sustaining and extending response to the child's behavior instead of a stopping and changing response. One day, one of the parents came in excitedly saying, "I sustained her! I sustained her! I was going to stop here but realized it was just my bias, so I sustained here instead."

The students became familiar with the terms and used them to describe their behavior. They began to identify what they were doing and became aware of inappropriate responses in terms of our goals and philosophy. We discussed the fact that where there are a lot of stopping and changing responses on the part of the teachers, this generally means that we are out of sync with the children's developmental levels and are experiencing behavior that the

Table 1

Sample Summary Form

Date _____   Person Observed _____

Time _____   Recorder _____

	Sustain	Extend	Change	Stop	Total
Instruct	5	5	4	3	17
Manage	3	2	7	5	17
Totals	**8**	**7**	**11**	**8**	**34**
% of Total Responses	24%	21%	32%	24%	

children cannot presently produce. Or we need to re-examine our goals, objectives, and values to see if they are appropriate.

There is no right amount of any kind of response. All the responses may be appropriate within the system, depending on the stated goals and objectives of the teacher or center. At the beginning of the year, for example, you may have more stopping and changing responses because you are setting up your classroom management systems. If at the end of the year, however, you have more management, and stops and changes, I would raise some questions. I believe that if a center is trying to have optimum development of children, then rules and management policies should be set up early in the year in ways that children and adults can understand. The management behaviors at the end of the year, then, should reflect sustaining and extending responses on the part of the teacher rather than stopping and changing responses.

I observed teachers, assistants, and aides in the classroom. I would sit for five minutes in the room to become acclimated to the classroom. Then I would code five minutes on one staff person, five minutes on the next, and five minutes on the third on a rotating basis, until I had done fifteen minutes of coding on each adult in the room. When I was coding for the study, I used only codes, but when I was doing staff training, I also wrote some brief descriptions to use as examples to share with the staff as we discussed successful and/or problem areas.

What did I find out about teachers' responses to children? I observed more than fifty adults in nineteen centers. In seven centers there were twice as many management responses as instructional responses, and this was in the spring of the year. The most instructional responses occurred in one-to-one activities and small group instruction; the most management responses occurred in the routine activities, such as snack and rest. In the centers observed, one-to-one activities included such activities as sewing on the sewing machines and making books.

Teachers who planned the classes for total group activity, had a high percentage of stopping responses. Teachers on the playgrounds also had a high percentage of stopping and changing responses. When children were all waiting at the table together for snack or lunch to arrive, teachers' responses also included a greater percentage of stopping responses than sustaining or extending responses.

There were a few exceptions in regard to snack and rest times. In one school, there was a high percentage of instructional extending and sustaining responses during rest. The teachers in this school were working individually with the children with toys, moving from mat to mat during rest. In another school, conversations were held among children and teachers during snack time. There was a high percentage of instructional responses here as well. In general, my observations supported and emphasized principles of early childhood, e.g. small group instruction, one-to-one activity, anticipation and planning by teachers. Where these existed, teachers had more sustaining and extending responses than stopping and changing responses.

This category system can also illuminate the discrepancies or consistencies between what a teacher suggests that she is trying to do and what she actually does. For example, one teacher suggested that she was trying to enhance a child's self-concept — that was one of her most important goals. The data from the observations indicated that she stopped and changed a child's behavior 60% of the time. The director later discussed with the teacher whether stopping and changing children's behavior tends to enhance or support the development of the child's self-concept.

Another teacher interviewed said she was hoping to help children become

creative and inventive. She sustained and extended the children in the instructional mode 75% of the time and seemed to be implementing her objective.

Using the Category System for Staff Development

What are the stops in using this category system for staff development? The first, of course, is establishing a positive climate with the staff. Next is to teach the staff the system so that they can use it alone and become familiar with the terms to develop a common language for discussion. The third step is to use it for group staff development.

- **Establishing rapport.** The first important consideration is to establish a supportive rapport with the teachers in your school. How can you establish the right climate for staff growth and development? I believe that each person comes in at a particular level, and it is my job to help them to grow as much as they want. My goals are: (1) to help them improve their responses to children so that they are in sync with the children's development level; (2) to help them produce many sustaining and extending responses; and (3) to help them feel human themselves with as little harassment in the day as possible. Once you have a rapport with the teachers and they know that you are working with them to improve their day as well as the children's, staff development usually moves forward smoothly.

I found that a system that worked well was to introduce the categories to the staff as a whole, invite them to use it individually and begin to talk amongst themselves and with me about it, without my doing any formal observations, although I did suggest what to identify as well as invite them to make changes, as described in the following paragraphs. After

they were comfortable with the system and had developed a common language, I moved to group staff development.

- **Introducing the system.** Once you have established rapport with the staff, describe the category system to the teachers. Invite the teachers to monitor their own behavior in the classroom to see what they are doing in the classroom in response to children's behavior. Teach them four terms — stop, change, extend, and sustain. Invite them to keep track of their own responses in their head, and then describe what their responses are to each other and you.

- **Identifying stopping and changing.** After the teachers have practiced just describing their responses, the next step is to begin identifying areas or children with whom they are using a lot of stopping and changing responses. Let them think about what's happening. What is causing these responses? Have them try to figure out how else they could plan that time or interact with the children to increase the amount of sustaining and extending responses. How else could they design that time to meet the child's needs and still keep things safe for all the children? Invite the teachers to try one change, and then keep track of their responses to see if the change reduced their stopping and changing responses.

- **Identifying sustaining and extending.** Ask teachers to begin to identify periods where they are doing a lot of sustaining and extending responses and children with whom they are making sustaining and extending responses. Ask them to see where they can increase their sustaining and extending responses. Suggest that they make one change, and monitor their behavior to see if they have been successful in increasing their sustaining and extending responses.

Group Staff Development

When teachers have used the categories to monitor their own responses for awhile, they are then ready to move to staff development as a team. They now have a common language that is easy to use.

Sometimes the discussion, depending on the development level of the teachers, can be around theoretical orientations — for example, in a child development classroom a teacher would be expected to demonstrate a considerable amount of sustaining behaviors towards children's activities. In a cognitively oriented classroom where a teacher sustains a child's own curiosity and inventiveness and extends his interest into other challenging areas, it is helpful to link objectives to kinds of responses. For example, as noted earlier, I encourage the staff to strive for sustaining and extending responses with the minimum of stops and changing responses.

Discuss a plan to collect general data on their responses. Reassure them that teachers' scores or responses will not be identified individually. Describe to them that for a reading on the center as a whole you would observe each adult in the classroom for between five and fifteen minutes. All the teachers' responses are tallied together to give a center reading on responses.

For example, if you were observing in the playground, you would report that as a whole we had 75% stopping and changing responses. There were some examples of sustaining and extending responses and you might cite these, without names. What do you think caused all the stopping and changing responses? Encourage the teachers to describe the problems.

Table 2

Examples of Behavior Categorization

SUSTAIN — The adult may make a neutral comment, a brief response, or participate without influence.

Instructional	Management
Context: Rest time. The child was playing with a boat on his mat.	**Context:** Rest time. A child was resting on the mat.
Child: "My boat is getting bigger."	The teacher patted her on the back gently.
Adult: "It sure is."	**Context:** Snack.
Context: Gym.	Teacher was handing out crackers.
Child: Nicole jumps.	Child: "What about Joey?"
Adult: Adult jumps.	Teacher gave Joey one and said, "I like the way you take care of your friends."
Context: Play.	**Context:** Rest. Child folds her mat.
Child: Child manipulated his toy.	
Adult: Teacher says, "It's working well."	Teacher says, "You know where it goes."

See if they begin to suggest alternatives. If they don't, ask if there are other ways to plan the activities to increase the sustaining and extending responses and reduce the stopping and changing responses. Relate the description to children's development. Relate the description to goals and objectives. It's important that the questions posed be searching, joint problem solving questions, not testing or inquisition types of questions.

Encourage the teachers to discuss where they have succeeded in the classroom and where they are still having problems. Encourage them to pick an area, by consensus, for you to observe, so they can begin to improve their responses based on

the data. For each area chosen, once a week perhaps, observe between five and fifteen minutes for each adult. Always use the compiled scores of the center as a whole. The teachers will themselves point out, as the scores are reported, where or why the stopping and changing responses occurred. They will begin to discuss what happened at that time. Questions like "Any suggestions?" or "Does anyone do it another way?" often encourage teachers to tell how they may design the environment differently.

Teachers usually plan to make one change. Then you can go back again to collect data to see if responses have improved as a result of this change.

Resources

Grossman, B., & Keyes, C. (1985). *Early childhood administration.* Boston: Allyn and Bacon, Inc.

Schwartz, S. L., & Mott, J. K. (1974). *Two coding systems to describe teaching behavior and pupil behavior: A Gestalt approach to teaching.* Paper delivered at the Annual Meeting of the American Educational Research Association, 1974.

Carol Keyes is the chairperson of the Early Childhood Development Department at Pace University in New York City. She is co-author of three books on early childhood and parenting. She is also active in the National Coalition of Campus Child Care.

Helping Teachers Grow: Confronting Inappropriate Teaching Behavior

by Kay Albrecht

"I have told Mary again and again that she needs to get down at children's eye level and she still doesn't do it!" It seems so simple. You know what you want to have happen. You share that information with the person who can make it happen. And nothing happens.

Although the center director's job has many frustrating aspects, confronting inappropriate teaching behaviors in a manner which produces change is an ongoing challenge. Many a director has been frustrated when her guidance to teachers about appropriate and inappropriate teaching skills fails to have the desired impact. Let's take a look at a design for helping teachers grow by confronting inappropriate teaching behaviors in a way that is most likely to produce change — and, in the process, improve the teacher's skill and the center's program quality.

Confrontation usually has a negative connotation. In many minds, it is associated with conflict. But confrontation is different from conflict. Constructive confrontation is a way to help calibrate perceptions of one's own strengths or limitations (in this case in teaching competence) with the perceptions of others (either supervisors, clients, or peers). When approached correctly, confrontation can be healthy, stimulating, and change-producing.

Five Steps to Growth

Confrontation which results in growth has five steps. First — identify the behavior you want changed. Nailing down the problem by specifying which specific behavior you want a teacher to change can be difficult — but if you can't do it, you are not ready to confront. Second — identify and describe how you want the new behavior to look. Specifying the change you want is the goal of this step. Third — identify how the change is to be brought about. This critical third step is what causes many to flounder. Developing the plan for bringing about change and identifying who will play what role in facilitating the change is difficult. Fourth — determine how the change will be measured. Consider including specifications about time, quantity, and quality. And fifth — identify how successful change will be measured, by whom, and when.

An example to illustrate the steps:

1. Identify the problem. Mary doesn't get down on children's eye level (an important teacher competency which facilitates positive interactions among children and teachers).

2. Identify and describe how the new behavior should look. When interacting with children, Mary will bend over, stoop, get down on the floor, or sit on the hassocks which bring her down to the children's eye level.

3. Describe how the change will be brought about. Every time I pass Mary's classroom door and think that she should be sitting, bending, or stooping to interact, I will signal Mary by pulling on my ear. The purpose of the signal is to make Mary aware of where she is in relation to children.

4. Determine how the change will be measured — in time, quantity, and quality. After two weeks of signaling, I expect Mary to be bending over, stooping down, or sitting while interacting with children at least half the number of times I pass by her classroom. After a month, Mary should be bending over, stooping down, or sitting while interacting with children on three out of four times.

5. Determine how success will be measured. When Mary is at children's eye level during 75% of her interactions (based on a one hour observation) or when she no longer needs signaling to sensitize her to where she is in relation to the children in her classroom (she is at eye level when interacting 75% of the times I pass her classroom), we will assume that Mary has mastered this skill.

Prerequisites to Constructive Confrontation

In order to help teachers grow, it must be clear to everyone involved what teaching competence means. The best way to make sure everyone knows is to have a clear program philosophy statement from which a list of philosophically compatible teaching competencies or skills are identified and then used in self and supervisor evaluation.

To find out if your philosophy is clear and understandable, ask your teachers to write it down for you in their own words. Then ask them to make a list of skills that teachers who follow the philosophy must have in order to implement a quality program. The results will give you insight into the clarity of your philosophy and the ability of others to interpret what the philosophy means.

Constructive confrontation works best when it begins early in the teacher-director relationship. If you have a staff member who has been with you for three years and has never been given any feedback on her teaching competence, it will be much harder to get the process of change started.

Constructive confrontation of teaching skill deficits requires that equal attention be given to skill strengths. This does not mean beginning confrontation sessions by identifying one or two teaching skills that are a part of the teacher skill repertoire. It means regular and frequent positive feedback as skills are demonstrated.

When skill strengths are recognized, the next step of working on skill deficits emerges naturally.

Kay Albrecht, Ph.D., is the former executive director of HeartsHome Early Learning Center, Houston, Texas, and senior partner in Innovations in Early Childhood Education. Her specialties include teacher training and curriculum development. Her latest book, Innovations in Infant Curriculum, is in press with Gryphon House. In 2000, she served as the academic dean of the World Forum.

Making Constructive Confrontation Work

- Break things down into manageable components. It is ineffective to start with "You're a bad teacher." Pick one skill to focus on at a time, allow a reasonable time for improvement, then pick another, and so forth.

- Pick discreet skills that can be taught. For a good list of *teachable* skills, see "Self-Evaluation — Early Childhood Teacher," (*Exchange*, April 1989). Stick to skills that are *teachable*. Avoid personality traits or personal style issues.

- Start with teaching behaviors that really matter. Skills that focus on interaction among teachers and children, curriculum, and parent-teacher interaction are some of the skills that make the most difference.

- Focus on outcomes. The process of change will happen more readily if the outcome is specified while the path for accomplishing the goal allows for flexibility, creativity, individuality, and spontaneity.

Helping Teachers Grow: Separating Competency From Compensation

by Kay Albrecht

Teaching competency can be viewed as a continuum — you can have a little of it, some of it, or a lot of it — and there is always room for more competency growth. Compensation, on the other hand, is usually finite — there are only so many salary dollars to go around. Standard practice in most work environments is to conduct evaluations (read: performance reviews) annually and to conclude with a salary change discussion.

This type of system works well for businesses which are static over time or whose employees need a fixed set of skills. But the world of child care is never static. Children develop daily and change in the process. Classroom dynamics vary depending on group size, composition, the day of the week, and the weather! Early childhood teachers need an ever-changing array of teaching skills to be able to handle both the variability of teaching responsibilities and the synergy of classroom groups. When they are having trouble, teachers cannot wait until an annual review to get help. They want and need new teaching skills when challenges present themselves — not at some undetermined point in the future.

In the child care setting, annual discussions of competence, and then compensation, seem inappropriate. A better approach is to adopt a performance review system that separates the two. It might work like this:

Competency and compensation evaluations follow different schedules. Compensation is discussed upon hiring and then again on a semi-annual or annual basis, with the outcome of the review being the determination of salary or wage change and the development of measurable performance objectives. Compensation discussions take place between the teacher and the person responsible for the overall program, usually the director.

Competence, on the other hand, is reviewed at the end of an alignment period, say three months, and then again at four to six month intervals, with the outcome being an improvement or training plan. Competency discussions might take place among any number of program staff including program coordinators, lead teachers, teachers, and assistant teachers, or even between mentors and protégés. Therefore, an employee hired in January would

have competency reviews in March and September and compensation reviews in June and January.

How does separation of competency and compensation help teachers grow? Let's first look at how this distinction helps teachers grow in competence. It helps teachers see competence as a continuum. When viewed as such, teachers are continuously challenged to learn new skills or get more information about teaching. It also recognizes the developmental nature of teaching — that the skills you need now may not be the ones you need later. In other words, it reminds teachers that you don't arrive at competence, you strive for it.

The separation also allows feedback to be frequent and direct and begins the feedback process early in the teacher-center relationship. This sets the stage for an ongoing dialogue which allows teachers and managers to determine variations in perception and to correct misconceptions before they become problematic. But most importantly, separating competency from compensation keeps us from accepting poor performance in the classroom because we don't have the resources to pay for outstanding performance. It forces us to continue to accept the challenge of turning the teachers we have into the teachers we want.

On the compensation side, separation of competency from compensation has many advantages. It allows teachers and directors to disconnect growing competency with increased compensation and instead connect increased compensation to the larger context of the center. Whereas competency discussions focus on an individual's teaching skills, compensation discussions focus on the individual's connection with and contribution to the center as a whole. Many variables are taken into consideration including regularity of attendance, initiative, progress toward completion of additional training or education, possession of special skills, contributions to the management and operation of the program, administrative or other responsibilities, ability to communicate the *center culture*, special training or certifications, assignment of hours, and teaching competence.

When this separation occurs, directors are free to pay those who contribute the most higher salaries. Rather than giving each employee a small raise after an annual review, available salary resources can be concentrated to give larger increases to those employees who contribute the most to the center.

The separation also creates a win/win situation at compensation review time. Either the teacher gets a

---

Characteristics of Competency Reviews

Focus on classroom and teaching competence

Conducted by a variety of center staff

Results in an improvement or training plan

Focus on "teachable skills"

Characteristics of Compensation Reviews

Focus on the teacher's relationship to the whole center

Conducted by the center or program director

Results in the development of performance objectives

Includes personal and professional skills as well as teaching competence

Includes a discussion of salary change

---

salary increase or she finds out what she must do to insure an increase at the next review. When teachers know what must be accomplished (in addition to continually increasing teaching competence) to raise their salaries, they are more likely to be able to do so.

The distinction also allows us to keep up the fight for better salaries and more benefits for all early childhood staff. It keeps the dilemma of finite resources and infinite needs in front of us. Today's children can't wait for society to decide to place a higher value on the teachers of very young children. What we can do is insure that those resources are put to the best possible use.

Kay Albrecht, Ph.D., is the former executive director of HeartsHome Early Learning Center, Houston, Texas, and senior partner in Innovations in Early Childhood Education. Her specialties include teacher training and curriculum development. Her latest book, Innovations in Infant Curriculum, is in press with Gryphon House. In 2000, she served as the academic dean of the World Forum.

Looking Inside:
Helping Teachers Assess
Their Beliefs and Values

by Paula Jorde Bloom

Directors often lament how difficult it is to change teachers so that teaching practices are more developmentally appropriate and interactions with parents and other staff are more professional. The reason for the difficulty is that change efforts typically focus on increasing teachers' knowledge base. Clearly, knowledge is important; the workshops, the college classes, the books and articles are essential to expanding teachers' repertoire of instructional strategies. But knowledge is only part of the equation when it comes to helping teachers grow in professional competence. Directors must also help teachers become reflective practitioners. And reflection begins with an examination of one's own belief system.

Teachers' attitudes and beliefs about children provide the foundation for their philosophy of teaching. Because beliefs are grounded in one's values, they have a strong impact on shaping behavior. Teachers' values also govern how they will react when confronted with the inevitable ethical dilemmas that occur from time to time.

The assessment tool found within this article was designed to help teachers reflect on their attitudes and beliefs about children, parents, and their role in the classroom. The information gleaned from this self-assessment will help directors better understand the undergirding values and beliefs that drive the teaching practices they observe. Without

clarification of these values, it is difficult to help teachers set goals for changing attitudes and behaviors.

This assessment can be used in a variety of ways. In the interviewing and hiring process, it can be used to help understand the belief system of prospective teachers. This information is essential if directors want to ensure that the beliefs and values of new staff are consonant with the shared beliefs and stated philosophy of the center.

The assessment can also be used as a springboard for discussion at a staff meeting. The director can distribute the assessment to teachers a few days before the meeting. Teachers can complete it at work or take it home

where they may have fewer distractions. In either case, it is important to tell teachers that there are no right or wrong answers.

The completed assessments can be collected prior to the meeting and the responses to each of the eight questions in Part I noted on a large piece of newsprint. It is not necessary to indicate which teacher made which comment. The eight sheets of newsprint can then be displayed on the walls in the room where the staff meeting will be held. The results of Part II can be summarized by simply noting the number of times a trait or characteristic was noted by teachers as being an important outcome of children's experience in the program.

If an open, nonjudgmental atmosphere exists during the staff meeting, a lively discussion should ensue about how each of the responses relates to the written philosophy and educational objectives of the center. A word of caution, though. When we discuss beliefs, we tap into teachers' core value systems. Tact and sensitivity to differing points of view is essential.

It is critical in such discussions that the director, as facilitator, avoid any hint of moralizing, criticizing, or judging the comments made by teachers. If teachers feel threatened,

Values Clarification*

Values are enduring beliefs — ideas that we cherish and regard highly. Values influence the decisions we make and the course of action we follow. Some values we prize more deeply than others; they become standards by which we live. The purpose of this assessment is to help you assess the values and beliefs that guide your teaching attitudes and behaviors.

PART I.   **Complete the following sentences.**

1. I think children are generally _____

2. When children are unhappy, it's usually because _____

3. I get angry when children _____

4. The most important thing a teacher can do is_____

5. Children should not_____

6. All children are_____

7. I wish parents would_____

8. When parents_____ I feel _____

PART II.   **Circle the five traits and characteristics you would like children to be as a result of their preschool experience with you.**

adventurous	appreciate beauty	determined
affectionate	inquisitive	energetic
polite	respectful	friendly
altruistic	self-starter	obedient
caring	sense of humor	spontaneous
honest	industrious	persistent
assertive	creative	proud
confident	independent thinker	risk-taker
cheerful	desire to excel	open-minded

* From: P. J. Bloom, M. Sheerer, and J. Britz (1991). **Blueprint for Action: Achieving Center-Based Change Through Staff Development**. Published by New Horizons, PO Box 863, Lake Forest, Illinois 60045. Reprinted with permission.

they will either shut down and refuse to share their inner feelings about these important issues or they will get defensive and assume a confrontational posture. Both are counterproductive to the goal of the group exercise.

Through an active, reflective listening process, the director can assist teachers in identifying and articulating the beliefs and values that undergird their teaching philosophy. The goal is to help teachers reflect on the source of their beliefs and begin to discuss how important parents, religion, early school experiences, and educational training are in shaping one's values. When conducted in a nonthreatening way, such group discussions can help teachers gain greater insight into how their beliefs guide what they do in the classroom every day.

Subsequent staff meetings might tackle thornier issues related to teachers' values and beliefs about the curriculum, instruction, and the teacher's role in promoting children's learning. For example, teachers can be asked to share their beliefs regarding the extent to which they believe child care experiences impact children's overall development and learning. Recent research in this area has found that many early childhood teachers in this country embrace the belief that children's learning is largely determined by influences outside the center, in the genes and social background of the children. This belief is in sharp contrast to teacher beliefs in countries like Japan where teachers at all levels of the educational system believe that achievement is a product more of effort than inherent talent. Teachers in Japan tend to believe their efforts in promoting student learning can make a difference.

Below are several statements that can serve as discussion starters about different values and beliefs that undergird educational practice. Teachers can brainstorm to generate additional statements to add to this list.

- Practice makes perfect.

- Telling is teaching.

- Parents don't value teachers' knowledge and expertise.

- Boys are naturally better at math than girls.

- Competition is necessary to motivate learning.

- The teacher is an authority that should not be questioned.

- Responding too quickly to crying children will spoil them.

Paula Jorde Bloom holds a joint appointment as director of the Center for Early Childhood Leadership and professor in the Department of Early Childhood Education at National-Louis University. She is on the Management Committee for the Illinois Director Credential.

Ongoing Growing

by Connie Jo Smith

You are excited because the Child Care Resource and Referral Agency has scheduled a well-known speaker for their upcoming Saturday conference. You enthusiastically offer the opportunity for staff members to register and hear complaints that Saturday is the only day they have to spend with their children.

You receive a cash donation to provide training for the center and are exhilarated. You ask for input about the topics and presenters. The session is scheduled for Tuesday evening after the center closes so everyone can attend. Staff members who worked the last shift are tired and hungry. Staff members who opened at 5 a.m. had to drive back to the center and it is getting close to their bedtime.

You schedule a training during the afternoon nap and arrange for volunteers to cover the classrooms. The training is close by so you can be reached. Several regular and competent volunteers show up and are pleased to help, but some volunteers do not show.

You advertised for hiring substitutes for training times. The toll on the budget will be significant and so far not enough people have applied to cover every classroom.

Do you want to provide professional development opportunities for your staff but have found more obstacles than solutions? Many child care programs are experiencing bountiful challenges.

The considerations surrounding training are limitless and sometimes overwhelming. As with every challenge, there are no magical answers; but by expanding our thinking on what professional development is, we may be able to find new solutions.

Professional development is often seen as a workshop where a group of people share ideas and learn new ones. Workshops can be very valuable and there is a place within professional development for them. Group sessions may be best for some required training. But what else can professional development be? Thinking about the ways young children learn may help open our eyes to other ways adults learn, too. Let's look at some ways adults can learn from doing.

Providing each staff member regularly paid professional development

time during working hours shows a commitment to quality. Arranging for part-time staff or well-trained, familiar substitutes to cover is likely to enhance the professional development program. Selecting topics and approaches by balancing individual needs and interests with center requirements and goals will allow individualization and facilitate team spirit.

Learning Center

Design an adult learning center for reading, viewing videos, listening to tapes, using a computer, thinking, and sharing ideas. Use an office for planning, a lounge, or a parent room. Perhaps there is a corner in the kitchen. Areas could be open for other purposes on a scheduled basis.

If space is limited, look for places where magazines, books, videos, audio tapes, and a laptop can be stored and checked out by staff and parents. If no space is available, consider scheduling staff development time at the end of work shifts so staff can go to a public library or home to work.

If you have a professional development work area and materials, examine how frequently and how well they are used. Just as we evaluate children's learning centers, it is important to measure the effectiveness of adult space and materials. Ideas from staff may make the space more comfortable and resources more beneficial.

Resource Review

To extend the use of professional resources, try highlighting a specific article, chapter in a book, videotape, or audio tape. Give assignments to review the material by a designated date. It is important to provide a method for processing the information. Schedule time for each teacher to discuss their reaction with someone or record their thoughts in a center professional journal. A worksheet developed for everyone to complete and place where they could see each other's ideas is another way to process information. Blank tapes and a recorder can be made available for comments on the assignment.

By focusing all staff on the same information, you give them something in common and facilitate a sense of community. Sharing ideas across shifts enhances communication and relationships with the total staff. If the center is part of a larger program, think about arranging for the sharing to occur across centers.

World Wide Web

A tremendous resource for professional development is the Internet. Providing access to the World Wide Web is one way technology can connect staff to professional development opportunities.

Allot time for staff to research and discover sites. Bookmarking pages that they recommend others visit could be a way to share their discoveries. Specific web addresses might be assigned for review.

Joining a listserv group is an exciting way to share expertise and turn to other professionals for help. (A listserv is an electronic discussion group. People communicate through e-mail about a specific topic, like early childhood. Through a listserv, one can get lesson plan ideas, participate in philosophical debates, find out about conferences, and much more. Information about ERIC sponsored listservs is available at ericeece.org.) The experience of using a computer and learning about the Internet will be professional development in itself.

Distance Education

Other ways technology can support professional development is through distance education. Participating in educational television training programs and registering for correspondence college classes are examples. Another opportunity is interactive distance learning through Early Childhood Professional Development Network (ECPDN) [(803) 252-0630], which offers a variety of satellite early childhood education training courses and resources, with credit options. The National Head Start Association (NHSA) Heads Up! Network provides training through a satellite television network created specifically for the Head Start and early childhood community. See their web page at www.nhsa.org or call (800) 438-4888 to subscribe.

Visiting Far and Near

People can learn from others within the same center, across town, throughout the state, or beyond. Arranging for staff members to make visits encourages the exchange of information and ideas.

Identify each classroom's strong point and let other staff observe that strength. Another approach is to pair staff and let them visit each other's classroom and give feedback. Still another approach includes encouraging visitation in all classrooms using a prepared observation form to guide the visit toward a non-threatening observation. The form may ask the visitor to identify toys/materials the children used frequently or to note something that they had not seen before.

To identify other sites for visiting, contact your child care resource and referral agency. Your state department of education may have model preschool sites identified that would welcome your visit. Some colleges and universities have classrooms open for visitation. A list of NAEYC accredited centers can be obtained by calling (800) 424-2460. The child care licensing office may also have suggestions.

In addition to visiting centers, there are community experiences that could enhance what staff offer children. Visits to art museums, theater productions, and concerts broaden staff experiences. Look around your community to see what may have been overlooked as professional development opportunities.

Mindful Questions and Answers

Great expertise often is right under your roof, but finding time to exchange ideas in an organized approach can be difficult. One way to get ideas flowing and integrate training into the process is to have a place where a question is written and staff members respond throughout a determined time frame. Reading each other's comments keeps communication flowing.

Questions could come from situations where input is needed to make a decision. "What new classroom materials would you like us to buy? Please tell why you want whatever you list." Questions may be ones you want to get staff thinking about. "What is the most important job a preschool teacher does?" Decide how often questions will be changed and who they will come from and inform staff.

Creating a designated place and time for questions makes it systematic. Asking only one question at a time allows the activity to focus all staff on the issue and encourages more thoughtful answers. Look at your space and see what would work in your center. Again, if you are part of a larger program, explore ways to rotate questions and answers to broaden the experience and encourage program wide connections. This approach may also be helpful in obtaining parent input.

Documentation

As creative approaches to professional development are implemented, creative ways for documentation may also surface. Programs may be required to prove to funding sources and licensing representatives that training has occurred. Look for ways to document all of the terrific learning that is occurring in less traditional styles.

Connie Jo Smith has served as the early childhood education specialist for Training and Technical Assistance Services at Western Kentucky University since 1977. She has firsthand experience as a teacher of young children, a child care and Head Start director, and an adult educator. Her extensive experience training Head Start and child care staff provides valuable insight into the field.

All Dressed Up and No Place to Grow!

by Pauline Davey Zeece

Michelle and Eric looked forward to the in-service training. The week-long workshop lived up to its promise to provide insight into child behavior management; new activities for the entire center; and creative ways to group children effectively. The two teachers returned renewed and ready to try some of their newly learned ideas and techniques. They were especially interested in setting up some of the language-based small group activities, but these required additional materials, lower child-adult ratios, and teacher planning time. None of these resources were available.

Frances was a "fixture" at the local Head Start program. Her first involvement was as a parent participant. After volunteering in the classroom for four years, she was hired as a classroom assistant. Through dedication and hard work, she gained confidence and courage to approach her director about supporting her efforts to complete her GED and then earn a college degree. Frances did well in all of her college classes, but she especially loved the ones related to children's literature. One day she approached the educational coordinator and asked if the program could invest in some updated children's books and related materials; she was told there were no resources in the budget for such items.

Training enriches a program and its staff. It not only helps employees to better understand their roles and responsibilities within an organization, it also creates the potential for people to grow in new and exciting ways. In-service opportunities provide ways for staff to extend their understanding of a wide variety of topics and enrich the program resource base. But too often they return to a program after inspiring training experiences only to discover that there is little support or minimal resources to put their new information or plans into action. Such staff invariably find themselves frustrated, discouraged, and *all dressed up with no place to grow.*

How then can directors support staff in their professional and personal development and still maintain a solvent operation? What can directors do to increase the chance that training opportunities turn into positive outcomes for an entire program?

Following are ten tips for making the most of training experiences. See what you think.

1. Conduct an all-agency training audit.

Neugebauer (1998) suggests that the budgets of most child care programs are precariously structured with little room for mismanagement or error. This implies that training decisions must be well thought out.

Training, any training, takes resources. Even if the training itself has been donated, the staff release time and follow-up activities should be considered and calculated as a training-related expense.

Information from an annual training audit can be used to profile the resource output for training activities, to predict and plan for current and future needs, and to demonstrate the priority budget percentage training and staff development hold within a program.

Calculating the amount of staff time and the cost of trainers and materials provides a way to complete a cost-benefit analysis.

Audit Enhancers:

- Survey staff individually. Be sure to include all members associated with your program.

- Complete training statistics for areas, components, and categories of cost.

- Develop an annual and a multi-year overview of trends and make this information available to everyone.

2. Create a training accountability chain within the agency.

Everything that happens within a program impacts on its effectiveness. Training is directly and indirectly related to the nature and quality of services provided to children and families.

It may be difficult to monitor all training-related activities unless this job is formally designated within your program structure.

Creating a system that tracks and records all activities as they occur helps to ensure a better match between staff needs and system capabilities. Available resources can then be directed toward the integration and implementation of new ideas, new techniques, and new approaches.

Knowing firsthand about staff training also provides an effective staff development and performance evaluation tool.

Chain Builders:

- Create a structure to record, monitor, and report all training activities and information.

- Ensure that reporting is multi-directional and user-friendly to staff and stakeholders.

- Accept or designate responsibility for all training-related decisions and articulate these to staff.

3. Provide information about and expectations for training and training-related outcomes at hiring, in-service, and staff performance reviews.

Training and in-service opportunities may be used as an effective recruitment tool. The benefits of a well conceptualized and individualized program can offset a lower salary structure, especially for staff members who are pursuing a formal education or certification.

Creating a formal expectation about outcomes related to training also engenders a reciprocal responsibility. Staff are expected to attend and use training opportunities to augment good performance or to improve deficient effectiveness; administrators are expected to provide ways for training activities to be available and actualized — or at least discussed!

Staff goals can then be tied to training opportunities and evaluated in regularly scheduled performance reviews.

Expectation Makers:

- Provide an overview of training opportunities and benefits during

the hiring process and use training as a marketing tool.

- Articulate expectations about training outcomes and follow up.

- Use training information as one measure within performance evaluations — including your own! Celebrate successes and discuss disappointments.

4. Support and plan for training that affords opportunities for personal and professional growth. Help everyone see how these are related.

After conducting a training audit, a seasoned director was surprised to learn that one employee had participated in over 200 hours and one had utilized only three hours of training. Three other employees had attended the identical training sessions for three consecutive years. Most disturbing, however, was the discovery that few people could tie their training choices to the program mission.

Some staff were able to align various training opportunities to the needs of a specific child and/or family, but none could articulate how all of their training choices fit together in a personal and professional growth plan. People need to expect that their talents and time spent in training helps to move a program toward its objectives (Bloom, Sheerer, & Britz, 1991).

It is worth the time to explore how training is utilized and perceived within a program. Healthy, effective workers must be able to balance the professional and personal parts of their lives — at work and at home. Training that facilitates the development of such a balance benefits everyone.

People Growers:

- Ensure that all training opportunities are tied directly to the program mission.

- Allow for a balance of training that strengthens the personal and professional goals of all staff members.

- Encourage risk taking in training selections. Reward efforts that move people out of their comfort zone while keeping them within their own long-term development goals.

5. Provide mechanisms for immediate feedback and reflection. Be sensitive to the initial enthusiasm and potential frustrations engendered in learning — help staff think about Plan B.

New ideas and activities can energize a staff and motivate everyone within a program. Learning new strategies for lingering problems or new approaches for worn-out routines is not only exciting but useful.

When staff are unable to discuss or try out what they have learned, disappointment, frustration, and/or anger may occur. Difficult feelings may also arise when training is inadequate or ill-targeted or when staff feel too busy or overwhelmed to do one more thing (even when it is exactly what they need).

Providing a system that encourages staff to develop individual training plans and to reflect on training experiences creates positive outcomes. In this way, workers take control of their own learning opportunities and their own learning.

Reflective Planners:

- Provide a mechanism for immediate feedback and for longer term reflective planning.

Individuals involved in child care and early childhood education need to keep abreast of research and information in the field by attending workshops, lectures, conventions, organizational meetings, and other means. . . . The way an employee is treated greatly influences personal performance. If staff is treated as self-directed, creative, and self-controlled, he or she is likely to respond as a productive, important member of the team.

— Barbara J. Taylor

- Encourage staff to discuss the selection and outcomes of the training opportunities with others.

- Provide a formal system for helping staff to determine what they NEED and what they would ideally LIKE TO HAVE to implement their training-inspired ideas and activities. Encourage the development of alternative approaches.

6. Create a resource base for implementation of prioritized training information (e.g., release time, planning time, materials, extra help, unusual opportunities).

Most people attached to a child care program are vaguely aware of the financial limitations that surround programming decisions. Disclosing the resources available for training opportunities encourages staff to creatively strategize and prioritize about the best use of resources.

Creating a data base about past, present, and future opportunities optimizes planning efforts. Differentiating and selecting between mandated and elective training helps staff retain control of their own professional development. In large programs, staff can participate in planning for training opportunities within program areas, components, or teams. In smaller programs, training can be planned directly with each

employee. Providing a range of training opportunities and a variety of training formats and venues further assures a good match between staff goals and program objectives.

Resource Creators:

- Provide accurate, timely, and complete information about all training opportunities. Clarify required versus elective training; provide a balance of professional and personal enhancement opportunities.

- Institute brainstorming sessions to discuss such things as release time, coverage, materials, and unusual training opportunities.

- Track the best AND worst of training opportunities (and everything in between) and create an agency data base; collect and share information about and with other agencies to extend the data base.

7. Facilitate the development of training interest groups.

The synergy within any well-functioning group is related, in part, to a shared understanding about how and why a program does business. When staff attend training opportunities together, common reference points and collaborative learning occur.

Providing opportunities for people who share mutual interests across jobs builds strong intra-programmatic linkages. A teacher may tie information to the classroom, a food service worker to menus, and a social services coordinator to the larger community. Yet when attending training together, information is dissected and applied in a comprehensive way.

Creating training interest teams also provides legitimate ways in which people who work together can build meaningful ties. Oftentimes the most scarce commodity in a program is the luxury of "extra" time — or any time to do anything else but work. Training offers people the opportunities to foster and build healthy personal and professional relationships.

Training Team Builders:

- Utilize information from staff surveys and training audits to develop a profile of shared interests within the program. Convey these to the staff.

- Create opportunities and provide resources that foster training team building. Reward teams for their efforts and achievements.

- Extend the expertise of well-developed training teams to other programs; sponsor and participate in inter-programmatic training opportunities.

8. Consider the development of all-agency "expert teams."

Just as every child and family in a program has strengths and gifts to share, so does every staff member. The development of an agency expert team is based on this premise.

Asking staff to identify their special interests and talents is the first step in the creation of a team. There may be an initial level of discomfort or even mistrust until people realize that EVERYONE in the program will be acknowledged and supported in

the development of an area of expertise.

Teams can then be created based on this expertise.

The fundamental difference between a training interest team and an agency expert team rests in the notion that the expert team will be called upon to provide leadership and guidance in a specific area to others in the program. Such a team is recognized and respected as the best source of information on a given topic or area.

Expert Team Developers:

- Work to identify interests, talents, and potential expertise in all staff members. Support and nurture the ongoing development of such expertise. Remember the old adage shared by many consultants: "You need to travel 60 miles to become an expert!" People may need to be convinced that they can develop expert teams within their own programs.

- Help others to recognize that such talents cross job descriptions and responsibilities and are strengthened by an inclusive approach. Recognize and reward efforts toward staff-developed goals related to expert team membership.

- Create opportunities for individuals and groups to build pods or areas of expertise. Provide regular, legitimate, and well-supported opportunities for staff to use their expertise to make real contributions.

9. Model the wise selections and application of training opportunities.

Directors serve as models for a whole host of things — whether they want to or not! Assuming the leadership

position within a program extends to everything that goes on.

Participating in training says to the staff: "Everyone in this program has something to learn, something to share, and something to celebrate."

Developing a well-conceptualized and well-suited personal training plan creates opportunities for personal and professional growth; participating as an equal partner within an expert team creates participatory management at its best.

Model Directors:

- Show honest enthusiasm for training efforts.

- Require the same of themselves as they do of all other staff members. If an expert team concept is adopted, be the example rather than the exception.

- Use training resources ethically and responsibly, especially as these are related to your own training. If your training choices involve trips to Hawaii and other staff members involve trips to the local library, think about the impact on the program. Using a disproportionate amount of training funds on a select few also creates difficulties if such allocations are viewed as preferential or unfair.

10. Help staff to recognize that gradual implementation is not a rejection of an idea or opportunity but a function of real-world programming constraints.

Being honest and realistic about what can and cannot happen builds trust. When people know what to expect, destructive game playing and passive aggressive actions are less likely to surface.

This does not mean that there still might be frustration or disappointment, but this can be tempered with alternative plans over which employees have some control.

Typically, staff members have a wealth of knowledge about how to phase in a new idea or approach or how to develop alternative materials — such information may be buried beneath many layers of tradition, habit, or even program mandate.

Pragmatic Directors:

- Recognize that training is not a luxury but a necessity within a dynamic program. Seek creative, alternative approaches and training opportunities for everyone. Make those who provide training accountable before, during, and after training is provided. Require and conduct an evaluation of all training that takes place in your program and summarize effectiveness by category/topic, trainer, and employee or category of employee.

- Accept staff enthusiasm about new ideas as an asset; validate their feelings when resources are not available to put training ideas into place.

- Allow staff to take the lead (and sometimes even the primary responsibility) for balancing the training budget and implementing appropriate training follow up. Be sure to provide appropriate release time for such an activity.

The methods of strategies employed in a training program depends on goals for program and staff; the amount of time and resources available; and the nature of the content selected (Sciarra & Dorsey, 1998). It also depends on the willingness of a competent director to ensure that life after training will be productive for everyone!

Sources and Resources

Bloom, P. J., Sheerer, M., & Britz, J. (1991). *Blueprint for action: Achieving center-based change through staff development*. Beltsville, MD: Gryphon House.

Neugebauer, B., & Neugebauer, R. (1998). *The art of leadership: Managing early childhood organizations* (Chapter 7: Managing money). Redmond, WA: *Child Care Information Exchange*.

Sciarra, D., & Dorsey, A. (1998). *Developing and administering a child care center*. Albany, NJ: Delmar Publishing.

Taylor, B. (1997). *Early childhood program management: People and procedures*. Upper Saddle Ridge, NJ: Merrill.

Pauline Davey Zeece is a professor in the Department of Family and Consumer Sciences at the University of Nebraska in Lincoln.

Chapter 4

Motivating
and
Supervising Staff

You Say Staff Deserve Respect? Energize Your Words With Action!

by Karen Stephens

Whether they represent folks in rural areas or big cities, political leaders in the spotlight routinely pronounce children as our nation's greatest resource. And now with hard-core brain research echoing their claim, the "pols" pronounce even louder how vital quality early childhood programs are to our country's welfare. They couch their support in terms of investing in our future workforce, our future bevy of taxpayers. Rarely is it frankly said it's simply the right thing to do.

And so leaders continue to skirt comprehensive measures that would put money behind their rhetoric, behind our children and programs that serve them. You know the economic culture in the United States as well as I do. If one truly believes in something, they back it with greenback. So far, our nation has been mighty measly. We've yet to muster collective commitment to children.

And, by extension, our country has been measly with its child care providers. Oh sure, people of note now proclaim child care is a noble calling, not merely babysitting. (How long did it take us to get THAT idea across?!) And they publicly commend child care folks for the lasting contribution we make to society. Astute leaders even cite studies that reveal the best path to quality child care is to maintain a well educated and trained staff.

But coming through with the resources to compensate quality caregivers — well that idea seems to cool as fast as news camera's spotlights dim. Perhaps positive steps have been made in your program; but on a national scale, the necessity of taking a vow of poverty to work in child care still reigns.

So while you and I and our fellow child care directors wait for voters to hold leaders accountable for their rhetoric, we're left shouldering the task of maintaining a stable child care workforce for American families. You may say I'm being overly dramatic, even pessimistic. I say I'm being realistic.

So how do directors motivate professionals who are usually undercompensated (I'm talking minimum wage even with a four year degree); their skills typically underestimated

(Oh, you're so lucky to sit around and play with kids all day); and their commitment often discounted (So when are you getting a real job?)?

I certainly don't have all the answers. In my 20+ years in child care, I've participated in innumerable salary surveys and equity wage initiatives. Some have even come through with meaningful results. But I still rarely see professionally trained child care providers paid as well as their public school counterparts.

I'm not naive. Even when better pay becomes a reality, it still takes more than money to motivate and retain well qualified staff. In fact, all things being equal (if that ever happens), intrinsic motivation is far more influential on staff performance and longevity. And the proof is visible in child care programs everywhere. Considering the average child care provider makes less than $15,000 annually, I'm not amazed 40% of us leave the child care field annually; I'm amazed 60% of us stay in it! Intrinsic motivation is the key.

So, over the years, I've tried to come up with a plethora of tangible ways to help staff feel great about the job they're doing. To feel great in their hearts and minds. I've tried to show respect for their knowledge and to appreciate their talent. And I don't take for granted their dedication to children and families. Some strategies have been simple to carry out; others require more effort. And I must warn you, some may be hokey, but they've all been effective.

I'll share my ideas below. Hopefully, they'll trigger your own imagination. Despite the miles that distance us, together we can work to keep our nation's child care infrastructure — our staff — stable, experienced, motivated, and proud. Until child care professionals receive proper monetary compensation, the least we can do is feed their generous spirits with respect and appreciation.

Tangible Ways to Show Staff Respect and Appreciation

1. Post staff photos near entrance. Include position title, length of service, credentials, and brief biography.

2. Include staff profiles in program newsletters. Distribute newsletters not only to parents and your board but also to program funders and supporters.

3. Include staff in community meetings whenever possible. Introduce them, with title, to *movers and shakers* in attendance. Recognize staff at appropriate events, such as program dedication ceremonies or other public functions.

4. Supply each staff member with a professional business card for networking purposes.

5. Post announcements for parents whenever staff acquire in-service training or renew certificates such as in first aid training.

6. Recommend qualified staff as workshop presenters and training consultants.

7. Send staff's *parents* clippings of program news coverage. (Yes, I'm serious. No matter what your staff's age, they always like to make their parents proud.)

8. Send staff's hometown newspapers press releases, such as announcements of your program's accreditation.

9. Publicly (as well as in evaluations) give staff credit for program improvements. If someone comes up with a creative idea or solution, they should bask in the glory!

10. Organize *regular* events for *team bonding*. Team spirit and camaraderie solidified when we instituted monthly staff dinners. It's a great tradition.

11. Recognize and utilize each staff member's unique talents. I have a teacher with a strong background in physical education. I turn to her for recommendations on new gross motor equipment; she knows I count on her expertise. Another teacher is a wizard with children's computer programs. She's our leader when purchasing decisions are made. AND she gets a subscription to a newsletter on children's software so her input can be well informed. (Meaning, I try — even in small ways — to help her be successful in her job.)

12. Take time to regularly observe in classrooms. At least yearly, *write up* your observations for the room's staff to read within a few days. The speedy feedback is always appreciated. The process is time consuming, but it allows you to document for personnel files as well as to congratulate staff on skillful child guidance or inventive curriculum.

13. Provide one-on-one mentoring when possible. If not, try to find a mentor to fit a staff member's needs. Is a teacher having trouble arranging his environment? Help him with new

arrangements or ask for another staff member's expertise.

14. Encourage staff's hobbies and interests. Is a teacher into bunnies big time? Go ahead and buy a bunny wind sock for her play yard. The kids will learn about wind and she'll appreciate the individualized attention.

15. Make copies of complimentary letters from parents for staff keepsakes.

16. Solicit staff input on decisions that affect them. For instance, they can identify best times to hold parent-teacher conferences.

17. Before preparing supplies and equipment budgets, ask staff to submit a list of recommended purchases.

18. Provide staff with articles, videotapes, or conference information that address topics of special interest. Are teachers interested in learning about the Project Approach? If so, secure funds to send them to a workshop. (My personal dream is to find travel funds so our teachers can visit the Reggio Emilia programs in Italy!)

19. Encourage staff to serve on professional boards and committees. Recognize their efforts when talking to staff, parents, and board members.

20. Compliment staff when they participate in wellness and stress management programs. Literally, they deserve a pat on the back for staying healthy!

21. Recognize staff talent in simple and spontaneous ways. When I go to a conference, I bring something back from the exhibitor's venue. One year, my treasures included a white rabbit puppet that popped out of a magician's black hat. I left the puppet as a surprise on the teachers' desk. An attached note said I marveled at the

magic they do with kids. Yes, it's sappy and sentimental, but the teachers appreciated the thought all the same — and who doesn't need another puppet for the classroom?

22. Provide staff with as much personal space for organization and planning as possible. In days of old, our teachers had lockers, not an office. We've made a bit of progress since then, but not lots. Now four head teachers share a cramped office with one desk, a file cabinet, and a computer. Their office has a love seat for comfort, but also stores our children's library, two refrigerators, and its walls are stacked — literally to the ceiling — with junk supplies creative teachers love to squirrel away. They don't have the separate work stations, staff lounge, or make-it-take-it resource room of their dreams, but they know I'd jump for space that would give it to them.

23. Provide staff time to observe other programs. Mutually decide with staff where they'll observe, why, and when. Arrange for substitutes so staff can leave without burdening those left with the kids.

24. Once a year, take a *fun and interesting* retreat or staff trip together. Visit an outstanding children's museum or go hear a famous children's author speak. Staff will appreciate the time you take to facilitate and organize their enjoyment.

25. Committed caregivers get a lot of enjoyment out of being partners with parents as they nurture children's development. To provide time for the communication the partner requires, bring in extra staff or volunteers at the beginning and ending of the day (that's when parents are most likely to be in the classroom).

26. Bring in a bouquet of wildflowers or a new compact disc to classrooms *just because*. Employees and children respond to aesthetics.

27. Involve staff in any changes in their work environment. We recently renovated one of our site's play yard. I can't tell you how many times I volleyed construction ideas between architects and teaching staff. I continually asked if a purposed design would help or hinder our teachers' job performance. And boy did it pay off! Our program ended up with a much better play yard because the people who used it day in and day out provided guidance. And the staff were pleased to be included in making decisions with other professionals. (In truth, they prevented the committee from making numerous design mistakes!)

28. Serve on committees that organize a community-wide child care provider recognition day. If there isn't one already, start one yourself. Staff will note your efforts to celebrate the important work they do.

29. Teachers love books. Make it a program practice to treat them with birthday or holiday gift certificates to a bookstore. Whether they purchase a book for relaxation or for reading to the children, your program will win either way.

30. Occasionally surprise teachers with helpful supplies that are *tools of the trade*. This could be a big-ticket item, like a laminating machine. But most likely your budget will better afford something simple, like notepads with motivational sayings. "To teach is to touch the future" is a perennial favorite.

31. Encourage and facilitate your program staff and parents' involvement with Worthy Wage Day!

32. Buy each program site a subscription to the newsletter *Rights,*

Raises and Respect — the biannual publication of the National Center for Early Childhood Workforce, $30/year. Send fee to: NCECW, 733 15th Street NW, Suite 1037, Washington, DC 20005-2112.

33. Nominate deserving staff for awards bestowed by the community or profession.

34. Ask staff for recommendations of curriculum books to add to their resource library. (And if they don't have an on-site resource library, create one. Our staff's is located in my office.)

35. Reimburse staff for part or all of their professional dues to organizations, such as local affiliates of the National Association for the Education of Young Children (to identify your local, call (800) 424-2460).

36. Reimburse staff for part or all of continued education costs, whether they be through conferences or college classes. Be sure to recognize staff each time they complete a course that improves their job skills.

So there you are, 36 tangible and specific ways to value your staff and the life-affirming work they perform. As you put these ideas into practice, you'll put action behind your hopes and dreams for children. It's the ethical thing to do — the right thing to do. And may the rest of the world follow your lead.

In 1980, Karen Stephens became director of Illinois State University Child Care Center and instructor in child development for ISU Family and Consumer Sciences Department. She writes the weekly newspaper column, "Keeping the Young at Heart," and is the author of the high school textbook, **The Child Care Professional**.

How to Implement an Effective Bonus System in Your Center

Ideas from the Exchange Panel of 100

The greatest management principle in the world:
The things that get rewarded get done.
— Michael LeBoeuf

One of the first things that Nancy learned when she went to work at Buttons and Bows Child Care Center is that you achieve better results in working with children if you reward their desired behavior than if you punish their undesired behavior. Yet when Nancy was promoted to center director, she left this principle in the classroom.

When staff members started becoming lax and dispirited in their performance, Nancy responded by establishing new rules and tightening their enforcement. By focusing on the negative, Nancy only succeeded in driving staff morale to an all time low. Had she not forsaken her early childhood training, she probably would have spent more time reinforcing the good things that were happening.

One step Nancy might have taken would have been to implement a bonus system to reward the types of behavior she preferred. Such systems are commonplace in most industries. However, due to lack of money, bonus systems are not employed widely in the child care world. Few centers can afford to provide teachers with the base salaries they deserve, let alone award them with bonuses.

Even with scant resources, however, over 50 percent of **Exchange Panel of 100** members have implemented bonus systems in their programs. The results have been encouraging. Panel members report noticeable improvements in staff morale, performance and retention. In this article, panelists will share their suggestions on how to implement a bonus system.

Step #1 — Fix Your Purpose

Awarding a bonus is not a magic cure for all ailments. In order to achieve results, a bonus system must have a single purpose. This purpose should be clearly defined from the outset, narrowly focused, and achievable.

The goals of bonus systems implemented by panel members fell into the four categories below. Under each category are listed examples of specific objectives of some of their systems.

1. **Improving Individual Performance**

- Discouraging absenteeism and tardiness

- Encouraging creativity in lesson planning

- Increasing genuine conversation between teachers and children

- Increasing the use of appropriate controls

2. **Improving Team Performance**

- Encouraging cooperative behavior among staff

- Encouraging team planning

- Encouraging staff members to help each other improve

3. **Increasing Staff Retention**

- Encouraging teachers to stay at the center

4. **Boosting Staff Morale**

- Boosting the sagging spirits of individuals

- Revving up the spirits of the entire staff

Types of Bonuses Offered by Panel of 100 Members

Money

- **On the Spot Awards.** When a supervisor spots an employee making a special contribution or an effort above and beyond the call of duty, she writes up a recommendation for a cash bonus, which, if approved, is awarded at the next staff meeting. Awards that different centers make are in the range of $50 to $150.

- **Teacher of the Month.** Teacher selected as demonstrating most achievement in identified areas during month receives a $25 cash bonus.

- **Special Achievement Bonus.** Staff members maintain bonus sheets on which they list special efforts they make during the year (extra training, collecting resources, helping train new staff, etc). At the end of the year the Board of Directors reviews these sheets and awards bonuses in the range of $200 to $600.

- **Longevity Bonus.** Once a year staff are paid a bonus of three to five cents per hour for the number of hours they have worked in the past year. The point at which this award is made is selected so as to encourage staff to hang in there during periods when turnover is typically a problem. Another center awards a $25 bonus at the end of the year to staff who have been with the program less than one year and $50 to those who have been there more than one year.

- **End of the Year Bonus.** Flat bonus to all staff. In some centers this is a flat amount (typically $25 to $50); in others, it's calculated as a percentage of one's salary (one center provides a bonus of 10 percent of one month's pay); and some base it on a percentage of center profits for the year).

- **Center of the Year Award.** Center that is most successful in achieving goals of the organization in past year is provided a cash award that staff can use at their discretion. Some centers use this for dinner out, others to buy a special piece of equipment.

- **Profit Sharing.** Some larger for-profit organizations reward staff members at various levels by presenting them with shares in the company, or with bonuses calculated on the basis of the profitability. One small center experimented with pegging all staff salaries to the center's financial performance (i.e. teacher and director salaries would rise and fall based on the center's annual bottom line).

Recognition

- **Employee of the Week, Month, Year Award.** Employee selected either by management or peers is presented with a certificate at staff meeting or staff party.

- **End of the Year Awards.** Staff votes for winners of awards in a number of categories (such as *best idea person, most supportive, hardest worker, most dependable, best cheerleader*). Awards announced and presented at annual dinner party. Some centers place pictures of award winners on special plaques displayed where all can see.

- **Special Effort Certificates.** Employees who display extraordinary performances or take on extra duties are cited at monthly staff meetings with the presentation of a certificate.

- **Feel Good Board.** Weekly notices on board in staff lounge recognizing individuals or teams for outstanding achievements.

- **Apple for the Teacher Tree.** When one staff member sees another performing well she writes a compliment on a red card shaped like an apple and adds it to a huge tree on the wall at the entrance for parents and staff to see. A rotating panel of three staff members selects one staff member for the **Golden Apple of the Month Award.** A gold apple with this person's picture sits atop the Apple for the Teacher Tree for one month.

- **Special Recognition.** Many centers recognize staff members on a regular basis in their center newsletters and bulletin boards. In others, special achiever awards are made in monthly board meetings, or in the form of letters of commendation placed in the individuals' personnel files.

- **Certificate of Service Pins.** At the annual staff party, staff members are presented with center pins for two, five, and ten years of service to the center.

The Gift of Time

- **Merit Days Off.** Staff members cited for special achievement have the opportunity to take one or two days off with pay.

- **Professional Days.** Special achievers released from daily duties to attend professional activities (conferences, classes, visits to other centers, or time away from the center to plan special activities).

- **Scheduling Priority.** Staff members qualifying (either due to longevity or special performance) receive first choice in selecting work schedules and/or in selecting vacation times.

- **Special Positions.** One center created a position of child development specialist with somewhat higher pay and responsibility than regular teaching positions. Teachers recognized for consistent exceptional performance are promoted to these positions.

- **Special Duties.** Teachers who are performing especially well are assigned special administrative and supervisory tasks for which they receive added pay.

- **Peer Trainers.** Top staff members are designated as training leaders for the staff.

- **Special Project Support.** Individuals or teams are awarded extra funding to carry out a special classroom project of their choosing.

- **Extra Supplies Money.** Team that is rated as most effective each month is given extra money to go out and buy extra teaching supplies.

- **Trips.** Top performers have all expenses paid to attend early childhood conferences or classes out of town.

Fun and Games

- **Staff Appreciation Banquets.** At the end of the year all staff are invited to attend a center sponsored banquet. Various festivities occur from director's annual report to presentation of special awards.

- **Employee Dinners.** Staff all go out together for a dinner at a local restaurant (or in some cases, at the director's house) for a purely social occasion.

- **Humorous Awards.** Some centers dream up tongue-in-cheek awards to present to staff members. Every staff member gets some award that pokes fun, in a good natured way, at some aspect of their personality or performance *(staff member who makes the most incredible messes, staff member who tells the best "night after" stories)*. Several directors write original poems that they read at the annual banquet which cite special contributions of each staff member *(Now Leslie's a jewel, and nature's her thing. Some homemade granola will strengthen her zing).*

- **Gifts.** Theater tickets, dinners out, magazine subscriptions, NAEYC dues, gift certificates. Some are given on employment anniversary, some at year end, and others on staff member's birthday. Some award gifts in lieu of cash to top performers; some present same gift to all staff members; and some present a hand picked gift for each staff member.

Step #2 —
Define Award Criteria

What does someone have to do to win the award? Who will pick the winners? How often will awards be given? How many will be given? Can someone win more than once?

These decisions should be made, and publicized in advance. In arriving at them, consider the following guidelines.

The behavior award should relate directly to the purpose of the award. If the purpose of the bonus is to encourage creativity, the award should be made on the basis of the creativity of teachers' classroom behavior. If retention is the goal, years of service should be rewarded. If cooperative team behavior is your objective, you would give a bonus to an entire team which performed well, rather than to individuals. An across the board bonus to all staff members at the end of the year will do little to improve performance, although it may give a shot in the arm to morale.

The award should be made in a timely manner. The closer in time an award is made to the behavior that earned it, the more reinforcing its effect will be. On the spot awards, in which a special effort is cited immediately, are clearly the most powerful in this sense. End of the year awards, on the other hand, usually are so far removed from daily life in the classroom that they can do little more than boost morale. (This is not to say that an end of the year morale boost is not of value, of course.)

The award system should be perceived as fair. Everyone should believe they have a legitimate shot at earning a bonus. When awards are announced, they should generally be perceived as well deserved. If staff members don't believe the system for awarding bonuses is fair, they won't be motivated to work hard to achieve them.

Step #3 —
Select Meaningful Awards

For a bonus to have an impact, it needs to be perceived as significant enough to justify any extra effort required to obtain it. The prospect of earning a $10 bonus is not going to weigh heavily in a teacher's decision to remain at the center another year. On the other hand, the prize of having first choice in work scheduling might well motivate a teacher to avoid tardiness.

Clearly, the bonus most likely to succeed is cash. As Oscar Wilde once mused, "When I was young I thought that money was the most important thing in life; now that I am old, I know that it is." But money is not the only effective bonus. In the July 1986 *Exchange*, Michael LeBoeuf outlined the "Ten Best Ways to Reward Good Work." These are the ten types of rewards ranked by LeBoeuf in order of importance:

1. Money
2. Recognition
3. Time Off
4. Ownership
5. Favorite Work
6. Advancement
7. Freedom
8. Personal Growth
9. Fun
10. Prizes

While centers may be hard pressed to come up with a big pot of money for bonuses, there are other items on the list where centers can come up with some meaningful awards. On the preceding pages are listed some of the bonuses that members of the **Panel of 100** have developed.

Exchange Panel of 100 members keep **Exchange** up-to-date on major developments and trends in the child care profession, and share ideas for resolving major challenges facing centers. Panel members are selected from among experienced directors to be representative of the overall profession in terms of organizational type, size, and location.

Staff Members on the Board of Directors — Centers' Experiences

A number of centers have written to Child Care Information Exchange and asked what the consequences are of having staff members from the center serve as voting members on the board of directors. To respond, Exchange interviewed teachers, directors, and/or board members from eight centers where teachers served on the board about their experiences with this process. The findings of this survey are as follows:

- **Staff participation is working better in centers where this was an outgrowth of the philosophy of the center than in centers where it was a response to a problem.** In a number of the centers, staff members and parents worked together in organizing the center initially and have continued to view the center as a collaborative venture. In these centers, staff members have served on the board from the start. Staff and parents generally take staff participation for granted and do not perceive their interests or motives to be in conflict.

In the other centers, staff members fought to have voting positions on the board out of concern that the board was not responsive to their interests. In some instances, this occurred after the board had poorly handled a staff issue. In others, it occurred after a period of growing distrust and poor communications between board and staff. In these instances, having staff members placed on the board did not really solve the relationship problem. Staff members and other board members tended to work together somewhat less comfortably as there were often lingering feelings of mistrust. The arrangement is often viewed more as a concession to the staff than as an expression of a commitment to staff participation.

- **The methods of election to and participation on the board vary considerably.** In most centers, staff members had one or two positions reserved for them on the board. In a few, staff held as many as eight positions, but in none of the centers did they represent a majority. In most of these centers, the staff members voted among themselves to fill these slots. In one center, the staff representative rotated every two months. In another center, staff members had the same right to seek election to the board as did all "members of the corporation." The numbers of staff on the board thus depended solely upon how many chose to run and how they fared in the election.

- **Staff members appeared more concerned with the overall quality of the programs than with their own personal interests.** In most of the centers, it was apparent that teachers' efforts on the board were directed toward improving the program much more than toward promoting the financial interests of teachers. Staff members believed that since they worked so closely with the program, the board needed their perspective in making plans and policies affecting the program. They helped remind the board of the urgency of day-to-day problems in the center. Also, if they were involved in making decisions, they believed they would be more committed to carrying them out. Staff members normally viewed the difference between having a voting role rather than an advisory role more as a matter of principle than as an issue of control or power. Most teachers also agreed that if the vote was taken away from teachers after they were accustomed to having it, staff morale would be damaged irreparably.

- **The centers had encountered few conflict-of-interest problems.** Several centers had board policies that prohibited staff members on the board from participating in debates affecting them as individuals. Thus a teacher on the board could be involved in a debate about a salary package for the entire staff, but not in one about a personnel action affecting only her. Surprisingly, most of the centers had no conflict-of-interest policies at all. Several directors explained that their centers did not have such policies because it was decided that it was no more a conflict of interest for teachers to vote on salaries and benefits than for parents to vote on fees.

In practice, the centers had encountered few situations where serious conflict-of-interest questions had arisen. However, none had been involved in having the board evaluate or take a personnel action against teachers or directors. It seems that these circumstances might cause significant conflicts if not prepared for in advance with formal policies.

- **Centers have encountered few objections from funding sources over staff participation.** An IRS official informed *Exchange* that there is no prohibition in the tax-exempt requirements against staff members serving on the board. Similarly, an HEW official stated that there is no specific Title XX prohibition against staff participation on the board. With one glaring exception, the centers stated that none of their private and public funding sources had raised conflict-of-interest objections. The one exception was the United Way. One center had its practice of staff participation on the board aggressively challenged by the United Way agency from which it received funds. In the end, a compromise was reached as the center agreed to specific limits on participation. A survey of other United Way agencies revealed that they generally will not fund organizations with paid staff on their boards.

- **Staff participation does not necessarily improve communications.** Even with teachers serving on the board, many centers found that communication problems between the board and the teachers were not eliminated. Only one of the centers had a formal process whereby teachers on the board conveyed news about the board to teachers and surveyed teachers' positions on board issues. In some cases, teachers even began to question whether those staff on the board were effectively representing their interests. Staff on the board sometimes had difficulty balancing the specific concerns of the teachers with the total perspective of issues as debated on the board.

Giving Your Staff
the Care They Deserve

by Leatha Ritchie

Much research has been done and many papers have been written about how to retain child care workers in an industry that historically has consistently high staff turnover. Specific qualities of a working environment can cultivate and maintain long term relationships between management and staff. Recommendations discussed in this article are based on conversations with and surveys of center directors and their staff where turnover is either extremely low or very high.

Of course, the first area of concern to all professionals taking care of and educating young children is pay. Whatever the reasons for low pay to these workers, it is unanimous among all advocates for the child care industry that higher pay would certainly help attract and retain long term employees. Admittedly this is true, but it will take many years to correct the low pay issue, so we must look for ways to keep staff with the salaries we can offer at this time.

The characteristics of a child care center where most, if not all, of the employees choose to stay and provide a high quality learning environment for young children are ones where:

1. **Care for employees as people, not just employees, exists.**

Each time I interview a center director or staff member of a center that has a majority of long term employees, the words "cares about me" or "really knows me" come up in one form or another. The directors of these centers can share information about all staff members that most supervisors would not want or need to know. This seems to be very important in the child care center. The types of loving, caring people that are so successful with children need to be cared for themselves. There is a family feeling in centers with low staff turnover.

2. **Communication is abundant, clear, and positive on all levels.**

Everyone is informed and asked their opinion in any matter that affects their job. There are numerous times during the week that management talks with employees about their jobs, their frustrations, and their successes. Regular staff meetings and impromptu mini-meetings are held when new decisions need to be made that affect the center or an individual classroom. In these centers there is little gossiping because everyone gets the same messages clearly from the correct source.

An important point to note is that not only is the communication free flowing from management down, but also from staff to management. In those centers where turnover is a problem, communication tends to be erratic or not clear. When employees do not feel they are getting the "straight answer," they will go elsewhere to find it. Sometimes rumor or speculation fills the need for communication, or employees go outside in search of good communication.

3. **Training for new skills and personal development is continuous.**

There are many opportunities to acquire new skills or brush up on old ones. Employees keep mentioning how much they have learned since they began this job and how much more they want to learn. The excitement for their work shines when they speak about trying a new technique or activity with the children, or their co-workers, that was successful.

The newest employees feel they are allowed to try their own ideas, but are coached when things do not work or need fine tuning. In centers that experience high staff turnover, the employees feel there is little or no coaching or training except when things are really a problem. Most new employees at those centers feel they are learning new skills mainly through trial and error.

Training needs continuous follow-up. No workshop is valuable if the attendee is not using the information on a daily basis to further succeed. Long term employees know that their center directors and assistant center directors will come back frequently to see how they are using the new information. Training in centers with low turnover comes from several sources: center management, corporate support, outside resources, and peers.

4. Values and goals are clear and everyone knows their importance.

When asked if they understand the center's mission, employees in centers with low turnover explain at length what their center wants to accomplish for the children, parents, community, and the company.

In high turnover centers, the employees generally say they are there to "take care of kids." The low turnover centers say that "taking care of kids" is a very small part of their work. They speak about their center being different than most. They talk about the people that educate children, not the curriculum used or the supplies provided. The employees at the low turnover centers know that the center is successful at reaching its goals because they are there and they believe in the center's purpose.

A striking difference in those centers with high turnover is that each teacher, classroom, or position works independently. Not only do they not feel a common mission for the building, but sometimes there are not common goals in a classroom. Often employees mention their positions as being less than or better than others. A frequent comment heard is that there is too much "interference" from other classrooms, their co-workers in their classroom, or even management.

People that work in professions that serve society need to see they are working towards clear goals that will result in making the world a little better. If the mission is not there, or if it is misunderstood, they will become frustrated.

5. Consistently high standards are expected and upheld.

Centers with a majority of long term employees seem to "have their act together." They clearly provide high quality care for the children, and the employees feel that anyone not willing to uphold that quality is quickly, but fairly, reminded of the goals. Most of the teachers I talk with believe they have autonomy in their work as long as they keep to the philosophy for nurturing and educating children.

6. Recognition and praise for success is continuous and public, while reprimand is quiet.

Each staff member has a realistic idea of their strengths and weaknesses. When asked how often they feel successful in their job, these people say, "many times a day"! In centers with tremendous turnover, the employees answer the same question with a resounding, "rarely"! When probing further to find out what makes them feel successful, it is clear that the supervisors are primarily responsible. Although they understand that their managers do not make them successful, the employees are sure their managers remind them of their abilities. Episodes of public praise are recounted, but staff also mention that they often get quiet suggestions for areas of improvement.

In centers where longevity is a problem, many employees mention not knowing whether they are doing a good job or not. Still others in those centers say they know they are not good enough. A major concern of all people in these centers is getting no positive or negative feedback from their supervisors. When talking with staff members in these centers, their view of professional strengths and weaknesses is not realistic.

7. Close and consistent supervision by management takes place.

The staff feel support from their center director and assistant director continuously and consistently. These managers typically practice MBWA (management by walking around). The directors are always in and out of rooms, frequently there as problems arise, and are available for parents at any time. There are few surprises. If one of the staff members is not performing up to standard, the director and assistant director are always monitoring the situation, constantly coaching. The newest employees feel that the director is there to help them join the team as soon as possible. These centers also have regular staff meetings and frequent formal and informal training sessions for all employees.

In high turnover centers, the staff often speak of inconsistencies in the management team. One comment summarizes these feelings well, "some weeks she is on me about everything and then I can go for months and hear nothing." Often one staff member feels she gets more attention than others, both positive and negative. Employees are not sure what any one day will be like or what the mood of their supervisors will be.

8. Extra "pay" is given for extraordinary work.

In every child care center, there are days or weeks when everyone must give 110%. In those centers with low turnover, the employees willingly put forth the extra effort because they know it is appreciated, temporary, and not something anyone in the center would not do as well. The extra pay does not come in the form of dollars but in:

- hours off when needed and those needs can be accommodated;

- a surprise lunch out with or without the boss;

- an extra special gift that shows the boss knows them well;

- a break during a hectic day; or

- a chance to share knowledge or hard work with peers.

Special privileges in small or large doses are frequent after an especially hectic week or two.

In centers where turnover is high, there is a lot of conversation about long hours, menial tasks, "not my job" kind of statements, or "why don't we get paid for staff meetings." Again, the feelings of not being appreciated are all too frequent.

Leatha Ritchie is an area manager for Bright Horizons Children's Centers in North Carolina. Previously she was an area recruiter for Children's World Learning Centers in the Virginia-Maryland area. She has been involved in early education for 13 years.

Making Communications a Two-Way Street

by Roger Neugebauer

"What we have here is a failure to communicate." How often this lament is heard in child care centers. Because of the myriad interactions which must occur on a daily basis among the director, teachers, parents, and children in a center, a breakdown in communications can have a devastating impact. Before we take a closer look at what causes these breakdowns, and how they can be avoided, you may want to take a moment to assess the effectiveness of communications at your center.

Quickie Communications Quiz

1. Do your teachers freely inform you about their feelings, opinions, and suggestions?

2. Are you made aware of problems and conflicts before they reach major proportions?

3. Do teachers accept criticism without becoming defensive or emotional?

4. Are you frequently torn between being a friend and being a boss?

5. Do you actively seek out the ideas and opinions of teachers before making major decisions?

6. When listening to teachers, do you concentrate 100% on what they are saying?

7. Are staff meetings characterized by an active sharing of ideas among staff members?

8. Do the teachers understand what you do?

9. Do you understand the frustrations, needs, and interests of the teachers?

10. Are you usually able to make time to talk to teachers?

If you answered *yes* to all ten questions, chances are communications are flowing quite effectively at your center. If you recorded a few *noes*, there's room for improvement. If there were more *noes* than *yeses*, your communication system is in need of a major overhaul. For those experiencing communication problems, this article will identify the major obstacles to communications in child care centers and then describe a variety of techniques for upgrading communications. The ideas presented come from 35 child care directors from 21 states who were surveyed by *Child Care Information Exchange* for this article and from three organizational psychologists whose works are listed at the end of this article.

Communication Barriers

For communication to take place, not only must a message be transmitted by a communicator but it must also be correctly received by a listener. If the message is not understood, there is no communication. There is only noise. Between transmission and the reception of a message much can go wrong. In child care centers, the following were identified as the most frequent causes of breakdowns:

• **Protectiveness**. Directors sometimes withhold negative information from teachers for fear that it will hurt the teachers' feelings or that it will jeopardize their friendship. Likewise, teachers can be protective of the director. They may choose not to inform the director about a problem that will upset her. They may avoid giving negative feedback to the director about her behavior or decisions for fear the director will hold that against them.

• **Defensiveness**. Not only do individuals occasionally avoid transmitting information, but often they resist receiving it. When an individual is verbally attacked, a defense is instinctively mustered — the emotions become aroused, the adrenaline begins to flow, and the mind races to mount a counterattack or to close in for a retreat. If a director is sharing reactions and suggestions with a teacher, and the teacher perceives this as an attack, her defense mechanisms will spring into action. The director's message will be rejected. Likewise, if a teacher is giving the director feedback on a decision he made, and the director interprets this as a challenge to his expertise or authority, he will erect an emotional blockade. In child care, these defensive reactions to feedback are commonplace. Child care people tend to have a strong ego involvement with their teaching philosophy and style and are therefore quick to interpret feedback on their performance as an attack on their beliefs, their ego, their very person.

• **Tendency to evaluate**. In an interchange, we have a natural tendency to judge or evaluate the statements of the speaker. For example, suppose one teacher comments to you, "The cook sure outdid herself today." Almost invariably, your reaction will be to make your own evaluation in response, such as, "Yes, it was so good you almost wanted to eat it." In other words, the natural reaction is to evaluate a statement from your own frame of reference, not to try to understand the speaker's point of view. This is not communication in the genuine sense. As Carl Rogers explains, "There will be just two ideas, two feelings, two judgments, missing each other in psychological space."

• **Narrow perspectives**. A director from Hawaii observed, "Director

and teachers can fall into limited-vision interest groups, with teachers seeing most clearly their own needs and those of their classroom and students, and the director seeing primarily the 'larger picture,' the interests of the whole school that may seem to overarch the needs of any part of it." Both perspectives are incomplete and impede communications. For example, a director may attempt to convince teachers of the budgetary reasons for her decision to reduce teachers' lunch breaks by 15 minutes. The teachers, not being aware of the complex pressures and instructions the director had to contend with in putting together the budget, may perceive that she is uncaring about the strains they work under. The director, not having to work in the classrooms, may not understand why this break time is so crucial. Communication does not occur because neither party understands the other's frame of reference.

• **Mismatched expectations**. Our ability to receive messages is limited by the fact that we tend to hear only what we expect to hear. As the organizational psychologist Peter Drucker explains: "The human mind attempts to fit impressions and stimuli into a frame of expectations. It resists vigorously any attempts to make it 'change its mind,' that is, to perceive what it does not expect to perceive." For example, if a director has an image of teacher aides as being unskilled, and never expects that they are capable of offering useful suggestions or insights, she will tune out whenever they talk and not hear any valid ideas they do express. If teachers go into staff meetings expecting them to be boring and irrelevant, they will not be sufficiently motivated to pay attention for those relevant ideas that do come up. If staff members expect to disagree with everything

one teacher says on discipline techniques, they will not hear ideas she expresses even when they fit in perfectly with their own approaches.

• **Insufficient time**. Last but not least, communication is impeded in child care by the lack of time available for in-depth communication. Teachers usually do not have the time (or energy) to attend frequent or prolonged staff meetings. Directors often become so preoccupied with paperwork, unexpected crises, and outside meetings that they have little opportunity for one-to-one discussions with staff members.

Ideas for Improving Communications

From his experience at the Peahi School in Hawaii, Stephen Gockley found that "true communication is not an easy task and requires continual attention." Certainly the list of barriers described above underscores the many ways in which breakdowns can occur. But many child care centers have experienced success in establishing effective open two-way communications by utilizing the techniques described below.

• **Make openness a valued commodity**. Directors often give mixed messages. On the one hand, they say they want communications to be open, while, on the other hand, their actions deliver messages that discourage openness. For example, they may fail to act when teachers bring problems to their attention, or they may be hostile to teachers who provide negative feedback on their performance.

To encourage open communications, the director must reward, not punish, the disclosure of feelings, opinions, or difficulties by teachers. The most effective reward is for teachers to see positive results from their openness.

At the Peahi School, for example, because when problems surface they are dealt with immediately, staff members feel more assured of being heard and understood. A director can also reward openness when it occurs by expressing that she appreciates how difficult it is to share negative or sensitive messages and thanking the teachers for their openness. Appreciation should also be expressed for incidents of sharing feedback among teachers.

Mari Chang, from The Good Years in Hilo, Hawaii, has found that it is also helpful if the director sets an example of being open and honest. The more the director provides feedback and ideas to teachers, the more likely they are to feel comfortable with sharing with the director and each other.

• **Take expectations into account.** Before delivering a message, a communicator needs to determine the expectations of the intended recipient. If the message is at odds with these expectations, the communicator must find some way to "break through the recipient's expectations and force him to realize that the unexpected is happening" (Drucker). One way to do this is to force people to examine their own attitudes, stereotypes, and expectations at the outset of discussions so that they will be more sensitive to the barriers these mindsets create. A director would do well to discipline herself to analyze her own expectations prior to every interaction.

If the people don't want to come out to the park, nobody's going to stop 'em.
— Yogi Berra

A second way to break through is to send an unmistakable signal that "this is different." This can be done simply by announcing the unexpected message at the outset of the discussion. Or it can be accomplished by breaking people out of their routines by providing a change of pace in the format, the tone, the time, or the setting of interactions. For example, the Children's Learning Coop in Tucson, Arizona, holds an all day Saturday workshop on staff communications. A topic of deep interest to the staff, such as discipline or racism, is selected and approached from a very personal perspective under the leadership of an outside group communications expert. This workshop is used to set the tone for weekly staff meetings which use an open or consensus model. During the week, all staff members can enter items on the agenda. At the outset of all meetings, there is a check-in where each staff member makes a statement about how they are feeling. Other centers break routine by holding staff development workshops at retreat locations.

• **Encourage active listening.** Many communication barriers can be removed, not by the director's becoming a more eloquent persuader, but rather by all staff members becoming more effective listeners. In order for new ideas, negative feedback, or positive suggestions to be communicated, there needs to be a climate created which is neither critical, threatening, evaluative, nor moralizing. Such a climate can be created through *active listening*. The purpose of active listening, as defined by psychotherapist Carl Rogers, is "to see the expressed idea and attitude from the other person's point of view, to sense how it feels to him, to achieve his frame of reference in regard to the thing he is talking about."

Since we were given only one mouth but two ears, perhaps we were meant to listen twice as much as we talk.
— John Samaras

The first step in the active listening process is to listen for the total meaning of the speaker's message. This total meaning involves not only the actual content of the message but also the feeling behind it. For example, the total meaning of the sentence "We sure have a wonderful director" can be radically different depending upon whether it is uttered in a relaxed matter-of-fact tone of voice or in an animated sarcastic one. Likewise, let's say a teacher charges into the director's office and bellows, "I can't understand why this center squanders its money on this useless magazine." The director might safely reason that the teacher would not get that worked up over the expenditure. Rather, her real message may be that she is upset about where money is not being spent, i.e., her salary.

Once the listener forms an initial opinion about what the total meaning of the message is, the next step is to check this out with the speaker. This can be done by reflecting back the message as perceived. Thus, in the latter example above, the director might respond, "I take it you're not pleased with the way money is allocated around here." This gives the speaker the opening to speak more directly to her real message.

The active listening technique can enable a director to more clearly keep in touch with the opinions and problems of the staff. It can also make staff more comfortable about sharing information with the director.

Communications can be even more effective if all staff members are trained and encouraged to engage in active listening. One way to do this is to call time out in a heated discussion in a staff meeting and require all staff members to rephrase the message of the previous speaker (to that person's satisfaction) prior to stating their own position. This helps staff members develop the ability as well as the habit of actively listening to understand the point of view of others.

There is no such thing as an open mind — every person has a set number of ideas.

— John Samaras

- **Opening multiple communication channels**. The more avenues a center provides for communication to take place, the less likely it is that important messages will be withheld or get lost in the cracks. One common approach is to set up a system for written communication. Diane Lowson reports that the Holy Innocents Pre-School in Lahaina, Hawaii, has a notebook in the classroom in which teachers write down interesting things that parents and children say to share with each other. The North Pocono Preschool in Moscow, Pennsylvania, has *mailboxes* in which the

director, Gail Laskowski, can leave messages and feedback for teachers. At the same center, suggestion forms are kept in the staff room so that teachers can submit anonymous suggestions. In other centers, teachers have notebooks in which they can write out questions, criticisms, or opinions to the director. All these written systems provide another option for staff who are too busy and to those who are too timid to communicate messages face to face.

Another approach to eliciting communication is through the use of written evaluation tools. Sara Kent got communication flowing at the Family and Child Development Center in Barium Springs, North Carolina, by having staff members anonymously rate how effectively the center was functioning in areas such as communication, decision-

making, and planning. Staff members discussed the results and used them to develop a set of goals for staff training.

Many directors take specific steps to encourage one-to-one interactions. Esther Stone of the Foothills Christian Day School in Pasadena, California, holds monthly "private talks" with each staff member to discuss school and/or personal matters.

Other directors seek to increase communication through more formal structures. Sue Biddle of the McNeilly Day Home in Nashville, Tennessee, found that it became impossible to communicate frequently with staff members when the program expanded to more and more areas. Her solution was to hire a program director to maintain daily communication with staff members. Lorraine Morse of the Villa Morse College Child Care Center in Erie, Pennsylvania, reports that the center was able to upgrade communications by establishing and

---

Strategies for Better Communicating

Michael LeBoeuf, in Working Smart (Warner Books, 1979), recommends the following strategies to be a more effective communicator:

- **Ask questions**. Many of us are reluctant to ask questions of someone when we aren't sure what the person means. This is usually born out of our fear of appearing stupid. However, a lot of confusion can be nipped in the bud by simply asking someone to repeat or rephrase his statement.

- **Don't overcommunicate**. It's possible to say too much and, as a result, confuse the listener. Saying too much keeps your major points from standing out by surrounding them with excess verbiage. Worst yet, overcommunicators are just plain boring.

- **Communicate your ideas at the proper place and at the proper time for maximum useful impact**. The location and frame of mind that you and the other party are in have a great deal to do with how well your ideas will be received and exchanged.

- **Give those you communicate with your undivided attention**. Most of us can do only one thing at a time well. Shuffling papers, answering the telephone, staring out the window, and tapping your pencil communicate a mood of indifference. If you take the time to communicate with someone, give him the interest and attention that you would have him give you.

writing up a formal communication network. This network spells out the limits of authority and the channels of communication for all positions in the center. This helps keep information flowing by making it clear who is supposed to be supplied what information.

Helpful Resources

Drucker, Peter F. *Management: Tasks, Responsibilities, Practices*. New York: Harper and Row, 1974.

Leadership — Reprint #1. Redmond, WA: *Child Care Information Exchange*, 1994.

Rogers, C. R. (July/August 1952). "Barriers and Gateways to Communication," *Harvard Business Review*.

Schein, E. H. (1969). *Process Consultation*. Reading, MA: Addison-Wesley Publishing Co.

28 Fun Ideas to Motivate Your Staff

by Sandy Roberts

We hear the usual voices, we use the same words or phrases, we do some things the same way every day, and we so often overlook the obvious. For example, I placed an ugly broom in the corner of my office one day, forgetting to put it away when I was done with it. Throughout my day I didn't have time to get back to the broom. Day after day the broom just stood in the corner — a rather unpleasing sight to visitors, yet eventually it became just a part of the office and I never noticed it. One day a staff member was looking for a broom and I answered her request with, "I have no idea where one is, I haven't seen one around here." There the broom stood, in plain view, yet I didn't see it.

The following ideas were developed to be used as motivators to your staff and to enhance their understanding of their role as teachers. The ideas are meant to be helpful in heightening awareness of each staff's personal daily behaviors. Use them to encourage your staff to take a close look at their daily routines and verbal interactions with children and co-workers. They're fun activities that will hopefully make your staff's daily routines not so routine any longer.

1. Name Tags. Place art materials in the middle of the floor and ask staff to make name tags that tell something about themselves without using their names. Give them a chance to explain their tags to the group and have them wear the tags the rest of the day. When children ask about the tag, it gives the teacher a chance to talk about herself and promotes a positive self-image.

2. Treasure Hunt. Have staff collect items from around the school that reveal something about themselves. They need to say where the item came from and how it relates to them. This helps them to pay close attention to their surroundings and aids in observation skills.

3. Personal Recordings. Have staff tape record themselves during the day. Ask them to take the tape home and listen to it. They should jot down things that were said in a negative way and write a positive way they could have said it. This helps teachers to become aware of what they say and how they say it.

4. Don't Say NO. For one entire day staff members may not say the word "NO." They are to say it in another way. If "NO" is said, a piece of masking tape is to be put on the "NO" sayer's shirt. People are amazed at how much tape they are wearing by the end of the day!

5. Observe a Candle. Give a small unlit candle to each small group. Each group is to write down as many observations about that candle as they can. Then do the same for a burning candle. Ask the groups to discuss their observations. Say to the group, "You have many of the same observations yet many that are different. It is the same way with observing young children. We all see some things that are the same and some things that are different. Study a child in the same way."

6. Back-to-Back Observations. About halfway through the meeting, ask each staff member to sit back to back with the person next to them. Have them write the answers to these or other questions.

- What is she wearing?

- What type of shoes is she wearing?

- What is something she said during the meeting?

- What color eyes does she have?

- What is her full name?

- How old is she?

- Write ten things you observed about her today.

7. "A Teacher Is . . . ." Have staff give *one* word adjectives to finish this sentence. This will be silly, fun, and yet very serious. You'll get an idea of how staff are feeling.

8. Skills and Talents. To foster staff awareness of others' skills and talents, have staff stand in a line according to their feelings about their ability in music (towards the front of the line represents they feel they have a strong ability in the area). Follow the line idea for abilities in art, science, circle time ideas, etc. This allows the staff to know who to go to for support knowledge.

9. Clarity of Instructions. Give one group very vague instructions, and give another group too many instructions.

Written instructions to Group 1:
You have received inflated balloons. Greet the other group.

Instructions to Group 2: You have received thumbtacks, pipe cleaners, and tissues. Move around in a triangular motion, covering the entire area. If someone should come up to

---

Watch what you say:

"I've told you a hundred times not to do that, now look what has happened."

"How many times do I have to tell you . . . ?" (Do you really expect the child to answer that one?)

"I don't know why you act like that."

"Why did you spill your milk?"

"If you do that again, you'll have to sit out for the rest of the day!"

"I know how you feel." (Do you really?)

"Don't you ever listen?"

"Do you do that at home?"

"When are you ever going to learn?"

"Why do you do that?"

"Can't you ever sit still?"

"Do you want me to pinch you?"

"Just a minute, OK?"

"Don't you ever do that again, or else. Do you understand?"

---

you, you are to say "What?" or ignore them. If they keep bothering you and actually touch you in some way, pop their balloon with something. If they still insist on talking to you, give them your tissue, but be sure they take it in their left hand.

If they put it in their right hand, wrap the pipe cleaner around their right ring finger. If someone says something to you who has a pipe cleaner on their finger, begin playing patty cake with them. If another person says something to you, just sit down. This is to show, by extreme, how too many directions may be overwhelming while not enough direction can be frustrating.

10. Back-to-Back Drawings. Two people sit back to back. One person is given a blank paper and a box of crayons. This person is the *receiver*

and may only say the words "go on" or "repeat." The other person is given a piece of paper with a picture drawn on it. This person is the *giver* and must give verbal directions to the receiver to enable the receiver to draw the same picture. The giver may not say what the picture is, such as "draw a cat." The giver must give verbal directions such as "draw a circle in the center of the paper" or "draw a triangle on the upper left part of circle." He must not say "draw an ear on the head." If the receiver does not understand, she may say "repeat" — nothing else. When the receiver has drawn the giver's direction, she must say "go on." You'll find, when all is done, that the pictures are not the same.

It is impossible to place blame on who made a mistake. Both people feel they did the best they could — listening and speaking; but communication is difficult and inexact.

11. I Am Unique. To help staff discover each person's individuality, answer the following questions:

- What kind of car do you drive?

- Where is your dream vacation destination?

- What are your two favorite pizza toppings?

- What is something that really bothers you?

- What is something you enjoy?

12. Black Box. Set a box in the middle of the floor as you begin a staff meeting. At some point in the meeting, ask if anybody has anything to add or any questions. You can bet they'll ask about the box. This creates an opportunity to remind staff to "teach for the moment." Kids want to know "what's that?" — don't ignore their wonderment. Until they know what that new thing is, they won't be able to concentrate on you. The contents of that box is a wonderment to the teachers. Place a box of M&Ms or a coupon for a lunch inside the box for whoever asks about the box first.

13. Follow Directions Test. Write a 30 question test or survey about anything. Tell the teachers to read over the test, answer the questions, and hand it in before the meeting is over. On question 19, write: "Do only question 27." On question 27, write: "Please write your name on the top lefthand corner of this page and give it to the director." See how many people actually follow the direction about reading over the test first.

14. Staff Survey. Some questions might be:

- The people in my job who make me feel the best are those who . . .

- The most important factor affecting morale on my job is . . .

- The greatest satisfaction I get from my job is . . .

- If I could make one change in my work, it would be . . .

- The most irritating part of my job is . . .

- When something at work really aggravates me, I usually . . .

- When I can't get help with problems at work, I usually turn to. . .

15. Inventing Games. Ask staff to develop a few *games* to help get a point across. Staff will discover that the best way to work on problems or concerns is to ask those they work with every day. If a teacher is concerned that she gets easily frustrated and raises her voice too much, ask co-workers to develop a positive game that the whole group can work on together. This will show support for co-workers and the concerned person will know he is not alone. A game is also a good way to help with a problem in a fun, relaxed atmosphere with peers.

16. Marble Jar. Place a glass jar and a box of marbles in the staff room. Each time a staff member has had a good day or she handles a problem effectively, she is to put a marble in the jar and tell why. All the other staff can clap or cheer. When the jar is full, the staff can have a party! (Then start all over again!)

17. We All Need Space. To find your personal comfort space, try this. Have two staff members stand facing each other. One is not to move; the other begins saying the alphabet and, with each letter, moves closer and closer. See how far you get through the ABCs.

18. Look Ma, No Hands! Ask staff members to try telling a story while sitting on their hands.

19. Explain Yourself. Ask staff members to share their feelings and tell why. Say "I (feeling) when (behavior) because (concrete effect on you)." Example: I get excited when you share your feelings with me because it makes me feel like your friend, or, I get upset when you yell because it bothers my ears when we're inside. Language use is very important and this idea should be practiced frequently.

20. Job Description. Post the following in your center:

You — The Excellent Preschool Teacher

Individual with early education background; loving; caring; outgoing; silly; enjoys playing in mud, wet sand, and shaving cream; loves crawling around on hands and knees, meowing like a cat, or slithering like a snake; has a calm speaking voice; has eyes in the back of her head; changes wet pants or diapers with a smile; can do plumbing (broken, clogged toilets, etc.); reads endless stories with zest; can do manual labor (shoveling snow, hammering bookcases, fixing broken tables, bikes, and so on); creative; imaginative; fun; is able to hug a child who has a slimy runny nose and clean up vomit; artist; scientist; interior decorator; psychologist; mathematician; puts in long hours; enjoys parent contact on a regular basis, informally and formally; spends many an evening working on school projects well into the wee hours of the morning; can do ten things at one time (calm a crying child, talk calmly to an upset parent, take a phone call); never tires of giving a hand even when not asked; responsible for lives of young children all day; takes criticism with a smile; accountable for every word and action; does volunteer work; always busy; receives little benefits and annual salary, well let's say that's little too. Your biggest reward — a young child smiles at you.

21. Testimonial Writing. Each staff member writes her name on a piece of paper. These are put in a can. A name is picked from the can weekly at the staff meeting. One by one, staff state positive things — attributes and favorites of the chosen one. The statements are written on chart paper which is signed by the group, displayed, and then given to the honoree. The procedure can only enhance a positive self-image.

22. Back-to-School Headbands. Have staff play this *get to know you* game. Teachers write their names on construction paper headbands. Collect all headbands in a box. One teacher chooses a headband and puts it on without reading the name. He sits in front of the class and asks questions answerable by "yes" or "no" until he guesses his headband's identity.

23. Suggestion Apples. Give each teacher an *apple sheet* the first day of school. Let them write a letter to you suggesting projects, discipline, meeting suggestions, and any ideas that might make the year interesting. Use the letters to help plan the year!

24. Expressions. Explain these to the kids: He's in the doghouse. You're behaving like a fish out of water. She thinks she's hot stuff. He's all steamed up. I'm sitting on pins and needles. I'm all thumbs. She spilled the beans. Keep it under your hat.

A questionnaire to get staff thinking about what they do, how they do it, and why they do it:

How do I react when I'm rudely interrupted?

Do I tune into what children are feeling?

Do my words match my actions?

Can I admit mistakes and recognize my limitations?

Can I separate the act from the child?

Do I teach for the teachable moment?

Am I tuned into the children's special needs?

Do I avoid showing favoritism to meet my own needs?

Am I enthusiastic about teaching?

If I were a child, would I like me to be my teacher?

---

25. Finish the Definitions. Delight is. . . . Relief is. . . . Imagination is. . . . Loneliness is. . . . Discomfort is. . . . Appreciation is. . . .

26. Reading Material. When you want staff to read information in a magazine, place a dollar bill (gift to finder) in the magazine article. You can bet that the person who does read the article will read other assigned readings, as will others who hear about the dollar.

27. Special Days. Find a calendar that has a special event for every day. Example: June 5 is *Doughnut Day* — be sure each staff member is wished a happy Doughnut Day and give them a real doughnut. June 15 is *Hug Holiday*. Show the others you appreciate them and give a free hug away! The staff will catch on quick and start giving hugs to the kids. *National Hat Day* — all wear a special or silly hat. *Birth of the Safety Pin* — use a safety pin to attach a special message to each staff member. *Joygerm Day* — make a tag for each staff member and catch them smiling during the day; give them the tag and let them know they are now a member of the Joygerm Club. (**Copycat Magazine** has a good calendar of special days and events.)

28. Positive Words. To enhance positive vocabulary, ask staff to write 100 different ways of saying "Very good."

Sandy Roberts is the director of Rainbow Express Preschool in Lansdale, Pennsylvania. She has been in the child care field for 20 years.

Substitutes — We're the Real Thing!

by Bonnie Neugebauer

The life of a substitute is not an easy one — the very word suggests someone who is not the real thing, someone we must put up with for the interim. The word, usually shortened to "sub," even sounds awful — rather short and low.

Yet it would be hard to come up with a person more sought after than a reliable, effective substitute caregiver. Early childhood programs will desperately search — even beg, borrow, or steal — to find a substitute. But on the job, substitutes often feel neglected, even exploited.

As I worked as a substitute teacher in early childhood programs, I discovered that I sometimes felt most valued before I entered the center. An affirmative response to a plea for help resulted in all sorts of joyful, enthusiastic gratitude — I was made to feel important and helpful. After I began my day's work, I often found myself abandoned, saddled with the worst jobs, and floundering to really take care of children with minimal information and support.

To give a sub his or her due, I would like to focus attention on some often forgotten truths about life as a substitute:

A Substitute Is a Real Person

This seems like a pretty straight forward point; but if you are not given a bathroom break, then someone has forgotten that you are real. It's awkward to be unsure, fumbling; but there is much that a center can do to enhance the effectiveness and foster the sense of belonging of the substitute.

A Substitute Has Real Needs

A substitute needs to understand the context. No one works effectively in a small, isolated space. Without some sense of the big picture, all of us tend to lose our sense of direction — we feel lonely, unsupported, forgotten.

A first time substitute needs a tour of the center. Show her where different age groups meet and how various rooms and spaces are used. Point out the bathroom. Introduce him to other staff, making special note of people he can turn to for specific kinds of help. Help him see how all the pieces of your program fit together. This is also a good time to fill a substitute in on the center philosophy and a few important rules.

Leslie, the director, mails a substitute packet to me, with the appropriate forms for me to fill out. She asks me to arrive 15 minutes early so that I have time to ask questions and read the routine and instructions for individual children before I begin working.

A substitute needs to feel competent in his working environment. Have someone orient the sub as to where supplies and equipment are located. Clearly define procedures for using and returning toys and equipment. Outline expectations for end of the day clean up. Look at the center from the substitute's point of view when labeling mats and storage and designing charts for routines.

A good way to tell if a classroom is efficiently planned and well labeled and organized is to watch a sub at work. How many fumbles to diaper a child? How many false starts in the search for scissors?

A substitute needs to feel the flow. Map out the routine for the day so that the substitute feels on top of things rather than scrambling behind. Children usually have a pretty good sense of the flow, so they can be helpful. However, a substitute who is dependent on the children for basic information feels vulnerable.

In this program there are nappers, half nappers, and no nappers, which I learn the hard way. My assignment is to get about 18 children to sleep. The mats are already positioned, thanks to the departing teacher. As the children come in from outdoors, we sort through pillows and blankets, do the shoe and bathroom routines, read stories, and relax to soothing music. Just as peace is settling over the room, Paul begins to cry, "I'm a half napper. I'm not supposed to come in yet."

A substitute needs to know how to prepare. Before the sub arrives, she should know exactly what to bring.

A group of 25 three and four year olds is having lunch outdoors in the sunshine. It's a beautiful day, and the children are enjoying all the nooks and hidey places in the bushes for small lunch groups. In this program the children bring their own lunches — no one told me to bring one, so I hungrily join the conversation at the picnic table.

Once you have given instructions, don't change the rules.

I am asked to bring an art activity for pre-kindergartners, but find myself in the three year old room. I don't know where any of the supplies are. Jonathan wants to paint, but I can't find any paper. Finally I discover a stash of old letterhead and tape a sheet to the easel.

Several times I arrived at a program at the appointed day and time to the surprise of the director who had forgotten that she had hired me.

A substitute needs to know your expectations. Clearly define your

expectations for how the substitute will function. Make it easy to fit in and feel competent.

The infant room enjoys a ratio of one caregiver for three babies. Kay is in charge with Rose as her assistant. So I am assigned to care for Caitlin, Graham, and Zoe. Special instructions for each baby are posted near the daily chart. Nap times are staggered, so that most of the time I am watching only two babies. All time not spent in routine care is to be spent playing with the babies.

A substitute needs to feel respected. Once you have hired her, support her in doing her job.

*Nap time. I tell the children that I will read them a story, we will listen to a tape, then we will drift off to sleep. After nap time I promise to read another story. I'm just to my favorite part of **Where The Wild Things Are** when Pauline walks by. "That's not how we do it! Play a record for them."*

A substitute needs to be identifiable. Make sure that everyone else knows that the sub is a sub. Knowing this will enable parents and staff to adjust their expectations and respond supportively. No one wants to be put in a position of feeling embarrassed or inadequate.

I am asked to arrive during nap time, so I sit quietly in a room of sleeping children. It's hard to stay awake. I can hear noises overhead as other groups are working away. A teacher comes by to check that all is well. A mother arrives to pick up Gina. I don't know the names of these children! I don't know where Gina is and I can't find her.

Post a notice on the door identifying the substitute — who she is replacing and the hours she will work. Be sure she wears a name tag that clearly identifies her to parents as a substitute — this enables parents to refer to her by name.

A substitute needs to belong. This is one of the trickiest issues to resolve. A substitute is a temporary part of your program so the issues of belonging are different. There is no history, no peer group (in a way), no future.

Somehow you must make the substitute feel that there is a place for him in your program — even if for only a day. Being sensitive to his needs, clear and generous with your introductions, and supportive in your expectations will help you accomplish this goal.

If you are nurturing a long term relationship with a substitute, consider ways to include her in your staff meetings, training sessions, and staff and parent social occasions. The more a substitute feels part of your program, the more committed she will be to continuing her role or becoming a permanent employee.

Part of belonging in an early childhood program is being able to call children by name. Devise a way of helping a substitute learn the children's names quickly. The best idea I've encountered is to put masking tape name tags on all the children before the sub arrives. Include the children who will be on the playground if that is to be part of the day's duties. Children expect immediate name recognition; having to refer to a wall display just doesn't work.

And perhaps most important and most often overlooked, give your substitute time to say goodbye. Often subs just disappear during nap time or into another responsibility. Making sure that substitutes mark their place with children bestows respect on the feelings of both.

A substitute needs to be a substitute. A sub should not be expected to replace a regular teacher in knowledge and ability to perform without time to learn and observe.

Do not ask a sub:

- to diaper a child who is wary of strangers until they have had a chance to get to know each other,

- to take all responsibility for playground duty unless that is the job you have outlined beforehand,

- to take the children outside the center unless accompanied by regular staff,

- to administer medications,

- to work all day without a break,

- to perform all the onerous tasks — unless you never want to see him again,

- to know policies and procedures if you have not given her the opportunity to learn them, or

- to instantly take the place of a regular staff member in knowledge and ability to perform.

A Substitute Has Hidden Potential

Just like everyone else, a substitute will need to talk about her experiences in your program. It's been a stressful day and whether it went well or not, your substitute will be eager to share her adventures. Whom she chooses to talk to and what she chooses to say is up to her but not totally out of your control.

Think of a substitute as a marketing tool. Whether you like it or not, your substitute is going to be doing some word of mouth marketing for your program. Armed with the information he has gathered — facts, impressions, experiences — he will be talking about you. Make sure that your substitute feels part of your program so that he feels invested and speaks from that perspective. If you

---

Prepare a Substitute Information Packet

If possible, mail this packet to the substitute so that he can come prepared. Include the following information:

Expectations —
Hours and days to be worked
Pay rate and how payment will be made
What to do upon arrival — whom to report to, where to stow personal items
Breaks — when, where, how
Age group of children

Basic rules —
Smoking
Telephone privileges (include staff phone number if applicable, when phone can be used, any special dialing procedures, whether incoming calls can be accepted and where messages will be posted)
Food (any special foods that may or may not be eaten) also times when it's acceptable to eat

Guidelines —
Discipline — time out/cool off, etc.
Drop off and pick up procedures
Health issues, list of children with special health considerations — food allergies, medications (who and what to administer)
Curriculum — which activities are fixed and which are open to choice

Responsibilities —
Daily routine
Any activities or materials that the substitute should bring/prepare
Clean up — how to know when work is done

Directions —
How to get to the center by car or bus
Which door to enter
Where to park

---

give a sub the opportunity to share his experiences and insights with you, he leaves your center feeling valued and will be more likely to put the best light on things.

Think of a substitute as a short term, inexpensive consultant. During her day in your program, the sub will have gathered all sorts of impressions. Because her perspective is different, she will see different things. Some of her observations will be valuable and some will be irritat-

ing. But all of her observations will give you information about your program.

Anika's parents arrive during their lunch hour to be with their six month old. She is sitting in an infant seat, playing with the mobile overhead. Her parents crouch down beside her and talk to her. They play with her fingers, but they do not pick her up. Why?

You might even offer to pay a substitute for an additional half hour of time to ensure that she will fill out a questionnaire about her day. Or, if time is possible, pay a substitute for a few minutes of direct feedback in conversation with you.

Of course, the substitute carries her own baggage, so you must keep this in mind. Some comments will point to bias, inexperience, or attitude — you can put these into perspective and still find the insights and truths in this one person's feedback.

Think of a substitute as a resource. If you know of special interests and talents, encourage the substitute to share them in the classroom. She might be a gardener, a storyteller, a carpenter, or a musician. This is a wonderful opportunity to bring new experiences to the children; and it gives the sub a special way to become part of things.

A substitute usually has knowledge about other programs in the community. Ask her how other centers solve particular problems and accomplish specific activities. Encourage her to share her valuable expertise.

A Substitute Responds to Love

If you love your substitute, make it as easy as possible for her to be effective. Prepare a substitute information handbook (see box on page 147), orient her on site, give her support on the job, and let her know that her good work just might have saved your day. A good substitute is indeed the real thing — a necessary and valuable component of a quality child care program.

A Million Dollars for Sam's Other Shoe!

an excerpt from the diary of a substitute

3:00 PM.   *My afternoon assignment is the Panda Bears (the three year old room). I walk into a blur of activity. Several children on risers are watching a squirrel's antics through the window. One boy is clutching his blanket and crying, "Daddy, daddy!" One child in the midst of it all is sleeping.*

Brenda, the morning Panda Bear teacher, announces, "Hi friends, this is Bonnie. She's going to be with you for the afternoon. Isn't that great?" No one responds. Brenda ticks off the names of the children: "This is Caitlin, and Quinn, Drew, Renko, Sam, and Emily (sleeping) . . . oh, you're not going to remember them anyway!" She pulls me to the side. "This is Drew (the boy with the blanket). He's new and having a rough time. And you have to watch him. He's always wandering off. Usually I find him near the bathroom. And this is Jennifer, our teen aide. Sometimes she needs guidance in how to talk to the children. So keep an eye on her, too."

Brenda shows me the schedule:

3:00 to 3:15	wake up
3:15 to 3:30	snacks
3:30 to 4:00	stories
4:00 to 5:00	playground
5:00 to 5:30	free play/parents begin pick up
5:30 to 6:00	clean up

"Oh, and by the way, I can't seem to find Sam's other shoe." Brenda looks at her watch and rushes out the door.

I offer to put the laces back in Caitlin's shoes, but she refuses help, not at all sure about me yet. The cook brings in squares of cornbread and cups of milk. There aren't enough for everyone so Jennifer goes off to find more. Snacks are quickly devoured and everyone is asking for more. Emily sleeps on. Quinn is struggling with her shoes and socks. Renko insists on another piece of cornbread. Drew wants more milk. There isn't any more milk. I help Quinn with her socks. Jennifer shoves Emily gently with her foot, "Wake up, Emily." Emily sleeps on. Sam is walking around with one shoe. As his weight shifts from one foot to the other, he notices: "Shoe?" He looks at me, and I quickly scan the room for hiding places.

I put out Duplos for the children who have eaten, clear some of the mess

away, give my piece of cornbread to Renko, and look around for Drew. He's not there. Jennifer is sent to find him, as I begin to search for the shoe. Caitlin and Sam are squabbling over the Duplos because they each want to use the same piece for the tail of an airplane. Jennifer returns with a crying Drew. I hold Drew in my lap, arbitrate the Duplos dispute, and give Jennifer verbal instructions to take over the shoe hunt.

Emily finally wakes up and looks around, bewildered. Jennifer helps her with shoes and socks and gives her her snack. Drew joins the Duplos play. I look for the shoe.

It is now 3:45. We must be back in by 5:00 for parent pick up. Sam cannot go out without his shoes. The kids are getting antsy. I find two empty glue containers, a bag of paper scraps, and a stash of raisins, but no shoe. Jennifer is reading to Emily. I'm getting frantic. "Forget storytime, Jennifer! Help me find the shoe!" My perspective is slipping.

I see a certain look in Renko's eye and feel an instinctive need to involve the children in the hunt. "Does anyone have an idea where Sam's shoe might be?" Jennifer: "I'm sure none of them would hide it; and besides, they're not smart enough to do something like that." I send Jennifer to the office to ask for a spare shoe of any sort so that we can go outside and begin to rally the children to the bathroom. Drew (surprise) is already there.

Now no one wants to go either to the bathroom or to the playground. The office can find no shoe. Okay, so we won't go outside. Jennifer plays Duplos with some children, and I get out **Caps for Sale**, one of my favorite read-a-louds. Jennifer comes over to listen. "What caps are on top of the grey caps?" I ask. Jennifer responds: "The red ones." "Oh, you've heard this story before, Jennifer. Does anyone know where the monkeys are?" Jennifer: "In the trees!"

Every now and then someone stops by to see how I'm doing, asks about Sam's shoe, looks around a bit and leaves. We're obviously into problem ownership. So we spend the time until 4:40, now and then looking for the shoe. I get out my collection of jar caps and bottle lids and the children enjoy sorting through and playing with them. Jennifer decides the shoe could be in the sleeping mats so she sorts through all the mats, piling them all in the center of the room as she does so. While she is looking, Drew makes another trip to the bathroom.

We get out markers and scissors and glue. For a few minutes, everyone — even Drew — is happily absorbed in

artistic endeavors. The stack of paper quickly disappears, so I lift the roll of butcher paper in the corner — and out rolls Sam's shoe!

Hurray! We have ten minutes of outdoor time left. To hurry them on with coats, I suggest we make a list of things we'll look for outside:. "Let's see if we can find a slug, and what else? A worm, a round stone; and anything else? A puppy." Jennifer: "We'll never find all of those things." As I button Drew's coat, I easily notice that he has had a bowel movement. "Jennifer, do you want to diaper Drew or take the others outdoors?" She pats me on the shoulder, "He's all yours."

Managing From Afar:
Out of Sight, But Not Out of Mind

by Sarah and Robert Boschi, Richard McCool, Sue Portnoy,
and Arlein and Edwin DeGroot

It all used to be so simple. You had just one center. When a teacher was having a problem with a child, you went in and helped her out. When the bus driver called in sick, you drove the bus. When you announced new procedures for serving meals, you were on the spot to remind teachers to follow through. At the time it didn't seem simple at all, of course; but now that you manage centers in five different neighborhoods, you often think longingly of those days when you could work with all your staff on a face to face basis.

Styles of supervision that are effective in single site operations seldom translate well to the management of multiple centers. When you managed a single center, your success rested heavily upon the force of your personality and your attention to endless details. But such traits are not enough when it comes to managing from afar. The force of your personality is diluted when you only see staff members once a week; and trying to attend to all the administrative details of three or more centers would overwhelm even the most extreme workaholic.

Supervising the performance of staff in more than one location requires a unique set of skills. You need to be able to enforce your decisions without your presence, establish rules and procedures without creating a stifling bureaucracy, achieve consistent quality without sacrificing individuality and spontaneity.

In order to experience success in managing from afar, you need to learn how to accomplish results through a system. While the force of your personality will still have an impact, and your attention to details will still be well rewarded, what will make the biggest difference will be your ability to supervise staff through organizational structures and procedures.

What follows are a number of basic guidelines for success in managing staff from afar:

1. **Delegate responsibility to someone you can trust.**

In a growing organization, one of the hardest things for a director to learn is how to let go. A director who has done everything for years naturally resists giving away responsibility. "Who else can do this as well as I do?" is the typical rationalization. But as demands on her time increase, even the diehard entrepreneur eventually realizes that she can't do it as well as she used to. She needs to lean on others, especially in terms of supervising staff in different locations.

Identifying individuals that you can lean on with confidence must be done with care. You need to find individuals who share your values on working with adults and caring for children, who can take initiative, who can set priorities and stick to them, who can earn the respect and cooperation of the people they supervise, who can be trusted to carry on without close supervision. And most of all, you need to find individuals who you can relate with comfortably on a personal, as well as professional, basis.

What you don't need is a clone of yourself, or a *yes man*. You should not try to find someone who will do everything just like you do, or someone who can be intimidated into doing everything your way. As long as everyone's basic values are in accord, it is healthy for key management staff to follow different paths to accomplishing the same goals. This creates a constructive tension which helps keep you out of a rut and open to new ideas.

2. Develop management talent within your organization.

The best way to find second level managers is to look inside your organization. By promoting from within you can accurately evaluate how you relate to the people on a personal level and how they perform on a day to day basis. When you hire someone from outside, you can never be sure how they will work out in your setting.

You can slowly groom someone from inside by gradually giving him more and more responsibility. If he responds well, you know you've backed a winner. If he flounders, you can try someone else. Some organizations have created an assistant director position at their centers as a means of preparing promising individuals from their teaching staffs for management positions.

3. Turn over responsibility gradually.

Once you have identified a manager, you need to help her grow into the position. One common error is to move too rapidly from where you did everything yourself to where you dump all the responsibility on the new person. A person with a great deal of management potential may fall apart if given too much responsibility at once. You should adhere to the educational maxim that a person grows optimally when presented with moderate challenges which cause her to move just a little bit out of her comfort zone at a time.

It is healthy for key management staff to follow different paths to accomplishing the same goals.

By working closely with a new manager at the outset, you will give him the security of learning the ropes without the fear of making some horrendous mistake. Then, by gradually pulling back and leaving him on his own, you will give him the opportunity to build his confidence and develop his own style.

4. Provide all managers on-going support.

All managers, whether they are new to the job or not, can benefit from continuing support. At Palo Alto/Gerber Centers, for example, it was observed that center directors spent a lot of time on the phone with each other finding out how they handled certain situations, or simply letting off steam. To upgrade the kind of support that was going provided through this informal buddy system, a new position of executive director was created. Experienced directors were promoted to these positions, and each was assigned two or three centers. They call upon their center directors daily and offer whatever kinds of advice or support are needed. Since the executive directors are not formally supervising the center directors, but only offering them support, center directors feel free to admit their mistakes, to ask dumb questions, and to air their complaints without fear of undercutting their credibility in the organization.

If staff know that they can make an end run around their center director and get what they want from you, the ability of your center directors to supervise staff will be greatly diminished.

Another way to support second level managers is to protect their authority. When a parent comes to you with a problem, or when an old friend from the teaching staff asks for a special favor, it is tempting just to step in and take care of it as you used to do. But to do so would undermine the authority of your center directors. If staff know that they can make an end run around their center director and get what they want from you, the ability of your center directors to supervise staff will be greatly diminished.

5. Focus everyone's attention and efforts on the basic goals and policies of the organization.

The saying "If you don't know where you're going, you'll never get anywhere" applied particularly well in managing staff from afar. Having clear-cut goals provides a sense of purpose that helps focus the efforts of staff in various locations. You cannot be in every center all the time; but if staff have a clear fix on what they are supposed to accomplish, they can carry on confidently in your absence. If staff do not know what is expected of them, their efforts will be unfocused, inefficient, and often at cross purposes.

It is also critical to communicate to all staff the basic program and personnel policies. If center directors are aware of the organization's policies, they can use these as guides in implementing the day to day program. When issues arise they can use these policies as a basis for decision-making.

Communicating the goals and policies of the program to staff in all locations should start during the screening process. An important selection criteria should be that the candidates' teaching, philosophy and behavior is compatible with the goals of the center. Once hired, teachers should be given an orientation that emphasizes goals and policies. Then throughout the year all staff should be regularly exposed to training that emphasizes techniques for accomplishing these goals and policies.

The goals and policies also need to be reinforced in every way possible. They need to be distributed in writing to all parents and teachers. They should be posted in conspicuous locations in the centers. As head of the organization, you should focus your attention on these when you visit centers or meet with center directors. If you do not give priority attention to the goals and policies, chances are no one else will either.

Communicating the goals and policies of the program to staff in all locations should start during the screening process.

6. Utilize multiple channels for communication.

When staff are scattered in centers many miles apart, communication can easily fall apart. Yet communication is the glue that holds a program together. To keep morale high and performance improving, all sorts of information, from changes in the goals of the organization to ideas on making play dough, need to be communicated up and down the organization.

To ensure that communication is occurring, an organization should utilize multiple communication channels. The more important a message is, the more ways it should be transmitted. Above all, the more personal the mode of communication the better.

Teaching Centers Inc. holds two meetings a month for the entire staff — one for business and one for training. By making policy announcements in these meetings as opposed to issuing them in writing only, staff are given the opportunity to ask questions about points they don't understand and receive clarification, or point out problems with the proposals that can be discussed.

Weekly meetings with center directors are also a must. These meetings give the head of the organization (or her representative in larger organizations) the opportunity to communicate her current concerns directly. They also give the directors the opportunity to seek advice on unusual problems they are experiencing, and to give notice about any problems which may be looming in the future.

7. Develop a system for controlling center performance.

Once you have entrusted responsibility to dependable people and clearly communicated to them what their goals are, how do you make sure they are following through? Do you tightly monitor all aspects of center operations, or do you put good people in charge and let them do their own thing?

Clearly there needs to be some form of control to ensure that programmatic and financial standards are being complied with. But if controls that you impose are too demanding, you can stifle initiative and undermine morale.

The more important a message is, the more ways it should be transmitted.

To achieve the proper balance in setting up controls, try to impose only those controls which tell you whether or not the program is achieving its goals and complying with basic policies. If your controls indicate that these key requirements are being met, it should not be necessary to dig any deeper. If they are not being met, then you should take a closer look.

A center director should be able to feel confident that if her center is complying with established goals and policies her performance will be supported. If every decision she makes is second guessed and every aspect of the center's operation is put under a microscope, her motivation to take initiative and exercise responsibility will be diminished. As long as she is meeting her major targets, she should be allowed free reign to operate in a style that is comfortable to her. Overall results should be the criteria of success, not the means of achieving them.

8. Closely monitor key financial indicators.

One area where controls are essential is in terms of bottom line financial figures. Since all centers operate on such a close margin, the financial status of centers needs to be monitored on a regular basis. Money problems need to be caught and addressed early before they escalate to disastrous proportions. This does not mean that every penny earned or spent should be subject to approval by the central office. Once again, controls should focus only on key financial indicators.

A vital report is simply a tabulation of attendance and staffing. This report indicates whether or not a center is in compliance with licensing standards and whether or not the center is overstaffed (i.e. whether or not the center is spending more on salaries than it is taking in on fees). Organizations which experience frequent fluctuations in attendance may find it necessary to require these reports on a weekly or even daily basis. Others, where attendance is more stable, may only review these figures on a monthly basis.

Another key financial control is the monthly income and expense report. This report should be used to spot major discrepancies between what was budgeted for the month and what actually occurred. Unexpected drops in income should be noted, as should major increases in expense items. Such items would then be reviewed with the center director in an informal meeting. Any actions agreed upon in this meeting would then be monitored over the next few months.

9. Maintain frequent site visits.

Out of sight too often is out of mind. There is no better way to keep in touch with what is happening in the centers than to pay them periodic visits. These visits should be handled as informally and supportively as possible. If center directors come to view these visits as inspections, they will become defensive and uptight. As a result, it will not be a productive experience for anyone. Rather, these should be structured as opportunities to clarify policies, to discuss problems and success stories, and to review the needs of the center.

While the major purpose of the visit should not be to check up on the director's performance, you should not miss the opportunity to gather some informal feedback. When you drive up to the center, you may want to put yourself into the perspective of a parent dropping off her child. How does the outside appearance of the facility strike you? Is it well maintained? What about inside?

Does it appear messy, noisy, or downright hazardous?

It may be useful to actually use a checklist of key indicators (one that is written down or one that is kept in your head) for checking to see if the major emphases of your program are being adhered to.

One of the hardest things for a director to learn is how to let go.

Things to observe may include whether the children are engaged in appropriate activities, or whether the teachers are addressing the children appropriately.

10. Utilize a variety of tools for assessing program performance.

There are also a number of evaluation approaches that can be employed to check out center performance. The results of these evaluations can be helpful to the central office in its decisionmaking, but they can also be useful to center directors in helping them improve their performance.

Parent satisfaction is a key indicator of performance and needs to be regularly evaluated. Educo Schools send out a two page evaluation form to every parent every year. By offering rewards to the classrooms that have the most questionnaires returned, Educo has managed to achieve an 80% rate of return. These questionnaires provide valuable feedback on how the program is perceived by the parents.

Another means of measuring parent perceptions is to interview all parents

Try to impose only those controls which tell you whether or not the program is achieving its goals and complying with basic policies.

who withdraw from the program. While parents may be reluctant to fully discuss their reasons for departing with the center director, they do tend to be more open with someone higher up in the hierarchy. Again this information can be useful both to the central office and to the center director.

To get a fix on the staff perspective, Teaching Centers Inc. holds monthly teacher advisory committee meetings. One teacher from each center as well as representatives from the central office attend this meeting. Organization-wide issues that are on teachers' minds — problems, questions, suggestions — are discussed. (Problems that are unique to a particular center are reserved for discussion with the center director.) Minutes are kept, and every employee receives a copy of these minutes with their next paycheck. This forum helps to keep the central office staff in touch with emerging issues among the employees. It also helps the teachers feel more a part of the organization as a whole, and lets them know that their feelings and opinions are treated seriously.

Sarah and Robert Boschi are owners of Teaching Centers, Inc. in Wauwatosa, Wisconsin. Richard McCool is president of Educo, Inc. in Vienna, Virginia. Sue Portnoy is a regional manager of Palo Alto Preschools/Gerber Children's Centers, stationed in Scottsdale, Arizona. Arlein and Edward DeGroot are owners of Amrein's Child Development Centers in metropolitan Dallas, Texas.

Helping Employees Cope With Change

by Lorraine Schrag, Elyssa Nelson, and Tedi Siminowsky

• *In response to community demand, the ABC Child Care Center opened a room for infants. The new program was an instant success and soon had a waiting list. However, staff in the preschool room were less than excited. The director spent so much time in setting up the new room that she barely had time to help the rest of the staff with their problems. In addition, budgets for classroom supplies were cut to the bone in order to equip the new room.*

• *The head teacher in the four year old room quit after ten years of teaching at Happy Days Nursery School and was replaced by a new teacher. The rest of the teachers were upset that they were not considered for promotion and were threatened by the new teacher who arrived with lots of enthusiasm and new ideas.*

• *The arrival of the computers was greeted with delight by the children and with despair by the teachers at the Elm Street After School Program. The teachers were intimidated by the computers and were afraid that their rapport with the children would disappear in a rush of arcade fever.*

These are three typical examples of change and its impact on staff in child care centers. We teach children in our centers to be flexible, open, and creative. But when change occurs at the center, we often find that it is the adults who are the most inflexible and the most resistant to change. This resistance may manifest itself in anger, anxiety, bitterness, or despair.

Staff members who are unable to adapt to changes in their work environment may react by complaining to their co-workers, thus chipping away at staff morale. They may vent their frustration by refusing to go along with the change. Their anxiety or anger may cause them to perform below their ability. Or they may just quit, or perform so poorly that they end up being fired.

As a director you would like to avoid these reactions to change, but you know that you cannot avoid making changes. Whether your program is an expanding multi-site system or a small, stable nursery school, you will inevitably be introducing some magnitude of change into your organization. So the question is *how can you introduce change without upsetting your staff?*

The following are five suggestions on helping staff cope with change. They deal with ways to select and develop change-oriented staff members, and they offer some nonthreatening ways to introduce change. But implicit in all of them is the message from director to staff, "I value you so much that I'm going to do whatever I can to bring you along with this change."

#1. Building a Resilient Staff

The most direct way to minimize staff resistance to change is to build a staff that looks upon change as a challenge rather than as a threat. This involves not only including openness to change as a criteria in the selection process but also using staff development opportunities to strengthen the commitment of staff members.

Openness to change is not, of course, a trait that can be readily measured during the selection process. But there are some fairly reliable indicators to watch for. For example, it may be helpful to get candidates talking about what they did and didn't like about their previous jobs. If dealing with changes comes up in the negative category, this may be a meaningful clue as to what to expect. Also, candidates who are free flowing in their thinking, and who have many ideas to talk about other than that they really love kids, are likely to be able to deal well with change.

Exposing candidates to even a small deviation from the norm in the selection process can also demonstrate how they deal with change. For example, having candidates participate in a group interview as opposed to the expected one-on-one interview can show how they handle the stress of the unexpected.

It is important, once a teacher is hired, to carefully observe her during her probationary period to see how she handles change in practice. Observe how well she deals with small changes, such as being asked to change rooms to fill in for absent teachers. Another factor to observe is how comfortable new teachers are in discussing the problems and successes they are experiencing. Openness in discussing such issues is a positive indication that a person is open to change.

On an ongoing basis, any staff development efforts that get staff members more committed to the goals of the organization are likely to yield positive benefits in times of change. The more that staff members believe they are an integral part of the team, the more willing they will be to put up

with any discomforts brought on by changes. Staff, on the other hand, who have little commitment to the organization, who are just along for the ride, will react strongly to any inconvenience or stress.

#2. Avoiding Leadership Blind Spots

When the director of the Elm Street After School Program decided to buy computers for her program, she was sure the idea would succeed. She had researched the educational implications of computers; she had read hundreds of software reviews to be sure she selected programs that were truly educational as well as entertaining; and she tried these programs out on the computers she planned to buy to make sure everything worked as described. She even prepared carefully for breaking the news to the staff by pulling together the statistics and research to bolster her case.

When the teachers greeted her presentation with misgivings, she set up a computer and, with great enthusiasm, showed them two of the programs in action. Two weeks later, with the computers gathering dust on the shelves, the director wondered what had gone wrong — why had the staff opposed her great idea?

What went wrong was that the director had blind spots which prevented her from seeing what was happening. She was so preoccupied with launching *her baby* that she became oblivious to what was bothering the teachers. When teachers showed signs of resistance, the director responded by rolling out more artillery to win them over to her side. Instead, she should have tried to understand their concerns, to see what was happening from their point of view.

More often than not, when teachers resist a new idea they are not so

much opposed to the idea itself as they are anxious about the social consequences of the change. They may be concerned with how this change will affect their relationship with the children, whether it will keep them from working closely with teachers they enjoy, whether it will force them outside their comfort zone to work in an area where they lack expertise.

If the director is so preoccupied with the logistics of implementing the change that she fails to see such social and emotional impacts of change, no amount of haranguing on the merits of the idea will overcome teachers' resistance. When signs of resistance appear, the director may find it helpful to talk to concerned staff members on a one-to-one basis to explore their feelings about the change. An alternative is to pull aside teachers who have already bought into the change and ask for their views on what it is that is causing some staff members to fight the idea. Only when the director has overcome her blind spots and seen the root causes of resistance can she begin to work toward successful implementation of the change.

#3. Keeping Staff Informed

A large measure of the anxiety aroused during a period of change is caused by fear of the unknown. If a director decides to add an infant component and only announces this in a cursory way, staff members may well be consumed with a host of uncertainties: Will teachers be taken from our classrooms to staff the new program? Will this new program receive top priority for any new money for equipment? Will salary increases be put on hold while the new program is getting started?

Most of this anxiety can be dissolved by keeping staff informed both before and after the change. There may well be a temptation to withhold disclosing a plan until it is finalized, with the reasoning that there is no need to get staff all worked up ahead of time. However, more often than not, inklings of this plan will have leaked through the grapevine anyway. Rather than letting these rumors build erroneous fears, it is usually best to keep staff up to speed from the start on developments that will affect them.

When informing staff about an impending change, it is best to fill them in on the big picture. Let them know what has prompted you to think about making the change; how this change fits in with your center's current goals, or how and why you are shifting your goals; and what the advantages and disadvantages are to making the change.

Then, viewing the change from their perspective, describe how you anticipate this change will impact the day-to-day operations of the center and how it will impact them personally. Try to be as candid as possible in addressing any concerns people might have. If there may be some negative or unpredictable consequences, don't try to gloss over or conceal these. When staff find out later that you were less than honest with them, your credibility will be damaged, if not destroyed.

Sometimes it would appear that a new idea or a change in plans or policies is too complex to fully explain to all staff members. When economic pressures force a center to increase enrollment in the preschool rooms from 18 to 20, a detailed budgetary discussion of all the factors and alternatives may well be beyond the grasp of staff members who aren't versed in accounting. So the director may be tempted to say simply, "We need to do this for budgetary reasons — trust me!" If staff members are being forced by this change to work harder for the same pay, they may view this explanation by the director as somewhat

Who Can Cope with Change?

Some people have the ability to adapt to change, others do not. Larry Wilson, head of the Wilson Learning Corporation, has identified five attitudes shared by those who are best able to deal with change. If your center is likely to experience considerable change, you may want to keep these attitudes in mind as you select and develop your staff:

- **Challenge** — an openness to change. People possessed with this mindset view change as an opportunity, rather than as a threat.

- **Commitment** — a high degree of involvement in what one is doing. A staff member who believes in what the organization is doing, who is committed to the goals of the organization, is likely to be supportive of changes that improve the performance of the organization.

- **Control** — a sense of personal impact on external change. If staff members, through their ongoing relationship with the organization, feel as if they are not powerless in the face of change, that they will be able to influence the course of change, they will be more accepting of change when it occurs.

- **Confidence** — the recognition that no situation puts your personal worth on the line. Confident people are comfortable with who they are, with their faults as well as their strengths, and with others. They tend not to read into activities (such as organizational changes) implications about their worth. They are less inclined to avoid things that they may not do well, and they are more willing to take risks.

- **Connection** — the extent of interpenetration you are willing to establish between yourself, others, and your environment. Interaction with the external environment, or making connections, somehow appears to allow a parallel process to take place internally, enabling a person to develop an increasingly sophisticated system of adaptability to change.

less than satisfactory. While the director should not try to razzle dazzle the teachers with fancy charts and figures, she should take the time and trouble to translate the reasons into terms that all staff members can understand.

Helping staff fully understand change is not simply an act of professional courtesy. In general, it is in the best interests of the program to have teachers who understand what they are doing. A person who does not fully comprehend what she is doing will not be a fully productive worker.

She will not be able to exercise informed and intelligent judgment on what she is doing. If the after school teachers do not really understand how the computer programs the kids are using work, they will be handicapped in their efforts to help the children learn through computers.

#4. Involving Staff in the Change Process

An even better way to bring staff along with a change is to have them participate in the process of change.

There are two advantages to inviting participation. First, staff who are involved in planning a change have an ego investment in seeing that it succeeds. They will work hard to make their plan work. Second, by including staff in the planning process, you are multiplying the size of your solution pool. By having more minds focused on solving a problem, particularly minds of people whose work is central to the purpose of the organization, the chances of arriving at a successful conclusion are increased dramatically.

However, for participation to be effective, it must be true participation and not just a gimmick. Including teachers from the preschool room on a committee to plan the new infant room does not constitute participation if the director has already drafted the plans and just wants a rubber stamp approval. Asking for teachers' opinions on the new staffing structure in a staff meeting is not true participation if the director doesn't intend to take seriously what they have to say. Participation only works if those asked to participate feel like they are participating and not simply playing a game.

There are myriad ways to get people involved in the change process. One common way is to appoint staff members to serve on a task force. If a new head teacher is being selected, having other teachers participate on the screening committee can be very helpful. Having the support and agreement of the teachers who will be working with the new teacher minimizes feelings of resentment and promotes teamwork.

In other instances, however, appointing a committee is a poor excuse for participation. Unless they are given a very specific, achievable charge, committees often become cumbersome and indecisive. When confronted with a thorny problem, a director

may achieve the best results by picking staff members' brains on a one-to-one basis or by conducting brainstorming sessions at regular staff meetings.

Other informal types of participation can have valuable results. If a new head teacher is coming in, you can team her up with one or two of the more experienced teachers and ask them to teach her the ropes.

If you are moving to a new space, you can take field trips to the new space ahead of time so that teachers can start planning how to use it.

If you are adding an infant component, you can assign different staff members to be in charge of selecting equipment, buying books and materials, and designing the space.

#5. Providing Support

During a period of change, when staff members typically are most anxious or angry, the director is often the most distracted and, therefore, least available to relieve this tension. An integral part of the process of planning for change should be thinking through how extra support will be provided to staff during this period.

The most basic form of support that can be provided is to publicly acknowledge at the outset that staff members are likely to feel anxious, ignored, angry, or disoriented. Let them know that such feelings do not reflect a weakness on their part, but that they are an inevitable result of a turbulent, uncertain period. Assure them that someone will be available to listen to their concerns, to answer their questions, and to help them in any way they need to survive this traumatic period.

To underline your support, you should strive to maintain, even to increase if necessary, the frequency of staff meetings. You should schedule

specific times when staff members know that they can talk to you on a one-to-one basis. If you disappear from the face of the earth, and if standard communication forums are cut off during this period, staff will have limited productive means of expressing their feelings.

You may also need staff members to take on increased responsibilities as you may be distracted and unable to be as involved in the day-to-day operation of the program. If you see this happening, you should not let it occur by default. To avoid feelings of resentment, let staff members know ahead of time that they are being entrusted with increased responsibilities. Let them know that you are available if they have serious concerns, but that basically you expect them to act independently, and that you trust they can succeed. Then let them go. Don't be a Monday morning quarterback, second guessing all of their decisions. This is not the time to be hypercritical.

You will inevitably find that, having lain all the above groundwork, there will still be some individuals who will need even more direct support. Most individuals do want to deal successfully with change — it's all a part of growing up. As much as they may overtly resist change, there is a spot in them that wants to grow. What you need to do is to go for that spot, to find a way to get them excited about some aspect of what is going on. Encourage them to take that risk, and let them know that you are supporting them all the way.

If you can't get a teacher to work with the computers in the classroom, maybe you could get her to take a computer home to mess around with over the weekend. If you can't convince the cook that the new menu is a good idea, maybe you could get her to cooperate if you were able to work a kitchen aide into the budget.

Unfortunately, you will not be able to find that spot with all people. There will be some people who will not be able to deal with change no matter how much preparation and support you provide. They may not give you much feedback about how they are feeling or why they are having a hard time. They won't provide you with anything to hook onto to turn them around. Or they may be passive resisters — they may agree with everything you say but then go out and perform as they always have, totally disregarding the changed expectations.

Before investing too much time, you need to decide whether it would be in the best interest of the program to keep trying to turn these individuals around or to let them go. Sometimes those who are having a hard time with change will recognize that the stress is too much for them, and they will select themselves out of child care. Others will lack such self-insight and will need to be told that both in the interest of the program and of their career they are being asked to leave.

Throughout the process of change, your attitude as the leader in the organization is critical. If you approach change with enthusiasm and confidence, this spirit can infect your staff. If you maintain your focus on the goals of the organization throughout a period of change, people will not lose sight of the ultimate purpose of change. If you view your role during change as being a facilitator — one who carefully prepares the way, who keeps channels of communication open, who provides support wherever it is needed — you will make the change easier for everyone. If you respect your employees, you will take the time and effort to bring them along.

Chapter 5

Overcoming Challenging Situations

Understanding and Managing Negativity in the Workplace

by Linda Riepe

Every center seems to have at least one person who has a tendency toward negativism. You know the type, the person who creates and fuels the grapevine, complains about other staff not doing their share, and manages to pull others into the workplace black hole of despair.

In addition to up-front whining and complaining, this person is often the source of unsettling rumors. A few words out of context, a faulty perception of an encounter, or a perceived personal slight catapults them into action. Sadly, the fallout from these individuals raises the stress level of other staff, reduces productivity, and places roadblocks in the path of problem-solving efforts.

Why are child care centers fertile ground for this type of person? Lack of benefits, low wages, intense emotional and physical demands, and a perceived lack of appreciation from the public are contributing factors. Public opinion that child care is *just baby-sitting* strongly impacts the self-worth of many workers in this field. Among all types of jobs and careers, child care providers, who are doing the most important job next to parenting, receive the least amount of compensation and respect. Is it any wonder that staff burnout and turnover are high and that negative attitudes creep into the daily lives of workers?

While the problems may be indigenous to the job, the negativity and pessimism of staff members create a continual drain on the energy and resources of most programs. In seminars and workshops, participants share horror stories from their centers and anxiously seek solutions. Perhaps the first step toward managing negativity is the development of a better understanding of the underlying causes and typical characteristics of negative people. Clearly each center and individual has problems that are unique, but the basic reasons for this behavior are similar nationwide.

As child care workers, we understand the importance of approval and acceptance by others in the development and maintenance of positive self-esteem. Personal perceptions, accurate or inaccurate, come from the mirror image we see in the faces of others. In spite of ongoing efforts to educate the public, that reflection from society continues to be predominately negative. This public devaluation of our jobs puts workers in a defensive position that erodes self-worth.

Within individual programs, expectations from parents are high. Media coverage of claims about child abuse and molestation create an attitude of mistrust and suspicion. More and more of the children we care for are struggling with fears and problems related to poverty, crime, and uncertainty. Minimal levels of funding are barely maintained. We know from research and personal experience that *ideal* environments for children's programs often cannot be attained. Operational costs for such dream programs seldom match income levels. With all of these stresses, even the strongest personality may find optimistic attitudes hard to maintain.

At the end of the work day, many child care workers find little escape when they go home. Low wages force them to face the problems of supporting and managing a family with fewer resources than someone who collects trash for a living. Limited funds are available for fun and relaxation activities that might offer some relief. These problems may be magnified in the case of single staff whose lack of resources and energy also leave them isolated from typical support networks.

It is particularly sad that child care workers — the most caring, nurturing people in society — have little or no ability to nurture themselves. The unfortunate result can be a belief that problems or disasters are inevitable, unavoidable, and insurmountable. A sense of learned *helplessness* develops that strongly impacts their view of work and life in general.

When we understand that negativism is related to a sense of feeling helpless to find a solution or make a change for the better, it can change the way we approach and interact with negative people. These people tend to have lots of experience with failure, the logical result of which is a belief that nothing they do will affect outcomes.

To reverse that thinking pattern requires skillful intervention. The following ten strategies involve a combination of ways to change your own behavior along with the introduction of techniques that *disarm* negative responses.

#1
If you are working with a negative person, resist the temptation to argue or try to persuade them to accept your position or point of view.

Negative people are absolutely convinced that ideas and approaches won't work. They have a strong distrust of *managers* as a group. Often

they see an underlying motive of self-service in the actions of others.

#2
Do not rush into proposing solutions to problems.

One of the most common reactions to suggestions is playing of the *"yes, but . . . game,"* rejecting any solution offered. By playing that game, the person has a great deal of *negative* power over the manager. They keep you involved with guessing what they will accept as you try to find the right answer. For a negative thinker, no right answer exists.

#3
Be willing to accept them as they are.

Negativity is a personality and style issue based on a lifetime of experience. By consistently applying effective communication strategies, you may begin to see some *style* changes over a period of time. However, keeping realistic expectations about the overall impact you can make on any individual will help you deal with your own frustration.

Negative behavior is rarely limited to the work environment. Clearly, most of us have little or no impact on what happens in an employee's home, so it is important to keep the focus on how to manage the negative behavior at work. Understand that it is likely that these strategies will continue to be needed throughout your working relationship. With negativity, we are better off trying to manage one situation at a time while we hope for a long-term change in attitude.

#4
Ask them to state "specific" objections to the ideas and suggestions of others.

When they say something won't work, ask them to tell you the two

most important objections they have about the proposed approach or solution. When they are put on the spot to be specific, it is harder to be negative. It can break the pattern of the *instant negative response*. Additionally, it gives them some *positive* power or control over the solution. It is also a productive way to examine valid concerns or objections to ideas.

#5
Analyze the situation honestly in terms of worst case scenarios.

Often negative people are fearful of taking action without really knowing what they are afraid of. They grant an incredible amount of power to minor problems. When they learn to really look at the worst possible result or consequence, most problems and situations become manageable and less frightening.

#6
Use every possible opportunity to "empower" them.

Remember that negative behavior is directly related to a sense of helplessness and a perceived lack of power. Most people have previously made helpful contributions or developed good ideas. When approaching a new problem or task, draw on those past successes. Remember when you worked on the committee to . . . ? How did you turn that project into such a success?

It is helpful to be reminded of times when things worked out or when previous ideas led to the success of a project. Negative people often have experienced so few *successes* that they lose sight of success as a possibility. These individuals need reminders of good results.

#7
Help them think in shades of gray.

Negative people tend to see things as black or white. They have trouble accepting a temporary solution or anything less than *perfection* when it comes to problem solving. They have high standards for themselves and others. If the *perfect* or *ideal* solution cannot be found, it is easy to get stuck within the boundaries of the problem. Helping them identify partial or temporary solutions may be a useful way to move them from black to gray.

Another strategy is to put suggested solutions into place on a trial basis. Fear of making a mistake is reduced when solutions are not viewed as long term. The idea is to make decisions seem less monumental and threatening.

#8
Seek support from your most negative people prior to bringing the problem to a group discussion or meeting.

Generally this is most effective if it is done during a private discussion. *Nay-sayers* have a reputation to maintain with peers. By giving them the chance to express objections and feelings one to one, the need to do so in the group is reduced. Again, this is a way to empower the negative person and identify the *real* issues before attempting to solve a larger problem.

When you ask for a private moment with the person, it is a way to let them know you value their ideas and feelings. Draw out the specific objections/fears during that discussion and analyze each one together to defuse its importance.

This not only gives you more information about the person's concerns, it also allows you to garner needed support in advance. With fears set aside, they can help gain the support and acceptance of others they influence. Often the negative person has great ideas and is more likely to offer them up in private.

#9
Suggest that opinions and ideas on a problem or topic of discussion be submitted in written form prior to a meeting.

Ask for the rationale behind ideas/concerns and objections. Written words are perceived as more powerful to many people. When the negative person sits down to write about their feelings (accompanied by rationale), they have an opportunity to see that fears may be unfounded. It also allows them to assess real feelings without being *put on the spot* in a meeting. Many people feel more positive when they have the chance to be heard.

#10
Find ways to have fun!

Regardless of individual lifestyles and support systems, providing less serious moments and social time with colleagues lightens any job. Fun times can create enthusiasm, optimism, and positive attitudes. These characteristics are all part of the makeup of *successful* people.

Take every opportunity to recognize staff efforts and reward the behavior and attitudes you value. Success is the greatest motivator of all. Find ways to utilize individual strengths

rather than fight those characteristics. Even the smallest rewards and recognition are appreciated. Remember that rewards need not always come from management; peer rewards and recognition create harmony and good will.

You do not need a big budget to offer rewards, incentives, and recognition. Something as simple as a notation in the newsletter or on the bulletin board about the efforts of individuals can go a long way toward improving staff attitudes. If you don't know how to begin, try asking staff what motivates them or what would make them feel good about themselves and the program.

It is particularly sad that child care workers — the most caring, nurturing people in society — have little or no ability to nurture themselves.

The mirror image we see each day is reflected back in our work attitudes. If that image is negative, it will take some time to change it, but it can be done. Establish confidence with staff that you will listen, be empathetic, and supportive, and optimism will likely follow. Keep sight of the messages, benefits, and rewards we can and cannot control.

We are all working to gain better wages and acceptance from society, but the immediate solution may be within the walls of our own programs. The bottom line may be that child care workers need more nurturing than the average employee.

Linda Riepe has over 25 years experience in the field of early education. She presents workshops and writes articles on various child care topics in addition to her full-time position as coordinator of early childhood programs at Lane Community College in Eugene, Oregon.

Reading Staff Dissatisfaction Cues

by Kay Albrecht

Walk with me into a center—the air is heavy with tension, more children are crying than normal, an angry parent is waiting to see the director, and three staff resignations are sitting on the desk! The bewildered director asks: "How did this happen? Just last week we were humming along merrily — fully staffed, fully enrolled, and looking forward to a good month. What happened?" After talking with the resigning staff members and the angry parent, the director finds out that the center has been a boiling cauldron ready to overflow for weeks. Staff are unhappy; parents are perceiving the staff's dissatisfaction and identifying their own concerns; children who are normally just healthy, challenging children are pushing every limit — even the custodian isn't doing what needs to be done.

How did it go this far? What happened to unsettle the whole center system? Could this blowout and the fallout that will certainly result from it have been prevented? What cues did the director have of the impending disaster? It is my premise that there were plenty of cues. But for some reason, these cues were not received in time to do something about them. Let's take a look at some strategies for preventing situations like the one described above by insuring that the director is not the last one to know.

By definition, teachers and directors have different world views. Teachers have a micro view of the center world — they are sensitive to what goes on with their assigned children, the parents who come in and out of their classroom each day, the teaching team members who work together planning and then implementing curricula, and the world within the physical boundaries of their classroom. Directors have a macro view — they see the sum of the parts, the big picture, the way policies and procedures affect different children, families, and teachers; the impact of change in one sphere of operation on the other spheres; and the equilibrium of the whole center.

Because of this basic difference in orientation, staff are the perfect barometer of the center's overall health. Teachers aren't supposed to look at the big picture — they are supposed to focus their energy and efforts on the world of their classroom. When they do so and are satisfied with the results, children are busy and well cared for. If they are dissatisfied with the results, for whatever reason, this dissatisfaction will leak out of the classroom into the rest of the center. Let's look at some things the director can do to insure that staff dissatisfaction is uncovered and identified before it discombobulates the whole center system.

Observe for dissatisfaction cues — really observe — regularly. Directors need to be astute observers of the center milieu. But when they are looking for dissatisfaction cues, the observation needs to take a more focused approach. Don't try to observe for dissatisfaction cues when you are evaluating teachers, looking for classroom maintenance needs, checking for the lunch count, or passing through on your way to the restroom. Make this observation a participatory one. Go into the classroom and work along side of your teachers. See their jobs as they see it.

A personal example. Recently, a teacher was out due to a family emergency. Although we had a substitute, I wanted to help, so I went into the toddler room during the transition to lunch and nap. Frustration was not far away. I found out that I didn't know which lunch box belonged to whom (regardless of the fact we request that parents label everything they bring to the center), I was useless in helping toddlers get to sleep because I was unfamiliar with their calm down routines and couldn't identify which mat belonged to which child or locate the "right" blanket or security toy, and I was reminded just how hard it really is to clean up five toddlers at once after they have eaten lunch. But the real lesson learned was that a substitute in the toddler room has a really hard time being very useful. And, as a result, the remaining staff have a truly tough day because substitute help is so unhelpful!

Now, no center director can prevent staff absence. But the way substitutes are used and the extra support given classrooms with substitutes is definitely the purview of the director. Insight into the realities of the problem came from participating in — not just observing—how rough it was to compensate for an absent staff member.

Identify frustration points. Different teachers will become frustrated over different things. Knowledge of the "hot buttons" for each staff member is a critical piece of information for a center director. Unresolved frustration can be the source of much dissatisfaction. If you know what frustrates a staff member, you can

---

Surefire Signs of Staff Dissatisfaction

- Increases in tardiness or absenteeism without prior notification

- Lack of attention to details like where children's shoes and socks are located or what happened to the new manipulative toy

- Room arrangements that look just like they did last month or last year

- Defensive responses to feedback from peers, parents, or supervisors

- Changes in productivity levels as indicated by out of date curriculum plans or incomplete materials requests

- Lack of follow through in usual routines like playground pickup, returning toys to central storage, etc.

- Cabinets whose contents fall on your head when the doors are opened

---

work hard to prevent it as much as possible or at least anticipate its occurrence. How do you find out? Try asking! Add a question about "things that frustrate me" to your current teacher self-evaluation tool. Also, use a similar question during interviews with applicants for teaching vacancies.

Vary the techniques used to measure dissatisfaction. Put out an anonymous suggestion box in the staff lounge. Or hold a blank agenda staff meeting where you listen and teachers ask questions, raise issues, and confront problems. If you let the structure of the meeting emerge, rather than determining it in the beginning, you may get lots of data about frustration and dissatisfaction. Establish only one ground rule — if you bring up a problem, you must suggest at least one solution. This rule will keep

the meeting from becoming a gripe session.

Take action on dissatisfaction. Knowledge is the key to problem prevention. Now that you know some techniques for identifying staff dissatisfaction, use them to find latent crisis and to take action *before* dissatisfaction takes hold and permeates your center.

Kay Albrecht, Ph.D., is the former executive director of HeartsHome Early Learning Center, Houston, Texas, and senior partner in Innovations in Early Childhood Education. Her specialties include teacher training and curriculum development. Her latest book, Innovations in Infant Curriculum, is in press with Gryphon House. In 2000, she served as the academic dean of the World Forum.

Off-Site Stress and the Disadvantaged Caregiver: A Neglected Factor

by Paul D. Wessen

Overwhelming stresses outside the job setting appear to be one of the key reasons for lateness, absences, and unexpected quitting by disadvantaged child care workers. These workers often find car problems more anxiety-producing than any work-related problem, including getting fired. These are some of the findings from doctoral research conducted by Paul D. Wessen at Nova University in Fort Lauderdale, Florida. At Child Care Information Exchange's request Wessen prepared a summary of his study's findings and implications.

Studying the Disadvantaged Worker

The past several decades have witnessed the publication of a massive body of literature concerned with the motivations of personnel working on the lower levels of institutional and industrial hierarchies. Has this literature changed the attitudes and policies of institutional management? More specifically, have education's primary caregivers developed a stronger bond to the work site?

The answers to these questions lie in reports of ever-increasing absenteeism and rapid turnover, especially among newer and younger personnel. Although turnover among certified teaching staff is somewhat stable, absenteeism is growing to such proportions that at least one school system in south Florida has had to resort to the creation of a highly systematized and centrally staffed "department of substitution." The situation in non-public caregiving centers is much worse. Attempts to present children with ongoing developmental programs are constantly interrupted by teacher absences and the continual influx of new "teachers-in-training" who are trying to take the place of personnel who have left without notice. An investigation of the motivators of low-echelon caregivers indicate that American management has not yet evolved effective strategies for coping with employee disaffection compatible with changes in the general work culture.

The measuring instrument, developed by the author, used socio-economic status (as defined by federal guidelines) and the independent variable and motivational drives, based on Maslow's Hierarchy of Needs, as the dependent variable. The self-report consisted of a demographic checklist designed to rate the respondents' degree of socio-economic disadvantage and 100 pictorial items representing all possible forced-choice combinations to ten stressors commonly related to the work site, as well as ten common off-site stressors. For each paired item, the respondents were asked to select the stressor that would represent the least preferable occurrence. With the items pictured below, for example, respondents were asked to choose between a car accident and peer disapproval.

Findings Point to Non-Job Stressors

Several of the findings of the study are worth noting:

- Stresses not related to the job were much more anxiety producing for disadvantaged workers than were job-related problems. In a ranking of caregiver choices of problems to be avoided, the top six choices were non-job problems (see chart on page 170). Thus it would seem that the respondents are more highly motivated by off-site pressures than by on-site pressures. The top three rankings are economically dominated and represent a serious threat to the already tenuous financial stability of the disadvantaged low-income family.

- The lower workers ranked on a socio-economic scale, the more likely they were to be concerned with non-job stressors and the less likely they were to be concerned with job problems. Employers and supervisors, on the other hand, demonstrated significantly less reaction to external stressors. Their incomes are higher than those of their employees; thus they are better able to address problems by merely spending their way out of them — a recourse not available to most workers in this low-paid field.

- A positive correlation was also demonstrated between the number of socio-economic pressures individuals have and their employment effectiveness and longevity. Whereas the normal theory is that those who need a job the most will attend to it more faithfully, the opposite is indicated by the findings of this study. In fact it can be concluded that absences are often caused by individuals' adaptation to external stressors rather than by job dissatisfaction. Non job-related problems tend to distract individuals from their task and lead to early termination regardless of the fact that the resultant loss of income will likely exacerbate those problems.

- An unexpected finding was the lack of interest expressed by caregivers in further professional training. Employees surveyed did not demonstrate strong agreement with the statement — "More professional training would help me do a better job more

Disadvantaged Child Care Workers Rankings of Stressful Situations	
Rank	**Stressor**
1	Car damaged in accident
2	Home maintenance problem
3	Sick family member
4	Family dispute
5	Your child underachieving in school
6	Gossip about you by neighbors
7	Justifiable criticism for job error*
8	Unjustifiable criticism for job error*
9	Bad report to your personnel file*
10	Lost wallet
11	Peer disapproval*
12	Losing a raise you expected*
13	Losing a promotion you wanted*
14	Personal injury
15	No chance for advancement*
16	Being fired*
17	Having to do more work than your share*
18	Being sick
19	Missed opportunity for community service
20	Uncomfortable physical work environment*

*Job-related stressors

easily and give me more satisfaction." Employers, likewise, did not agree that further training would reduce absenteeism and turnover.

Implications Stress New Approaches

We are beginning to collect evidence indicating that utilization of the basic stressors of non-work life as the foundation of work-life motivators might promote sounder, more reliable, and more systematic staffing policies than those now produced by tenuous dependence on raises and promotions. Nonetheless, most management advice today still focuses almost entirely on aspects of the work environment as causes of staff management tensions. These strategies are at least moderately successful with middle- and upper-

class workers who have a measurable investment in the economic system. However, they offer little inducement to those whose living standards are marginal.

The findings suggest that management personnel in child care need to re-orient their perceptions concerning employee motivation. They need to become more aware of the limited problem-solving resources available to many of their staff members. In addition they need to adopt new strategies such as the following:

- Staffing designers should consider ways to make the job-site an integral part of employees' problem-solving resources. Staff motivation can be better tapped if staffing practices offer workers an increase in their problem-solving resources, rather than promises of raises or threats such as demerits in a personnel file. For example, centers in a community could band together to develop legal, family therapy, or car maintenance services, in addition to hospitalization, as part of a fringe benefits package. Or supervisors could be trained to be more supportive to staff with personal problems. This study, and other recent research, clearly indicate that a sense of being nurtured by immediate supervisors is a crucial element in avoiding high turnover rates for low-income, low-skilled employees.

- Training efforts should, as much as possible, avoid the trappings of "school." One likely explanation of caregivers' low interest in training might be their past unrewarding schooling experiences.

- Entry-level wages should be raised, even if the entire wage spectrum is not. Low wages offered by most child care centers do not impel new workers to view this occupation as a long-term career worthy of the time and effort of professional training.

References

Wessen, P. D. (1980). "Development and Implementation of a Psychometric Instrument to Assess Job vs. Non Job-Related Strengths Among the Disadvantaged." Unpublished doctoral dissertation, Nova University.

Paul D. Wessen is a doctoral candidate in Nova University's Ed.D. program in early childhood education and a co-founder of the Palm Beach County Private Child Care Operators Association.

Way Beyond Chicken Soup: Caring For and About Ill Employees

by Pauline Davey Zeece

What Personnel Handbooks Never Tell You

*They don't tell you about eye contact
and how easily it slips away
when a woman who lost a breast
says, "They didn't get it all."*

*You can find essays on motivation
but the business schools
don't teach what the good manager says
to keep people taking up the slack
while someone else steals a little more time
at the hospital.*

*There's no help from those tapes
you pop into the player while you drive or jog.
They'd never get the voice right.*

*And this poem won't help either.
You just have to figure out for yourself,
and don't ever expect to do it well.*

From: **Love and Profit: The Art of Caring Leadership**
by James A. Autrey (William Morrow & Company, 1991).

Understanding Illness in Child Care Settings

There is little else that tests the human fabric of a child care program or the stamina of a director like an experience with a seriously or terminally ill employee. By its definition, child care work is characterized as a compassionate and caring endeavor. The very nature of this business suggests that people of all ages (and their feelings) matter. Thus, the serious or terminal illness of a staff member presents a wealth of challenges and opportunities for an administrator. To deal effectively with employee illness, a director must ideally be both compassionate and pragmatic.

. . . the compassionate director

Dying, like living, is a unique journey for each one of us. Compassionate directors understand, assess, and act. They understand that the nature of illness and dying is unique to each person and each circumstance. They know that there is no one *right* way to deal sensitively with a struggling employee. They are willing to acknowledge when they are unsure of what to do to help — yet this does not daunt their efforts to determine what is the next best action to take.

Compassionate action wears many coats. Compassionate directors understand that support is much more than hand holding or crying. They recognize that sometimes the most powerful support comes in the form of doing business as usual or laughing at life in a child care program. Other times compassion is shared through sitting quietly and listening.

Caring does not mean compromising quality, only giving of self. Caring administrators watch for cues from employees about how and when they can make a difference. The workplace atmosphere is supportive of staff in good health and illness. They are realistic about what they can and cannot do in the context of their administrative role. They are willing to give of themselves without compromising their programs.

Sometimes the greatest pain comes from ignorance, not illness. Caring directors recognize that serious illness or dying can create discomfort for many people in a program. Sometimes this discomfort manifests itself in interactions which are hurtful to an ill employee. A child care worker recovering from a bout with cancer reported that the "courtesy committee" from her workplace informed her that there wasn't enough money to send her flowers — after all, she had been hospitalized so many times that year. Another colleague asked her in the presence of her young children how long the doctors thought she would survive. A director who has built and demonstrated a caring style can help an ill employee by putting the inappropriate actions of others in a different light — or simply by acknowledging and understanding the pain caused by such behavior.

Living, rather than dying, is the first order of business for all of us. Many systems (and the workers within them) are set up to deal with sudden death, rather than slow dying. When death comes in slow steps with ebbs and tides, ability to give support or show compassion may wear thin. This is especially true when remission or decrease in symptoms gives an ill staff member a renewed burst of energy or optimism. Co-workers and administrators may assume that the illness has gone away. Yet it may be difficult for an ill worker to say to others: "This is a predictable upswing, but the long term outcome of my disease has not really changed."

Prejudice about illness is a special kind of social cancer. Compassionate directors assess the ability of an ill worker to do his/her job and provide realistic feedback. They offer adjustments in job load or assignment when possible, but they do not make promises they cannot keep. They do not assume that a worker can or cannot do a job based on only a general or generic understanding of a disease or illness. They invest heavily in the power of positive thinking and assume that a worker will do well until an objective assessment (or the worker) tells them differently.

. . . the pragmatic director

Information helps, misinformation (or no information) hinders. Pragmatic directors also understand, assess, and act. Effective directors understand how laws, rules, and policies relating to illness impact on staff. They know what the child care system can and cannot offer, what the law does and does not mandate, and how policies do and do not accommodate illness. They are able to help an ill employee understand the scope of options available with regard to such things as health insurance, disability compensation, sick leave, and even death benefits.

Knowing an illness is important to the development of a helping strategy. Having a general understanding of the nature and typical course of an illness, condition, or disease can also be helpful. When directors know that an illness or its treatment can cause fatigue, depression, general or specific weakness, slowed speech or reaction time, limitations in motor movements, loss of appetite or hair, or eventual death, they can better help a worker who is struggling with such things in the context of the job setting. Understanding the symptoms associated with the progression of a serious illness or a degenerative disease allows

a director to offer support in more realistic ways.

It is helpful to have general emergency information for all program *staff* at quick access. In this way, hospital and medical personnel preference, special medication instructions, and family contacts can be shared with emergency personnel during an on-site crisis. Staff should be reminded regularly to keep all medication in a safe place, as young children find exploration of pockets and purses quite exciting. This is good practice regardless — with or without the presence of an ill employee.

The Impact of Serious Illness

Everything that happens in a program impacts in some way on its functioning. The illness of an employee is no exception. Competent administrators assess the affects of an employee's illness on the program, families, the employee, and the director.

• Impact on the Program

One of the most difficult parts of child care management can be balancing the needs of a sick or dying worker and the demands of everyday programming. In a very real sense, a seriously ill staff member can create a financial strain on a program if job responsibilities cannot be shifted or covered without hiring additional staff. Additionally, serious illness of a staff member may create feelings of distress, sadness, fear, frustration, and even resentment among co-workers. It may also provide an impetus for members of an organization to pool their collective kindness to help a colleague.

Distress and **sadness** may surface when people worry about an ill colleague. They may feel helpless as they watch an illness progress. They may feel sad at the prospect of losing a colleague and/or a friend. Some staff may feel guilty because they never liked the ill person when he/she was healthy. And they may feel frustrated simply because they do not know how to act or what to do. The effective director provides a mechanism by which all concerns about a program can be shared. When such a system is in place *before* a crisis occurs, distress about illness can be dealt with in the context of total program concerns.

Fear of *catching* an illness or becoming ill is not uncommon. This is particularly true with AIDS and cancer. Although such fears may be irrational, they can have devastating effects on all workers. For the ill employee, a colleague's fear may manifest itself in subtle avoidance or overt rejection. Recently a teacher diagnosed with cancer reported that a co-worker would not stand closer than three feet from him for fear of being breathed upon. Directors who model rational, typical, and compassionate behavior toward an ill employee send the message that this is the way business should be conducted.

Although fear is best conquered with facts, details about the personal lives of employees cannot ethically be shared without permission. Directors might find themselves unable to help dispel misinformation about the nature or course of a disease until a worker is willing or able to share facts about an illness with others in a program.

Resentment can also be part of serious illness in a child care center. Well-intentioned workers can burn out when they are asked to *cover* over an extended period for an ill colleague. Resentment may also occur when a sick worker receives what outwardly appears to be preferential treatment. This is especially true when people have only a vague idea about the nature or the course of an illness.

A director walks a fine line between asking others to help out and exploiting them. The key to this dilemma rests in establishing guidelines for managing absences b*efore* any serious illness occurs. Co-workers have differing abilities and resources to contribute during an illness. Some will be more willing and able to help an ill colleague than others. This should be respected. As long as staff do their own jobs well, they should not be forced to *help*. Genuine help comes from a personal kindness which cannot be mandated. Directors and staff members who are able to extend such kindness are assets to everyone involved with a program.

• **Impact on Children and Families**

Seemingly rational parents can become hysterical when they feel their children are in danger. For this reason, the serious, obvious illness of a worker can raise a variety of concerns among parents. Parents may worry that an ill worker cannot care for their children adequately. They may have concerns that children will worry when learning about illness or impending death. Finally, parents may have a fear that children will *catch* the illness or disease, even when this is not logical. But illness also gives parents and teachers the opportunity to model compassion for children. It provides a way for adults to introduce young children to all the concepts involved in the cycle of life.

Information and honesty are effective strategies for dealing with and helping parents. Fears are handled best when people understand what to expect and why things occur. The ethical dilemma for a director rests in the struggle between the privacy of an ill employee and parents' right to know. Personnel policies may dictate regulations in this instance, but conscience should rule behavior.

• **Impact on an Ill Worker**

The pragmatic director assesses the impact of serious or terminal illness on a worker to ensure the safety and well-being of everyone involved in a child care program. Almost all aspects of child care work require a minimum level of stamina. If illness (or treatment of an illness) does not interfere with normal functioning within the context of a job, it should not be used as a reason to request or demand that a staff member stop working. However, when illness prevents a teacher from doing a job well, a director is faced with difficult decisions.

Not all programs have the financial resources, the personnel, or the program philosophy to modify job expectations to meet the changing needs of an ill or dying worker. Yet, for some ill people, work is an impetus which is key to their immediate survival. Ultimately, this becomes a very difficult decision for a director. It is best made by determining the minimal acceptable performance necessary to keep children safe and a program running effectively and by weighing the costs and benefits of asking an ill employee to stay or leave.

• **Impact on the Director**

Managing serious illness in a child care program is similar to many other challenges. Yet the human dimension of this challenge makes it especially painful for some directors. Competent administrators invest in workers in a variety of ways: watching an effective, productive worker slowly die can be a great challenge. But dealing with those who are facing death can also be rewarding. The prospect of dying does not usually radically alter personality. Pain and drugs may alter reactions and abilities, but these do not affect the essence of who or what a person is. In fact, after coming to terms with a serious illness, most people die in much the same way they live. Thus, a pragmatic, but caring director can use such insight to help a colleague in need.

Avoiding Common Pitfalls

Although each person and each illness is unique, there are some basic pitfalls to avoid when dealing with an employee's serious illness. If you are unsure of what to say or how to act, ask. If you are uncomfortable but want to help, tell. If you care and the loss of health makes you sad, share. Here are some pitfalls to consider.

The *Back in '56, my Aunt Bessie* pitfall. It is not uncommon for people to try to out-story an ill person with an anecdote about a more serious illness. The anecdote is usually filled with gruesome details and sometimes with a melodramatic description ending in death. One of the most supportive things you can do for a seriously ill person is to listen and to focus on their thoughts and difficulties. Save the graphic description of Aunt Bessie's surgery for the family picnic.

The *I know JUST how you feel* pitfall. This is a modified version of the Aunt Bessie scenario. Instead of her dilemma, however, the conversation switches to your difficulties. Thus, when an employee discloses that her cancer has returned and that she is experiencing much pain, you might reply with information about your current health status. The point is not that it is wrong for you to disclose. In fact, your pain may be more severe. By redirecting attention, however, you give the message that you are not really that interested, and you may close the door to a necessary discussion about dying later on.

The *Sit down right here — oh my God you're dying* pitfall. Overreacting to an illness and overcompensating can also cause an ill person embarrassment and personal pain. Drawing attention distracts from the day-to-day business of child care work and can actually contribute to alienation among staff members. Instead of building a support network, this approach may inhibit its formation.

The flip side of this pitfall is not reacting or acknowledging when a worker's health interferes with job performance or not responding when it is obvious that a worker is on the verge of collapse. Ignoring potential crisis is inappropriate with or without the presence of a seriously ill employee.

The *I'm so sorry I said that — I forgot for a moment that you were seriously ill* pitfall. People need to laugh and argue and enjoy life to its fullest for every day that they are alive. You do not have to apologize for saying such things as "Let's do that next year" or "I could have *died* laughing when I listened to those children try to tell jokes." Being sensitive *is* important; being afraid to be yourself can be destructive. If you are concerned about a comment you have made, ask. But ask in private. Being part of the everyday workplace is important to many people as they struggle with a serious illness. It helps them to put life in perspective and to know that what they do has meaning.

And Finally

Over the last four years, three of my colleagues have struggled with serious episodes of cancer. They have taught me much about illness and

death — but most of what I learned from them was related to living well, rather than to dying. Two of these people have died and the third is currently struggling with another serious bout of cancer. I asked her to share with me some thoughts that I could share with you. This is what she said:

- *Support my need and my right to manage my own illness. Understand that this doesn't mean that I don't want your help or treasure your concern.*

- *Help me to be sensitive to how my illness affects others and then help me find the best way to say "good bye."*

- *Understand that although it is very difficult to share all the details of my illness with you, I still need to talk about it in my own way.*

- *Let me be angry and sad and let me rage and cry without feeling compelled to reassure me that everything will work out all right. Let me laugh and enjoy the happy things in life without you being surprised. What I seek most is to be at peace with my illness and myself.*

- *Recognize my commitment and my contributions to my profession and to my friendship with you. Let me know in little ways that my being here has made a difference.*

Pauline Davey Zeece is director of the Child Development Laboratory at the University of Nebraska-Lincoln and assistant professor in the Department of Human Development and the Family.

Older Child Care Staff: Asset or Liability?

by John M. Johnston

Many administrators are unsure whether or not it is in their program's best interest to hire older workers: those employees who are nearing or have passed retirement. Is the goal of providing supportive treatment of older employees worth the effort required? The answer to this and other questions about the value of older employees in child care programs depends on our understanding of the strengths, weaknesses, and unique needs of older workers; on our own perceptions and stereotypes about the capabilities and appropriate roles of older employees; about recent legal trends applicable to older employees; and about recent trends regarding older adults in child care programs.

Employment of older adults in child care programs can provide a number of benefits to the children and families they serve. The number of extended family households has decreased sharply during the past generation. Increased mobility, particularly among the more affluent middle and upper classes, has resulted in fewer opportunities for interaction between grandchildren and their grandparents. Employment of older workers in child care programs provides young children an opportunity to encounter the values and attitudes of another generation. When cared for by older adults, young children have many opportunities for frequent contact with older adults in play and routine settings. Meaningful interactions between young children and older adults will support development of positive attitudes toward the elderly and will help counteract the many negative stereotypes of older adults which young children encounter in our culture.

Current Trends

There are several trends in our society which support the need for early childhood program directors to consider older employees and volunteer workers. Inflation, the women's movement, and changes in family patterns have contributed to a sharp increase in the demand for child care services. Cohen, Hardgrove, and Rosen (1981) estimated that by 1990 75% of women with preschool children will enter the work force.

At the same time that demand for child care services is increasing, many early childhood program directors are reporting difficulty in obtaining staff. This is no doubt due, in part, to the traditionally low wage paid to child care workers and the failure of that wage to keep pace with inflation and the increasing cost of living. Recent scandals of child abuse in some child care programs have reinforced the public's already low opinion of child care programs and those who work as child care providers. As the early childhood profession matures, increases in licensing standards and standards for child care staff have reduced the attractiveness of child care work for many marginally qualified staff.

Further information of interest is available from demographic trends regarding older Americans. The older population — persons 65 years or older — numbered 27.4 million in 1983, or about 12% of the U.S. population. The number of older Americans increased by 6% since 1980, compared to an increase of only 3% for the under-65 population. The older population is expected to continue to grow in the future, with the over-65 population reaching about 21% of the population in America by 2030. These figures take on additional importance in light of the effects of economic pressure to delay retirement or, in the case of those already retired, to augment their real income. As child care administrators are well aware, employees with limited education and skills — many of whom are women — have a great need to continue working for financial reasons.

The trend toward increased legal protection for older workers is an important reality facing early childhood administrators. While in the past attention has been primarily on race and sex discrimination, the focus in the future will shift to age discrimination. The Age Discrimination in Employment Act as amended in 1978 provides specific protection against discrimination in employment decisions for employees and job applicants between the ages of 40 and 70. The effect of this act is to require administrators to make job assignment, promotions, pay raises, training opportunities, and all other personnel decisions without regard to the employee's age.

Understanding Age Stereotypes

Stereotyping is making judgments about others on the basis of their membership in a particular group. Age stereotyping involves making judgments about people based on how old they are. If an early childhood program director makes decisions based on the age of an employee, she runs the risk of making faulty judgments about individ-

ual differences in skills, knowledge, and attitudes. Such decisions can be harmful to children, the program, and the self-esteem of the employee.

Meaningful interactions between young children and older adults will support development of positive attitudes toward the elderly.

There are many clichés used to describe older employees in prekindergarten and child care programs: went into retirement but kept the job, you can't teach an old dog new tricks, marking time, fading fast, and slightly senile. While these are negative clichés we often hear, there are also positive examples: never too old to learn, the wisdom of age, not older just better, and has everything at her fingertips.

Stereotypes such as these are learned and used to organize our interactions with the world. The content of stereotypes is affected by the culture in which we were raised and live, economic factors, social factors, pressures from our families and friends. Stereotypes may be learned from inaccurate images presented in school, textbooks, and movies and television. Stereotypes are also learned from our own experiences with individuals representing the groups to which stereotypes are assigned and from attitudes and biases passed from person to person (especially adult to child).

Accuracy of Job-Related Age Stereotypes

The whole notion of age stereotyping suggests that all older persons share the same characteristics. Since this is not true, of course, judgments or actions based on age stereotypes may result in false impressions, poor judgments, and inappropriate assignments. Rosen and Jerdee (1985) summarize evidence reported in Doering, Rhodes, and Schuster's (1983) comprehensive review of the

scientific literature on the characteristics of older workers:

What emerges from this review is a picture of older Americans as a heterogeneous group, including many individuals who show commitment, loyalty, dedication, and good health; and others whose continued organizational contribution depend on job redesign or job transfer to reduce physical and stress demands, special precautions to reduce accident risks, and training and development to overcome obsolescence.

In their book *Older Employees: New Roles for Valued Resources*, Rosen and Jerdee (1985) report the following facts regarding the accuracy of job-related age stereotypes:

- **Morale, commitment, and involvement**

1. Older workers have higher morale and a greater sense of organizational commitment and job involvement than workers in any other age group.

2. Older workers tend to rate work as more important to their lives than do other age groups.

3. Workers over age 65 have the highest job satisfaction of any age group.

4. Older workers are much less likely than younger workers to report an intention to leave a job or to actually leave a job. This finding has particular implications for child care programs which are plagued by frequent turnover and the problems this causes for children and administrators.

- **Performance on the job**

1. There is little support for the common belief of significant drops in performance associated with aging.

2. Of particular interest to early childhood administrators are studies

which indicate that among groups of paraprofessionals, older workers actually outperformed younger workers.

3. In direct opposition to another common stereotype, rigid, dogmatic behavior is unrelated to age.

4. Chronological age is an inadequate basis for predicting vocational performance.

• **Health and well-being**

1. The net effect of changes in physical condition of bones and muscles due to aging is some loss in strength.

2. The immunity system is more likely to fail as the body ages.

3. Sensory losses are modest and correctable and do not impair job requirements.

4. Only about 8% of the population over 65 show indication of significant mental deterioration such as partial memory loss and slowing of reaction time.

Absenteeism

Rosen and Jerdee (1985) cite an important distinction between avoidable and unavoidable absences. When an employee takes a couple of days off for personal reasons (either reported or unreported), these are called avoidable absences. When an employee is allowed time off for reasons such as illness, these are called unavoidable absences.

1. Older workers have a much better attendance record with respect to avoidable absences.

2. When unavoidable absences occur, older employees lose more time than their younger counterparts.

3. The accident records of older workers appear to be better than those of younger workers.

Other Common Misconceptions

As Rosen and Jerdee (1985) note, misconceptions about the economic condition of older adults, their involvement in society, and their attitudes about work and retirement may also affect how older employees are treated and utilized in the work place.

1. A 1982 Harris Poll found that in all areas of economic life surveyed, older adults were in better condition than was perceived by others in our society. Fowles (1984) reports that the poverty rate for persons over 65 was less than the rate for persons under 65.

2. A 1983 Harris Poll indicates that older adults are more likely to be registered voters and to vote than the general population. Older adults were found to be more involved in charitable work than other age groups and that they belong to as many voluntary organizations as do other age groups. It is clear that older adults are involved with social and political affairs.

3. Older adults are commonly viewed as uninterested in learning or incapable of learning new skills and knowledge. This notion is clearly called into question by the more than 1.7 million adults over age 65 who are enrolled in post-secondary learning institutions.

4. In direct contradiction to the belief that older workers are eagerly anticipating their retirement, a 1979 Harris Poll found that over 50% of respondents indicated that they intended to continue working beyond age 65.

In summary, there appears to be many benefits when child care pro-

Judgments or actions based on age stereotypes may result in false impressions, poor judgments, and inappropriate assignments.

gram administrators employ older adults. Staff turnover, a perennial and difficult problem for many administrators, can be reduced by the employment and proper assignments of older adults. Not only are older employees more committed to and satisfied with their work, they are generally more committed and loyal to the organization for which they work. In paraprofessional job assignments, older employees will likely outperform younger employees. Finally, older employees are likely to have fewer avoidable absences than do their younger counterparts.

Staff Development and the Older Employee

It has been noted above that the stereotype of the older adult as rigid, dogmatic, and unwilling to learn new knowledge or skills is false. Cohen (1981) reports the results of a program involving the training of older adults to work in child care settings. All but three of these students were retired, and included former secretaries, a furniture salesman, a truck driver, a nurse, housewives, and a janitor. All expressed interest in working with children in previous years.

After receiving training, 75% took positions working with children on a regular basis as employees, volunteers, and foster grandparents. Follow-up research on these older caregivers found no significant differences between older adults and other staff in the characteristics of their responses to children. Moreover, both groups displayed similar caregiving behaviors and children initiated activities with them in qualitatively similar manners.

While a great deal more needs to be known about the training of older adults, a recent project training Hispanic older adults in child care work (Landerholm & Nelson, 1985) suggests that training approaches that permit self-paced learning and focus on experiential learning rather than abstract learning may be most compatible with the cognitive strengths of older persons.

Staffing and Older Employees

In current practice, prekindergarten teacher personnel are normally employed for the full length of the operating day of the program: half day for many nursery/preschools and full day for most child care programs. It is generally assumed that within each program most teacher personnel will have approximately the same work responsibilities. If prekindergarten programs are to meet the employment needs of many older adults, it may be necessary to employ workers on a variety of work schedules and to make an effort to match the demands of specific jobs to the abilities of the employee.

A review of the biological and psychological changes associated with aging cited earlier indicates that it may be necessary to focus on a notion of functional rather than chronological age. In such an approach, the levels of physical functioning which an employee must have to perform a given job are matched to that employee's level of physical functioning. This approach recognizes that there are certain capacities and limitations associated with various medical impairments and allows the administrator to assign an employee so that it will be advantageous to both the program and the employee. For

example, analysis of various jobs in a child care program may reveal that workers in the 16-24 month toddler room must have the capacity for frequent lifting of 25-30 pound weights, as is required for necessary diaper changes. Such a requirement is not necessary for teachers in the five-year-old room.

Older workers tend to rate work as more important to their lives than do other age groups.

Knowledge of this job requirement allows an administrator to assign workers based on their physical abilities. While a 70 year old may not be able to meet the job requirements in the toddler room, she may be perfectly able to carry out the work demands in the five-year-old room. The issue here is not one of preferential treatment of older employees, but rather one of utilizing older employees in ways that are beneficial to the program and to the older employee as well.

Since it appears that most older adults wish to continue to work in some capacity and to be contributing members to society, early childhood program administrators should consider alternatives to mandatory retirement, including options for part-time work and flexible working hours. Given the economic realities of an aging work force, and an increased demand for child care services and child care providers, early childhood educators and program administrators must collaborate on effective retraining programs suited to the specific needs of older adults. Effective utilization of older adults

will require attention to the demands of child care work in order to assure that older adults are placed in work settings that are rewarding to them as well as of value to the program. Many older adults have considerable potential for productive participation in child care programs, and their participation is needed.

References

Cohen, M. C., Hardgrove, C., & Rosen, K. (1981). *The Intergenerational Caregiving Program: A Replication Manual.* Sacramento, CA: California State Postsecondary Education Commission, Zellerbach Family Fund (ERIC Document Reproduction Service No. ED 212 367).

Doering, M., Rhodes, S., & Schuster, M. (1983). *The Aging Worker: Research and Recommendations.* Beverly Hills, CA: Sage.

Fowles, D. G. (1984). *A Profile of Older Americans: 1984.* Program Resources Department, American Association of Retired Persons, 1909 K Street NW, Washington, DC 20049.

Landerholm, E., & Nelson, N. J. (1985). Training Hispanic older adults in child care work. *Life-long Learning, 8*(7), 6-7, 26.

Rosen, B., & Jerdee, T. H. (1985). *Older Employees: New Roles for Valued Resources.* Homewood, IL: Dow Jones-Irwin.

Given the economic realities of an aging work force, and an increased demand for child care services, early childhood educators and program administrators must collaborate on effective retraining programs suited to the specific needs of older adults.

John M. Johnston is an associate professor of early childhood teacher education in the Department of Curriculum and Instruction at Memphis State University.

A Practical Approach to Resolving Inter-Staff Conflict

by Dr. Marjorie J. Kostelnik

*"Sticks and stones may break my bones,
but names will never hurt me."*

We have all heard children chant that sing-song phrase hundreds of times — and know it isn't true. Name calling, backbiting, gossip, and snide remarks muttered under someone's breath do hurt. They damage our self confidence and leave us in turmoil, unable to concentrate on issues outside the negative interaction. Unfortunately, many of us work in child care settings where this type of exchange takes place between staff members every day.

Discord among child care workers can pose a major problem for any early childhood administrator. Directors overwhelmingly agree that when dissension mars staff interactions, center morale is adversely affected and the quality of service to children and families impaired. Two types of dissatisfaction are most common. The first occurs when an employee perceives that he has not received the full rights or benefits guaranteed by the policies of the organization. Generally, the individual feels that some injustice has occurred relative to salary, promotion, working conditions or evaluation of job performance (Benton, 1972). These complaints frequently result in a grievance which is formally presented either verbally or in writing to a supervisor or governing board (Flippo, 1971). When a grievance is submitted, the director's role is relatively straightforward. There are usually specific rules and procedures he can refer to as a guide for settling the dispute.

A more insidious type of discord may result when staff members have complaints about the attitudes or actions of fellow employees which are not directly related to the center's policies. The discontent is not formally expressed. Instead it permeates the work place in the form of grumbling, sour looks, lack of cooperation, irritability, gossip, disparaging remarks, silent brooding, excessive lateness, absenteeism, and turnover (Benton, 1972). The source of dissatisfaction may be as concrete as feeling that a colleague is not doing her fair share of the work or as subtle as the feeling that her personal style is incompatible with the others on the team. Disagreements of the type just described are often defined as inter-staff conflict and may occur at any level of the agency.

Inter-staff conflict is much more difficult for directors to resolve than are grievances for three reasons: 1) the discontent is generally expressed in ways which are vague and diffuse, 2) it frequently exists as a long-standing undercurrent to daily interactions rather than resulting in direct confrontations, and 3) the real issues of the conflict may be obscured when the workers become preoccupied with particular irritants rather than concentrating on those central issues which may be at the root of the problem. Handling conflicts which take this form requires a high degree of patience, sensitivity, and skill on the part of the early childhood supervisor. The purpose of this article is to describe guidelines for reducing the number of inter-staff conflicts which occur in child care organizations which workers find impossible to resolve on their own. The following article will identify specific strategies supervisors can use when conflicts arise.

Realistic Expectations

In any organization there will be times when people rub each other the wrong way. The entrance of new members into a group, proposals for changing familiar practices, competition for materials and physical space, contrasting interpretations of professional responsibilities, differences in educational philosophy or style and the unintentional violation of implicit program traditions all serve as potential sources of friction among staff. As a result, it is impractical for program supervisors to expect that disagreements never occur. In fact, differences of opinion which are constructively expressed contribute to the continued vitality of an organization. For these reasons, a supervisor should not try to force unanimous agreement on every issue. However, it is appropriate to expect staff members to learn to settle their differences in ways that are neither harmful to the organization nor inhibit their ability to work productively in support of program goals.

A prerequisite to fruitful dialogue on areas of potential disagreement is an atmosphere in which open communication about concerns and differences is both encouraged and required. If this has not already been established, development of such an atmosphere will be a long and laborious process; it will not take place overnight nor can supervisors simply demand that it happen. Rather, they must set into motion a series of gradual changes which will lead to the ultimate goal of more constructive interactions among staff members.

Communicating with Staff

The first step in developing candid, constructive methods of communication is to model the behaviors you expect workers to eventually use with one another. This requires providing feedback to each staff member on a regular basis. Feedback is most effective when stated in positive rather than negative terms and when it describes some specific aspect of an individual's behavior rather than his personality. In addition, employees benefit when feedback is given in both positive and negative situations so they have opportunities to assess their

strengths as well as their weaknesses (Drucker, 1967). Most importantly, you must express any concerns you have about a worker's performance directly to the person to whom it pertains. You cannot expect child care personnel to confront one another about their differences if your own approach relies on using the "grapevine" as a primary means of communication.

Encouraging Staff to Communicate with You

Since communication is a two-way process, many supervisors find it beneficial to institute an open-door policy in which time is allocated for employees to approach them with ideas, concerns, or suggestions (Gellerman, 1966). However, it is not enough for workers simply to have access to the supervisor. They must also be assured of receiving an impartial hearing regarding their perception of a situation (Carvell, 1980).

Supervisors demonstrate objectivity when they remain calm even when criticized, when they refrain from immediately evaluating an idea, when they listen carefully to the employee's point of view, and when they take the time to consider several options prior to adopting a particular line of action (Strauss and Sayles, 1980). Numerous studies show that even when the supervisor reaches a conclusion which is contrary to workers' suggestions, workers are more willing to accept those results if they feel their position has been at least considered (Rothman, 1974). In addition, it is critical for staff members to be able to express themselves freely without risk of ridicule, censure or retribution. For this reason, the content of supervisor/employee discussions should be kept strictly confidential.

Finally, it must be noted that not all staff members will be equally com-

fortable discussing their feelings or concerns in such an open manner. Certain individuals may be naturally timid or fear future vulnerability. In cases such as these, the supervisor must make a special effort to interact with employees who are reluctant to take advantage of the open door policy (Strauss and Sayles, 1980).

Once workers have had opportunities to hear you give constructive feedback and have expressed their own reactions in the relative safety of the supervisor's office, the stage is set to encourage them to express their concerns directly to one another.

Facilitating Inter-Staff Communication

The ability and willingness to forthrightly and constructively confront fellow workers when problems first arise is at the heart of preventing or reducing inter-staff conflict. However, even caregivers who are able to clearly state their expectations to children are frequently uncomfortable attempting to do so with adults. The reason that so many "gripes" go "underground" is that people feel insecure discussing their concerns with potential adversaries. It seems easier and safer to complain to other co-workers who may concur with a particular point of view than to risk a confrontation which may end in failure, reprisal, or embarrassment.

Simply modeling good communication skills will not necessarily lead to adaptation of those strategies by child care personnel. The supervisor can, however, help employees learn particular skills that will enable them to communicate more openly and effectively with each other and thus ensure a more successful interaction. Covert means of communication will then become unnecessary. One excellent technique which contributes to this process is called a personal message.

Personal Messages

Personal messages involve describing complaints in terms of one's own feelings about a situation (Kostelnik and Kurtz, 1980). When workers use this strategy they then avoid making inflammatory remarks to the person with whom they are dissatisfied. For instance, if one employee said to another: "You never get your group to the buses on time," the person to whom this is addressed may react defensively. Defensive reactions do not lead to problem resolution. A personal message could be used to pinpoint the same problem in a less threatening way. An example would be: "I feel frustrated when I have to keep coming into the building to get children for the bus. I'm worried I'll lose track of who is and who isn't already on. I'd like to discuss some ways to make this situation more comfortable for me." Chances are the person who is still inside is also experiencing some frustrations. This personal message allows each worker to react to the "problem" (how to get all children on the bus quickly and safely) rather than attempting to avoid or affix blame. It may not be possible for the problem to be resolved at the exact moment it is expressed. Nevertheless, the way is now clear to continue the discussion at a later time in a productive manner.

The guidelines for teaching workers to use personal messages are simple. First, each personal message should begin with the word "I" rather than "You." Second, workers should identify their feelings in relation to the problem described. Finally, solutions should be viewed as a way to relieve workers' feelings of anxiety, anger or discomfort rather than simply adhering to their demands. In other words, the worker is saying "a problem exists which is bothering me," rather than "you are making a problem for me."

Problem Solving Skills

Workers who are able to identify and express their feelings to another person have made a good start toward relieving the tension of inter-staff conflict. However, confrontation alone does not lead to a resolution of the differences between individuals. They must go a step further and decide on a plan to prevent the problem from continuing and to avoid future difficulties. Workers' acquisition of basic problem solving skills is necessary if such a plan is to be developed and a carried out. Problem solving consists of the following steps:

1. Defining a goal.

2. Generating alternative solutions.

3. Weighing the potential benefits and disadvantages of each alternative.

4. Developing a plan of action based on one or a combination of the suggested alternatives.

5. Deciding on the strategies to be used to carry out the plan.

6. Determining the means by which the plan will be evaluated.

7. Implementing revisions as necessary.

Frequently when workers approach the supervisor with a problem they expect him or her to take primary responsibility for its resolution. The supervisor must shift this expectation to one of mutual problem solving in which the employee shares in formulating the solution which is finally selected and carried out. In order to do this, supervisors help workers find their own solution to a problem rather than dictate a particular answer themselves. Employees who are not used to this nondirective approach may become frustrated at

what they interpret as lack of decisiveness on the part of the supervisor. It will take patient explanation and encouragement for many staff members to accept the process. However, there is clear evidence workers ultimately value the opportunity to take responsibility for decisions which affect their performance in the organization (Rothman, 1974). One of the most effective ways to introduce problem solving of the type just described is to present specific issues to be discussed by the staff as a whole. This can be described as group problem solving.

Group Problem Solving

Group problem solving provides an excellent means for confronting and resolving operational issues such as how five classrooms will share the gym, methods for keeping the art closets organized, or deciding what piece of equipment to buy for the playground next year. Child care workers benefit when some portion of each regularly scheduled staff meeting is designated for this purpose. First, they have an opportunity to practice each step of the problem solving process. Second, workers feel a greater commitment to a plan in which they have some input. Finally, designation of an official time and place to discuss issues which concern organizational policies and responsibilities help alleviate the need for workers to utilize the more covert, strategies which characterize inter-staff conflict.

Group problem solving is not difficult to initiate if the following ground rules are observed:

1. All complaints should be phrased as personal messages.

2. Problems submitted for group consideration should involve procedural or organizational issues which affect more than one person. Inter-personal conflicts

which revolve around differences in philosophy, personality or teaching style should be taken up privately between the individuals involved.

3. Everyone should have an opportunity to contribute to the final plan which is developed.

4. Solutions which any one person vehemently opposes should be avoided. It is better to select a compromise about which everyone is a little less enthusiastic than to choose a plan some members find impossible to support.

Techniques to Facilitate Group Problem Solving

It helps to remember that the success of group problem solving is dependent on each person feeling that his or her ideas have been heard. Communication is inhibited when a few people dominate the discussion to the point that others become observers rather than participants. It is the supervisor's responsibility to elicit from each person in turn a reaction to the issue at hand or to a suggested alternative. In addition, direct statements such as, "If we adopted option two, tell me how you think this would affect your classroom," foster more active participation than the general question, "What do you think?"

A round-robin gripe session is a second strategy which generates interest in and commitment to problem solving in a group. In this procedure a time limit is set to identify problems (e.g., ten minutes). Individuals around the table have an opportunity one at a time to present an issue of concern to them. This may involve a major or minor irritant. The supervisor verbally summarizes each concern and writes it down. No evaluation of the concern should be made. Lengthy

explanations about probable causes are not necessary at this point nor are discussions of potential solutions. The purpose is to give everyone an opportunity to get their gripes out in the open. Continue around the group as long as time permits.

At the end of the stated time period, begin problem solving starting with the first concern. Work your way through the list in order. In this manner, each person knows their concern will eventually receive attention. Do not move on to the next item until some plan of action has been decided for the current issue under discussion. This plan may involve a solution, a compromise, or a strategy for gathering the information needed for discussion at a later date. Assign responsibility for specific aspects of the plan including who will report its progress at the next meeting. If by the end of the meeting, each item has not received attention, keep the list for the next time the group gets together. Set a specific date for this to happen. Staff members benefit from knowing there is a time table for dealing with issues of particular interest to them.

It also must be recognized that not everyone will be equally pleased with the approach that is finally selected by the group. A favorite idea or suggestion may have been revised in the spirit of compromise. While an individual may not oppose a plan strongly enough to veto it altogether, she may feel "cheated" in the bargaining process. When this happens the supervisor can offer comfort by acknowledging the worker's willingness to try an idea on which he is not completely sold. This acknowledgment goes a long way in helping staff members accept solutions brought about by group process.

Finally, it is encouraging to note that when workers have an opportunity

to practice problem solving in a group, they frequently are able to transfer many of the component steps to working out their concerns with staff members.

Personnel Policies

Expectations for staff in the form of specific personnel policies can now be developed that reflect the interpersonal skills they have learned.

1. Individuals experiencing an interpersonal conflict with another employee must bring it to the attention of that person prior to discussing the issue with any other staff member including the supervisor.

2. Problems related to program operations should be submitted to group problem solving.

When staff members approach the supervisor with complaints, the first step is to determine whether the problem is an inter-personal one which should be dealt with privately or is one more suitable for discussion by the group. In the case of an inter-personal problem, the individual should be directed to bring it to the attention of the other parties involved. Concerns related to program operation or management should be included on the agenda of the next staff meeting. Quick action in either case is imperative.

Occasionally, staff members will seek advice from the supervisor about how to present their concerns constructively. This is an appropriate request. However, the supervisors should refrain from expressing any opinions regarding the problem at this time. Instead, they should encourage the worker to pursue a solution to the best of his ability. Compliance with these policies should be recorded as part of each staff member's yearly evaluation. Continued failure to discuss problems with other staff members or frequent use of covert methods to express dissatisfaction may serve as cause for probation or termination.

There will be times when staff members try to resolve a problem using the guidelines suggested thus far, but are unable to reach a final agreement that satisfies all concerned. When this occurs, the preferred role of the supervisor is to mediate the conflict rather than impose sanctions on any person.

References

Benton, L. R. (1972). *Supervision and Management.* New York: McGraw-Hill Book Company.

Berkley, G. E. (1978). *The Craft of Public Administration.* Boston, MA: Allyn and Bacon, Inc.

Carvell, F. J. (1980). *Human Relations in Business.* New York: MacMillan Publishing Company, Inc.

Drucker, P. (1967). *The Effective Executive.* New York: Harper and Row.

Flippo, E. B. (1971). *Principles of Personnel Management.* New York: McGraw-Hill Book Company.

Gellerman, S. W. (1966). *The Management of Human Relations.* New York: Holt, Rhinehart and Winston.

Kostelnik, M. J., & Kurtz, P. D. (1980). *Communication and Positive Guidance Skills for Teachers of Young Children.* East Lansing, MI: M.S.U. Press.

Rothman, J. (1974). *Planning and Organizing for Social Change.* New York: Columbia University Press.

Strauss, E. B. (1981). *Principles of Personnel Management.* New York: McGraw-Hill Book Company.

How to Mediate Staff Conflict

by Dr. Marjorie J. Kostelnik

The preceeding article described various approaches for reducing conflict by providing staff members means and motivation for working out their own problems. Unfortunately, there inevitably will be time when staff members are unable to resolve problems among themselves. When this occurs the preferred role of the supervisor is to mediate the conflict rather than impose sanctions on any person. This article will describe a step-by-step process for achieving this goal.

Mediating Seemingly Irreconcilable Differences

The mediation method described below utilizes the same steps as those described for group problem solving. However, certain adaptations have been made for use with individuals who perceive the situation as irreconcilable. The model presented here has been used successfully with both adults and children, individually and in groups, as a method for helping them resolve conflicts as independently as possible (Stein and Kostelnik, 1982). Prior to using this approach within an organization, the supervisor should introduce it to staff members in a general meeting. Each step should be defined so workers know exactly what to expect.

Step One: Becoming Aware of Developing Conflicts Between Individuals

There are three ways in which a supervisor may be made aware of inter-staff conflict. One is the supervisor's own observations that discontent is brewing. If this is the case, it is a good idea to document incidents to use as evidence in confronting those involved. For example, "I noticed that when you left the building yesterday, you seemed very angry," or "This is the third time you've refused to ride in the van with May."

A second way in which supervisors are made aware of potential problems is when one or both of the disgruntled employees approaches them with complaints about the other. Finally, a third party may point out the dissension that exists between fellow workers.

Step Two: Initiating the Mediation Prorcess

However the supervisor discovers inter-staff conflict, he or she should approach each person separately and state that a problem seems to exist which he or she is anxious to help the parties resolve. Workers who enjoy open communication with the supervisor generally treat this as an honest inquiry related to their own well being rather than an accusation or the antecedent to punitive action.

If the workers feel that further discussion on their own is fruitless, the supervisor should announce that she or he is going to begin the mediation process.

Step Three: Airing Feelings

Conflict situations generate a multitude of intense emotions. Frequently, when those involved attempt to describe their perception of the problem, their response consists of denials, angry denunciations or accusations. Later, they may regret the vehemence of their initial outbursts. The central aim of Step Three is to give each worker an opportunity to express feelings openly without antagonizing fellow employees.

The most effective way to facilitate this goal is for the supervisor to utilize active listening skills while discussing the situation privately with each individual. Active listening consists of summarizing what another person says without evaluating the relative merits of the message conveyed. It forces the supervisor to recognize each staff member's view of a situation even when that perception is very different from the supervisor's own. Once each person has a chance to "blow off steam," they will be better able to view the situation more objectively and rationally. Once this has been accomplished, all parties should be brought together to pursue steps four through nine.

Step Four:
Mutual Clarification

All persons directly involved in the problem should be present for Step Four. The major focus at this point is clarification of each person's ultimate goal regarding the conflict. The supervisor should solicit from each person in turn, a statement of the situation from that individual's point of view. The ground rule here is that the situation must be described in terms of personal aims rather than phrased as an accusation about another person. An acceptable statement might be, "I wish I spent less time on classroom maintenance." An inappropriate remark would be "She makes me do all the clean up and saves the fun things for herself." The supervisor may have to frequently remind participants of this ground rule or help them phrase their statements accordingly by saying something like, "Tell me what it is you want rather than what you think she wants."

It is important to allow each worker ample opportunity, without interruption, to state his or her ultimate desire with regard to the problem at hand. The assurance that each

worker will have an opportunity to speak is critical. In order for the supervisor to be an effective mediator, staff members must trust her not to make an arbitrary decision in favor of one person or the other. The mediator establishes neutrality by withholding any evaluation of the merits of any position.

Paraphrasing each person's view to the other is another effective way to demonstrate impartiality. It ensures that the supervisor correctly perceives each worker's notion of the problem and helps clarify that position both for the worker herself and for the other person(s) involved. Individuals who are very upset may require several opportunities to describe their position accurately. It must be emphasized that depending on the level of the worker's distress, Step Four may take several minutes. In addition, staff members may need help from the mediator in articulating their desires. The supervisor should try to be as accurate as possible in paraphrasing by checking back with each person in turn.

Step Five:
Summing Up

Step Five occurs when the supervisor has elicited enough information to understand each worker's view of a desirable outcome. At this time the supervisor should define the problem in mutual terms implying that each staff member has a responsibility for both the problem and its solution. "From what you've said here it sound like you're both interested in fostering children's independence but have very different ways of approaching that goal. It is important that we work toward a strategy that will satisfy each of you."

Step Six:
Generating Alternatives

Generating several possible alternative solutions is the purpose of the

sixth stage of the mediation process. Suggestions may be offered by the adversaries themselves or by the supervisor. Each time a possible solution is offered, the mediator should paraphrase it back to both individuals: "Mary thinks you could allow the children to pour their own juice." At this point, each person is asked to evaluate the merits of the recommendation. "What do you think, Sarah?" "What do you think, Mary?" The mediator elicits as many divergent ideas as possible and should have no stake in which solution is eventually selected. Supervisors are cautioned that each worker should be a willing participant in the outcome and that no particular alternative should be forced on either employee. It is typical during this procedure for individuals to reject certain possibilities which they may later find acceptable. Therefore, when a suggestion is repeated, the mediator should present it, rather than assuming it will be vetoed again. If the workers are not able to originate alternatives, the supervisor should help them out by saying something like: "One compromise I can think of is _____ . What do each of you think?" The supervisor may also provide information which would be pertinent to any alternative such as "There is $20.00 left in he petty cash fund this month."

Step Seven:
Agreeing on a Solution

Staff members will reject certain suggestions outright, and will indicate that others seem more palatable. The ultimate aim of Step Seven is to get both parties to agree on a plan of action that is mutually satisfying. The role of the supervisor is to help them explore all the possibilities that seem most acceptable to them. The plan should not include any alternatives which either person fervently opposes. The final agreement usually involves some concessions on the part of each worker and so may not represent any action the individual would take if he did not have to consider another person's point of view. Eventually each worker will indicate that she can find a way to accept one idea or a combination of ideas. The mediator can facilitate compromise by paraphrasing points of mutual agreement. This process continues until the possibilities have been narrowed down to a workable solution. When this finally occurs, it is important for the mediator to identify that a resolution has been achieved. For example: "You think the children can pour their own juice as long as we buy some plastic pitchers first. And, we do have some money available for that purpose. It sounds like you've solved the problem."

Step Eight:
Reinforcing the Problem Solving Process

The purpose of the eighth stage is to praise each person for developing a mutually beneficial solution. The message to be conveyed is that the process of reaching a solution was as important as the solution itself. The way the mediator achieves this is to acknowledge the emotional investment each person had in the original conflict as well as the hard work involved in reaching an agreement. For example: "Mary, it was important to you that children have an opportunity to do more for themselves; and Sarah, your major concern was safety. You worked hard at figuring out how to approach both goals at the same time."

Step Nine:
Following Through

The conclusion of the mediation process involves helping the individuals carry out the terms of the agreement. This is accomplished by reminding them what the terms were, and if necessary writing up an agreement of how the plan will be carried out and evaluated. At this point records should be maintained to indicate the degree of success which is eventually achieved. If this plan begins to falter, bring the individuals together again to discuss possible revisions.

Pitfalls to Avoid

Reluctance to Take Action: Probably the most devastating mistake a supervisor can make is to avoid taking action for fear of offending someone or because a complaint seems too small to warrant administrative action. No matter how ridiculous or implausible a worker's concern may seem, it is very real to him or her and deserves prompt and serious consideration (Berkeley, 1978). Only in this way can minor irritations be reconciled before they develop into full blown arguments which are much harder to resolve.

Inconsistency: Another difficulty occurs when supervisors are haphazard in their approach to problem situations. Coming down hard on one staff member while being lax on another is a sure way to sow seeds of discontent among child are workers. It is important that supervisors be consistent and predictable in their reactions to inter-staff conflict.

Avoiding the Issue: In an effort to put a worker at ease the supervisor may initiate the mediation process by discussing some unrelated topic — the latest fashions, bowling or the weather. Although such an approach may momentarily relieve the supervisor's anxiety, it only serves to heighten the employee's distress, particularly if he or she has some notion about why the meeting has been requested. At times like this it is natural for the worker to wonder why the supervisor doesn't get down to business or to feel that a "cat and mouse" game is about to begin. Neither impression enhances the worker's view of the supervisor as an interested listener or possible mediator.

Taking Sides: In order to establish credibility and be accepted in the mediating role, the supervisor must be perceived as impartial. For this reason, he or she should avoid indicating initial agreement or disagreement with any position that is stated. This means paying strict attention to non-verbal cues such as nodding, smiling, frowning and fingertapping and refraining from verbal indications of support, sympathy, disdain or revulsion. Final judgment must be suspended until all sides are heard from and the facts are in.

Denying a Person's Perspective: There will be times during individual or group problem solving situations when a staff member expresses a point of view which seems ludicrous or untrue. In those circumstances it is tempting to try to correct that person's perception. For example, "I really don't think that's what Mary is trying to accomplish!" or "You shouldn't feel so upset about this situation," or "You know we divided the work fairly from the start." While any one of these statements may be accurate, they do not correspond to the worker's impression of the situation. As a result, what began as mutual problem solving will end in a fruitless argument. As hard as it may be, it is the supervisor's responsibility to exercise patience and to allow staff members to work through their own perceptions about the problem under discussion.

Masterminding: It is natural to want to resolve conflicts quickly. Sometimes to accelerate problem solving supervisors step in with their own solution rather than permitting staff members to work out the problem themselves. A related tactic is to force workers toward a preconceived conclusion by using leading questions such as: "Don't you think _____?" or "Doesn't it seem that you should _____?" or "Wouldn't it be nice if we _____?" If the supervisor has chosen to initiate the problem solving process, he or she should allow it to proceed to a mutual resolution. Otherwise, workers become frustrated as being led to believe that they are responsible for reaching a decision when in reality they must acquiesce to the supervisor's conclusion. When this occurs, the chances for continued conflict are high because staff members do not feel a real commitment to an approach that is dictated to them. In addition, coercive strategies do not help employees practice the problem solving skills they will need to reconcile future disagreements. Finally, the use of such directive techniques seriously jeopardizes the supervisor's effectiveness in subsequent attempts at presenting problems for mutual consideration.

Not Allowing Enough Time for Problem-Solving to Take Place: It is important that the supervisor allocate a specified block of time for group problem solving as well as for conflict mediation when the need arises. It is better to temporarily postpone attempts at resolution than to proceed when staff members feel rushed or distracted by other circumstances.

Summary

Because of the time involved, some supervisors may be reluctant to enact the problem-solving procedures described in these two articles. Instead they prefer to shuttle from person to person seeking compatible solutions. This approach undoubtedly works in the short run. However, it does not provide an opportunity for staff members to practice confrontation and problem-solving strategies. As a result, over time, the supervisor continues to bear the primary responsibility for conflict resolution rather than gradually shifting responsibility to the staff members themselves.

In my own experience I have found that enactment of the preceding problem solving approaches leads to more open and tension free early childhood programs. Staff members develop many of the necessary skills to resolve their own concerns as they arise. Eventually more and more problems are reconciled in their beginning stages making formal mediation less necessary. Also, staff members are more apt to approach supervisor-led mediation as a real

chance for mutual problem solving rather than the final step in an angry confrontation. If you are planning to initiate this procedure, it is usually helpful to alert staff in advance that this is the approach you will be using. It is also worth noting that it takes time and practice to develop the skills described in these articles. At first the results may be less than optimal because staff members are not used to a process which emphasizes compromise rather than winning or losing. However, the alternative is to continue acting as a judge or disciplinarian rather than assuming the role of model and teacher. The choice is up to you.

References

Berkley, G. E. (1978). *The Craft of Public Administration.* Boston, MA: Allyn and Bacon, Inc.

Stein, L. C. & Kostelnik, M. J. (1982). "A Model for Conflict Mediation in the Classroom," paper presented at the Midwest Conference of the National Association for the Education of Young Children, May, 1982.

How to Help Your Staff Cope with Conflict

by Tom Copeland

Directors and staff often find that dealing with conflict takes up a lot of time, without necessarily solving the problem. Here is one tool you can use to help resolve conflicts: The Three Choice Model.

Choice #1: I am satisfied with the way things are. I can live with what is going on, so I won't worry about it.

Choice #2: I am unhappy with my situation and I am on a path of trying to resolve the conflict. If my first effort doesn't succeed, I will try something else.

Choice #3: I will quit my job.

There are no other choices. Staff shouldn't complain about something unless they are trying to do something about it. Staff can use a coach (who may or may not be a supervisor) to help remind them about these three choices.

Here's how this works. Let's say there is a conflict over how many hours, at a minimum, staff must work each week:

Staff: I want to work fewer hours each week, but the director won't let me.

Coach: What are you doing about it?

Staff: I don't know. It's hopeless.

Coach: It sounds like you should quit your job.

Staff: Oh no! It's not that bad.

Coach: So, how are you trying to get what you want?

Staff: The director won't listen to me.

Coach: Let's talk about how you might negotiate this problem.

Staff: No. She won't listen.

Coach: So, maybe it's not such a serious problem and you should just be satisfied with the way things are.

Staff: No, I'm not happy.

Coach: Then you should quit.

Staff: No! You aren't being very helpful.

Coach: Okay, then let's talk about what you can do about it. Have you tried doing . . . ? Or how about this idea . . . ? What other alternate options could you propose?

Staff: That won't work. I can't change the rules.

Coach: Then you should relax and accept the way things are.

Staff: But I can't!

Coach: Then try to change things.

And so on.

At some point, the coach can summarize the three choices to the staff person and indicate that they need to choose among them in order to resolve the conflict. The coach keeps the discussion focused choices, until the staff person has acknowledged choosing one of them. The coach should refuse to encourage any other behavior outside of these choices (complaining without seeking to change, hopelessness, etc.).

The coach should not try to influence the staff person to accept one choice over another. The decision is up to each person to make. The staff person can always decide later to pick another choice. Once the staff person chooses one of the three choices, they are much more likely to be happy and the level of conflict should be reduced.

This model addresses one of the major creators of conflict: hopelessness. Directors who are in the habit of complaining about staff can use the same model. The director can seek out a coach from a friend, family member, or colleague not associated with the center. Directors can teach staff to use this model as a way to help solve problems. The role of the coach is critical to making this model work. Everyone is capable of being a coach for someone else.

Tom Copeland, JD, is the director of Redleaf National Institute in St. Paul, Minnesota. He conducts workshops for centers on legal issues and the ADA. Tom is a national expert on family child care business issues. His e-mail address is tom@redleafinstitute.org.

Overcoming the Fear of Firing

Ideas from 30 Directors

"It was obvious that this teacher could not relate well to kids. But I could not bring myself to fire her . . . and while I wavered, things only got worse for everyone in her classroom."

Having to fire someone is probably the most difficult action a director may have to take. It is an action for which directors can find endless excuses to avoid, as did the director quoted above. But it is an action which in certain cases must be taken.

To discover how directors can overcome their fear of firing and to learn what precautions to take and what mistakes to avoid in the firing process, *Child Care Information Exchange* surveyed 30 child care directors who had fired an employee. The suggestions that follow are based on their experiences and recommendations.

When is Firing Appropriate?

People who go into a social service such as child care typically care very much about individuals. However, directors are also responsible for caring for the organization as a whole and for the families it serves. When the needs of an individual staff member come into serious conflict with the needs of the group, the director must place higher priority on the welfare of the group.

The directors identified four areas where the performance of individual staff members most frequently detracts from the performance of the organization to the extent that firing may be necessary. The four areas, listed in order of frequency of occurrence are:

1. Poor work habits — Chronic lateness and absenteeism; shirking of job responsibilities; sloppy, careless work. One director reported firing a teacher who "sat most of the time and shouted across the room instead of going to talk to a child. I found her sleeping in the nap room rather than watching the nappers."

2. Sub-par job performance — Inability to satisfactorily perform job responsibilities; inability to develop necessary skills. Specific problems cited include "lack of behavior management skills," "inability to supervise assistant teachers," "lack of empathy and patience with children," and "inability to plan appropriate activities."

3. Unacceptable behavior — Behavior which is detrimental to children, staff, or the organization. Typically these behaviors relate to inappropriate disciplining of children such as "striking a child," "verbally abusing children," "locking a child in the bathroom," or "attacking children's self-images." Some directors also cited situations where staff members disrupted the organization by "refusing to cooperate with other teachers," or by "inciting disharmony and negativism among the teachers."

4. Policy violations — Unwillingness to conform to center policies and philosophies. A wide range of incidents were cited here including "stealing center property," "violating the confidentiality of parent conversations," "refusal to adapt to the curriculum approach of the school," and "coming to work intoxicated."

Potential Problems

The process of firing an employee is never a pleasant one. During the period when the director is weighing the decision and then waiting to announce it, he or she typically experiences considerable anxiety. The conference at which the employee is notified of the decision is often loaded with tension and tears or anger and ill-will. Then, if the employee reacts poorly to the action, the director may experience guilt.

Occasionally, more serious problems occur. When an employee perceives that she is being fired unjustly, she may seek to rally support among the other teachers and parents. This can lead to a period of internal conflict and leave a residue of hard feelings.

When there is a level of authority above the person who did the firing, such as an owner, a board of directors, a regional director, or a sponsoring agency, the terminated employee occasionally will appeal the decision. This appeal may proceed through normal channels such as a grievance procedure, or it may take a more personal direction. In one instance, an employee sent letters to every board member, claiming foul play by the director and demanding immediate reinstatement. In another instance, the spouse of a terminated employee appeared at the door of the center's owner threatening a law suit.

A confrontation may also occur if the terminated employee is denied unemployment benefits and appeal this ruling. In many states an employee who is fired may have a claim for unemployment benefits judged to be "unapprovable" if he was fired for gross misconduct or for misdeeds directed against the employer. The information for making this decision comes from the former employer. If the former employee appeals a decision, the director may then be required to attend a hearing. One director who attended such a hearing found it very unpleasant "to be discussing the employee's poor work record in front of her, her husband, and the hearing officer."

In some cases the repercussions are even more unpleasant. Several directors reported receiving angry or obscene phone calls at home from the terminated worker for weeks after the firing. One was physically threatened. In another case the former employee dedicated herself to spreading vicious rumors about the center and the director in the community.

Although such negative outcomes do occur when the firing process misfires, they need not be the inevitable consequence. Three-fourths of the directors interviewed indicated that the positive results of firing an unsatisfactory employee far outweighed the negative ones. In most cases the morale of the staff eventually, if not immediately, improved.

Laying the Groundwork

The directors surveyed had many recommendations for avoiding the negative consequences of the firing process. Many of these had to do with laying the groundwork, with actions that should be taken even before the final decision to fire is made.

- **Establish Guidelines.** All personnel working in a center should know, from the day they join the center, what actions or behaviors on their part can result in their being fired. These policies should be in writing, and they should be given to all staff members or posted in a conspicuous place. Staff members have a right to know these ground rules. Once they know them, their responsibility to abide by them should not be subject to questions at the termination.

Most centers surveyed have two categories of offenses in their policies. One category is for flagrant actions which are cause for immedi-

ate termination. Cited as examples of such offenses were striking a child, leaving children unattended, inflicting harsh punishments, gross negligence, and being intoxicated on the job.

- **Establish a Grievance Procedure.** If at all possible employees should have some means of appealing major personnel actions such as a firing. This may consist of a hearing before an owner, an executive director, a personnel committee, or a special grievance panel. Having such a procedure established in advance gives an aggrieved employee a clear recourse and helps prevent unnecessary parties from becoming involved in the dispute.

- **Review Performance Periodically.** Once employees' work habits or performances have degenerated to the point where a termination is warranted, it may no longer be possible for them to radically alter their behavior. If the director is concerned with the welfare of individual employees and wishes to help them avoid termination, she should perform periodic performance reviews for all employees. Poor habits and substandard performance should be brought to the employee's attention before it gets out of hand. In these reviews the director or supervisor should help the employee set goals for improvement as well as offer whatever support the center can muster. Progress toward meeting these goals should then be closely monitored.

- **Give Adequate Warning.** Nearly every director emphasized that there should be "no surprises." As soon as it becomes apparent to the director that an employee may need to be fired, that employee should be warned that such an action is being considered. This warning should be given in a private conference between the director and the employee. The directors recommend that in this conference the employee should be told:

1) the specific center policies the employee is violating or failing to adhere to;

2) objective examples or anecdotes which demonstrate this claim;

3) the specific changes required of the employee to avoid being fired;

4) how the employee's effort to make these changes will be monitored; and

5) the deadline for the final evaluation.

Some centers have a formal two or three step notification process. In one center the director is required to give a preliminary verbal warning, an initial written warning, and a final written warning before issuing a notification of termination. However, if a center has an effective performance review process, the early warnings needed to give the employee a fair opportunity to improve should be coming up in the periodic reviews.

Since warning conferences can become quite emotional, key messages sometimes fail to get communicated. Sometimes directors try too hard to cushion the blow by sugar-coating the warning. In one instance a director went to such lengths emphasizing the employee's strong points in addition to the problem areas that the employee left the meeting unaware that she was close to being fired. A second message often delivered unclearly is what specific steps the employee needs to take to meet the director's expectations. To avoid miscommunication, one

director suggested having the employee state his interpretation of the director's message to be sure he has an accurate understanding of it.

• **Keep Written Records.** As one director urged — "Document! Document! Document!" Keep a record of periodic performance reviews, incidents of unsatisfactory performance, conferences where warnings are administered or terminations are announced. Some directors also issue warnings and terminations in writing as well as verbally. Other directors, dealing with a particularly un-stable or vindictive employee, request that the employee sign a written summary of a warning or termination conference to attest to the fact that the summary is accurate (not that they necessarily agree with it).

Documentation such as this serves two purposes. First, it insures that the director's message is conveyed. All people's memories of conversa-tions are distorted by emotions and expectations. So it is quite likely that an employee coming out of an emotional warning conference will have a faulty memory of the specifics, unless the memory is aided by a written summary.

Second, documentation provides insurance for post-termination confrontations. If the employee challenges a firing, either before an owner, a board, or an unemployment claims officer, claiming that adequate warning was not given or that the reasons are groundless, a written record of the entire process should provide sufficient evidence to counter these claims.

• **Keep Employees Informed.** Another means of avoiding poten-tial confrontation is for the director to keep her employer up-to-date on the situation. For a director who is also the owner of the business, of

course, there is no one else to turn to. However, if the director answers to a board, an owner, an executive director, a regional director, or a sponsoring agency, the appropriate party should be consulted as soon as the possibility of a termination arises. The privacy of the employee must be respected, so prior consultations should be made in confidence. One director kept the board's chairperson advised, rather than discussing the situation with the full board. When the terminated employee appealed to the board, the chairperson was able to verify the director's account of the process.

Completing the Process

Once the termination process is set in motion, a clear conclusion is neces-sary. The following are the directors' recommendations on minimizing the negative effects of the final act on the employee, the director, and the organization.

• **Make the Decision Objectively.** It is, of course, impossible to remove all emotion from a termination decision. How you feel about the person, how the decision will affect the individual and his family, and how it will affect the staff all will influence the decision consciously or unconsciously. The director should not try to deny these emotions but should try to keep them in perspective so that they will not cause a bad decision to be made.

One way to keep issues in perspec-tive is to avoid making a termination decision while under stress or in a crisis. When a teacher arrives 30 minutes late thereby causing the director to miss a meeting, the director may in anger be tempted to fire the teacher on the spot. Weighing the incident later in a calmer mood, the director may realize that this was one of the few times the teacher had ever been late and that to fire her would be seriously overreacting.

Another technique for maintaining perspective is to list all the specific pieces of evidence where the employee is in fact violating center policies or failing to perform her work responsibilities. Then assess whether this list is serious enough to justify termination.

If the evidence warrants termination, the director should then weigh the other negative consequences of the termination — i.e., the impact on the individual, his family, the center, the children, the parents — to determine if the firing can be handled in such a way as to ameliorate these consequences. For example — Could the employee be slotted into a less demanding job in the organization? Could the terms of the firing be stated in such a way that the employee can receive unemployment? Could the employee be given an opportunity to save face by resigning first?

Another consideration at this point is setting the employee's last work day. In general it is in everyone's best interest for the employee to leave immediately. Once the employee is fired she may find it embarrassing to continue working at the center. In other cases an embittered person may make life miserable for the staff or the director by stirring up trouble in the final days. In such circumstances it may be best to pay the employee severance pay for one or two weeks rather than keeping her on the job. In other cases where feelings are less damaged, it may be helpful to allow the employee to stay on until she can find another job.

• **Notifying the Employee Directly.** Once the termination decision has been made, the employee should be told as soon as possible in a private conference. Preferably, this should occur at the end of the day to protect the employee from confronting the other staff members when leaving. Without prolonging the agony by chit-chatting about the weather, the director should tell the employee of the decision in clear and simple terms. If this meeting has been properly prepared for, the decision should not be unexpected. Any sugarcoating or beating around the bush will only confuse the issue.

The director should state the specific reasons for the termination. There may be other unsatisfactory aspects of the employee's performance, such as sloppy dress, bad attitude or poor relations with staff or parents; but if these are not the reasons for which the employee is being fired, they should not be mentioned in this conference.

The director should also be prepared to answer all the employee's contractual questions, such as what the appeal process is, when the last day will be, whether severance pay and unused vacation time will be granted, and whether the director will write a job recommendation for the employee in the future. All important points should, of course, be included in a termination letter given to the employee during the conference.

In certain circumstances the director may be inclined to offer the employee help in applying for benefits or in finding a new job. This fact should be stated. But the director should not press to offer help unless the employee specifically asks for it.

• **Announce the Action Honestly.** The other employees, and in some cases the parents, will have an extreme interest in the action. If they are not informed, eventually the rumor mill will begin generating distorted versions of what happened. Such rumors can have a negative impact on staff morale and staff-director relations. Therefore, the staff and parents should be informed about the termination as soon as possible and as honestly as possible without violating the former employee's privacy by revealing details.

If the employee was popular among the staff and parents, they may find fault with the decision. But the director should not attempt to regain their approval by revealing confidential information or by reversing the decision. More likely than not, however, staff members will be more relieved than angered by the decision. Twenty-eight of the thirty directors reported that staff members reacted positively to termination decisions.

Healing Staff After a Termination

by Diana S. Khanagov

"As a new director the biggest mistake I made was underestimating the impact of a termination on the rest of the staff," *says Pam Scott, a director of a human resources department for* *Integris. Whether it is a teacher who shirks responsibilities or* *reliable teachers dismissed because of downsizing, termination* *affects everyone.*

A director's response to situations leading to termination helps the healing process, The key is damage control. Establish a plan for corrective action before you need it. The corrective action plan serves three purposes: it gives employees opportunities to change; it demonstrates that the director can be trusted to handle matters fairly; and, as the process continues, it prepares other staff members for the termination of their teammate.

The physical, emotional, and mental well-being of children cannot be compromised; therefore, some situations and behaviors must result in immediate termination. These should be written in the center's policy handbook. But what about the caregiver having difficulty keeping up with requirements or adapting to the center's improvements for quality care?

Larry Harrell, co-director and owner of Southwest Child Development

Center in Oklahoma City, says: "Endangering or belittling a child means immediate termination. My wife, Jana, and I ask ourselves, 'Is this a person who will represent this center in a positive manner? Is this a one-time incident? Does this person need some training on a particular issue?' An important aspect for us is 'What is this person doing for children?' There are all kinds of avenues. We could cut back on hours, change their hours — give them a new routine. It's really hard to give up on a good staff person. If you've had them four or five years, you just don't want to walk in and fire them. Before I hired them, I had to believe in them."

Begin with a method for evaluation. Employees must know what is inadequate about their job performance before they can choose what is best for them, whether it be a change in their job performance or a change in employment. Shop around

for evaluation ideas. Ask other directors how they evaluate staff. Check resources such as the Internet and the library for books about management styles. Don't overlook books written for businesses other than child care. Borrow features from corporate job evaluations, then add features specific only to the field of child care. Whatever form you choose, the evaluation is a tool that tells staff how you perceive the quality of their work.

How far will you go to help an employee? Some directors help the teacher find extra training, troubleshoot problems, and create a plan of action. When opportunities for change have been exhausted, it's time to say good-bye. Keeping a teacher who performs poorly lowers morale and encourages resentment from teammates. Their continued employment sends the wrong message to staff who go over and above the standards you have set for the center.

According to staff members, one damaging result of dismissal is the corrosion of trust, the most essential element between employee and employer. Trust is compromised when staff members witness a director fire someone on a whim, reacting on impulse to a situation. One director created an unproductive work environment by threatening, "If you blink wrong, I can fire you." Staff members reported difficulty concentrating on work for fear of the rug being yanked out from under them. "If the director is trusted, then it's a ripple in everyday life. If the director is not the leader and is mistrusted, then a termination can turn into a mob scene. It takes about two years for the group to become cohesive again."

Staff members prefer to hear about the dismissal from the director instead of hearing it through the grapevine. "Don't act as if nothing happened. When our director was fired, there was no announcement. There wasn't any thought given to the feelings of the staff."

"Sometimes you hear it from the grapevine first, but the director should still tell the staff as soon as possible. Don't wait for the regular staff meeting."

How a director tells the staff is a matter of personal style. Strive for a professional, sincere explanation without gritty details and hints of sarcasm. Pam Scott says: "I would say, 'This was a business decision. We are here to care for children. We have standards that we can no longer compromise. This person decided that she could not meet those standards. I want to assure you that I got all of the information and facts before making this decision. I treated this person fairly.' The aftermath depends on how well the person was liked. A great person can do a bad job." Sometimes termination means losing someone who you value personally. "It's fine to acknowledge the person's good points, but it is still a business decision."

"Even if you don't give details, they will talk about it. Women have to talk about it to process it. They are

more likely than men to have deeper friendships with colleagues." Negative remarks about the employee's lack of work ethics interfere with healing. In the weeks following a termination, your team may find themselves picking up the ex-employee's unfinished business or discovering more inadequacies in the person's work habits. Negative comments prolong "getting back to normal" to a healthful, caring, productive environment. Constant energy spent on negative issues can result in low morale — which is even harder to overcome than the loss of a teammate. Instead, direct your staff's focus on working together efficiently to repair damages.

Some teachers may be relieved if the termination process created tension in the workplace or if they carried the employee's workload over a long period. No matter how lazy or adversarial the ex-employee, count on at least one staff member who enjoyed her friendship, understood her problems, and feels sorry for her plight. Some staff may struggle with issues of loyalty. However the lines of relationships cross, expect your staff to grieve over the loss. Stages of grief may include shock, anger, and sadness.

Two weeks after an employee was immediately dismissed, a remaining staff member said, "I think we're just now getting over the shock, now we're getting angry." Other staff members reported signs of depression, 'I don't feel like doing anything," and feeling nauseous when the new employee showed up to fill the position. "It's a dilemma because you don't want to blame the new person."

Pam Scott says: "Some staff even experience 'survivor's guilt,' especially if they contributed in any way to the person's job loss. Guilt keeps on giving. Spend time one on one. Reassure everyone that they have a responsibility not just to the person fired but to themselves and to the business. It's an ongoing process. Check back frequently asking, 'What other questions do you have?' and 'How are you feeling?'"

A decline in morale was commonly noted by child care staff. "Termination definitely affects morale. You begin to wonder — if it happened to her, it could happen to me." What's a sign of low morale? Several teachers reported a lack of interest in work that gradually diminished with time. Signs of lingering low morale are increased sick leave, arriving late for work, and a lack of interest in the workplace traditions, such as celebrating achievements, birthdays, and holidays. One agency that supports child care centers chose not to celebrate the holidays with their traditional office party for the first time in 25 years — no tinsel, no lights, not even holiday music. Not one employee attended the holiday party of another agency that lays off a large number of employees every December. The sarcasm behind the "get-over-it" attitude widens the gap between director and staff. Eventually it undermines morale.

Low morale is like stepping on a piece of gum. It's most likely to happen when you're not paying attention. And if you're really oblivious to gum on your shoe, it affects every place you walk! The longer low morale continues, the more difficult it is to clean up. Long-term low morale leads to an overall careless attitude that, without proper attention, becomes the norm. New staff detect it without any explanation from other staff. It is serious handicap for a team leader.

Expect some staff members to continue a personal relationship

with the ex-employee. A divisive misconception is that staff must choose sides, their ex-teammate or their director. Sometimes it's an unspoken request or a verbal threat. One director told staff, "You will reap the consequence if you continue to talk to this person."

Just as negative remarks about the ex-employee affect the work environment, so a continued friendship focused on contempt for the director or the workplace breeds bad attitudes. Negativity, on either side of the coin, feeds tension that ultimately prevents a caring environment for children.

Coach your staff to recognize harmful attitudes that compromise the goal of the team — to provide a loving, caring atmosphere where children can develop naturally. Encourage and engage in conversations and actions that build a stronger team. Begin by acknowledging what it means to lose a teammate. "The biggest mistake I made was underestimating the impact a termination has on the rest of the staff."

*Diana S. Khanagov is a freelance writer who lives in Midwest City, Oklahoma. She is a contributing author of **The Parents' & Teachers' Guide to Helping Young Children Learn: Creative Ideas From 35 Respected Experts**.*

The Exit Interview: A Tool for Program Improvement

by Glenn Olsen

It was the fourth teacher resignation in the past eight months. Two teachers had resigned in August and one had resigned right before Christmas. "What is going on?" Peg Jones, director of this child care program, was becoming more and more concerned about turnover. When she asked employees why they were leaving, the standard answer was always "for a better salary." But was that the real reason? Although Peg knew salaries played a part in the resignations, she thought the time had come to determine if there were other reasons as well.

Many child care administrators and boards never really know why people quit their jobs and often make little effort to find out the reasons. No one wants good teachers or staff to leave. Any departure is associated with emotional upheaval as well as significant expenses. What can a director do to understand why people leave?

One useful method is an exit interview. Exit interviews generally cost little in dollars and time, can be used for any type of organizational structure, and provide data that can be tabulated and analyzed easily. Yet exit interviews in the child care field are not common (Tenoschok, 1988).

Why Should We Take the Time for Exit Interviews?

According to Drost, O'Brien, and Marsh (1987), "This information [from exit interviews] can be used for reducing turnover; detecting unfair employment practices (e.g., sexual harassment); establishing a competitive compensation structure; and improving supervision practices, appraisal systems, training, and working conditions" (p. 104). Through interviews, consistent problems in working conditions may become apparent. If such problems are discovered and corrected, staff morale may improve and all employees become more satisfied. If exit interviews are used, recent studies indicate some methods may be better than others.

Is There More than One Way to Conduct an Exit Interview?

For child care programs, the following methods, used separately or together, may be appropriate:

• Personal interview before the person leaves employment

• Telephone interview three to six weeks after a person has left employment

• Questionnaire mailed, with a pre-addressed, stamped envelope, to the former employee three to six weeks after leaving employment

Research suggests that telephone interviews or mailed questionnaires are more effective than personal interviews conducted as the employee leaves an organization (Tenoschok, 1988). Former employees need time to become more objective about their departure. Face-to-face discussion right before leaving

Do's of Exit Interviews

- State how the information will be used.

- Express the confidentiality of the interview or questionnaire.

- Use a majority of open-ended questions.

- Use a structured interview format.

- Realize that the departing or departed employee may be reluctant to share information.

- Be consistent with the interview format used.

- Put the former employee at ease before asking the difficult questions.

- Use the information gleaned to improve hiring and training procedures and working conditions for employees.

- Conduct interviews for every employee who is leaving, not just those voluntarily resigning.

Don'ts of Exit Interviews

- Do not conduct an exit interview if nothing will be changed after the interview.

- Do not have the director of the center or the employee's supervisor conduct the exit interview.

- Do not put the contents of the exit interview in the personnel file; exit interviews should be confidential.

- Do not ask only closed-ended questions; include questions that allow an interviewer to probe.

- Do not conduct the exit interview on the last day of work because the timing and the employee's attitude may not be the best for such an endeavor.

- Do not include a discussion of any employee benefits. This should be done during a separate meeting.

- Do not use a simple check list. This does not allow the employee to elaborate on answers.

employment usually results in few critical comments about the organization from the former employee. Hence, low salary becomes the stated reason for leaving. "At the time of departure, for example, an employee is more likely to cite salary considerations and career advancement opportunities as the principle causes for turnover than she or he would be later. . . . Instead of uncovering salary and career opportunities as real concerns for leaving, persons conducting post-termination interviews have determined that the real causes of forced or voluntary turnover were often personality clashes with the supervisor, lack of respect for the supervisor, and disagreements over the way things were done — all management related topics" (Wood and Macaulay, 1987, p. 43). Exit interviews can be very effective, but they need to be used with some caution. See boxes for some do's and don'ts.

What Can We Do to Ensure a Successful Exit Interview?

For successful person-to-person or telephone exit interviews, interviewers should be credible, trustworthy, and trained in interview techniques. The most logical, although expensive, choice would be an outside consultant. A second choice for a credible interviewer could be someone on the board of directors who has not been associated with the employee.

Experienced interviewers start the interview by asking questions that require short, specific responses. They usually explain how valuable the interview information is to the center and then they lead with questions that ascertain factual data. The interviewer needs to make the person feel comfortable before asking them to respond to questions about why they are leaving. Standard questions should be asked for each exit interview (see example). The exit interview, with appropriate

Employee Exit Interview

1. Why did you leave the center? If there was more than one reason, please rank numerically, with 1 indicating the most important.

    _____ Continue my education
    _____ Obtained a better job
    _____ Moving
    _____ Health reasons
    _____ Retirement
    _____ Family circumstances
    _____ Dissatisfaction with center employment (salary, fringe benefits, supervision, etc.).

    If this question is ranked, please go to Question 2. If not, go to Question 3.

    Comments:

2. What were the area(s) of dissatisfaction at the center? If there is more than one reason, please rank numerically, with 1 indicating the most important.

    _____ Salary
    _____ Fringe benefits
    _____ Working conditions
    _____ Supervision
    _____ Form of work
    _____ Other _____

    Comments:

3. How would you rate the following at the center?

	Excellent	Good	Fair	Poor
Orientation to the center	_____	_____	_____	_____
Working conditions	_____	_____	_____	_____
Fringe benefits	_____	_____	_____	_____
Salary	_____	_____	_____	_____
Staff communication	_____	_____	_____	_____
Strength of educational program for children	_____	_____	_____	_____
General morale	_____	_____	_____	_____
Supervision provided	_____	_____	_____	_____
Staff evaluation procedures	_____	_____	_____	_____

    Comments:

4. How would you rate your supervisor on the following topics?

	Excellent	Good	Fair	Poor
Provides clear instructions	_____	_____	_____	_____
Gives equal treatment to staff	_____	_____	_____	_____
Knows accomplishments of staff	_____	_____	_____	_____
Maintains consistent application of policies	_____	_____	_____	_____
Provides positive feedback and recognition	_____	_____	_____	_____
Resolves complaints and conflict	_____	_____	_____	_____
Welcomes/invites suggestions	_____	_____	_____	_____
Follows through on suggestions	_____	_____	_____	_____
Develops cooperation	_____	_____	_____	_____

Comments:

5. If you could change any two things about the job you held at the center, what would they be?

6. If you could keep just two things about the job you held at the center, what would they be?

7. Would you consider working for the center again? Under what circumstances?

8. What does your present job offer that the one at the center did not?

9. What were some of the duties of your job at the center that you liked performing the most? What did you not like about performing those duties?

10. What were some of the duties of your job at the center that you liked performing the least? What did you not like about performing those duties?

11. Give an example of an incident which occurred at the center which was especially satisfying to you.

12. Give an example of an incident which occurred at the center which was not satisfying to you.

13. Would you recommend the center to a friend as a good place to work? Why or why not? What constructive comments would you have for making the center a better place to work?

probing questions, should take no longer than 45 minutes to an hour to conduct. The center director or board needs to determine what interview technique to use.

What Can We Discover?

Peg Jones and her board of directors decided to use telephone exit interviews with those individuals who had left in the previous year. They also decided to interview all employees who had left the child care center in the previous five years to determine if any patterns in turnover would appear.

The results of the exit interviews verified that salary was, indeed, one of the major reasons for employee resignations. Based on these data, Peg continued the evaluation of teacher and staff salaries. However, several other previously unknown issues were identified. Peg discovered that, prior to her assuming the position, former teachers and staff were concerned about the lack of communication between themselves and the previous director. Communication, however, was not identified as one of Peg's weaknesses. Rather, she was perceived as being too controlling and unwilling or unable to delegate enough responsibilities to the teachers. From this information, Peg

learned that her supervision of staff needed improvement.

Peg shared the exit interview results with the board and teachers in order to solicit their support in making changes. She has begun to change the way she manages the child care program and hopes the improvements will increase staff morale, solve some of the teacher dissatisfaction, and reduce turnover.

Exit interviews will not solve all problems of staff turnover in each child care program. As Sherwood noted, "An exit interview program will not, of course, be the magic cure for all employee problems, but it will help you maintain morale, minimize turnover, improve hiring efforts, and correct unsatisfactory work conditions" (p. 750). The exit interview is just one of several management tools that can help an administrator be more effective and responsive to teachers and staff. For the benefit of the children who are served, lowering employee turnover in child care programs must be accomplished. The exit interview may be a step toward that goal.

References

Drost, D., O'Brien, F., & Marsh, S. (February 1987). "Exit Interviews: Master the Possibilities," *Personnel Administrator,* pp. 104-110.

Sherwood, A. (September 1983). "Exit Interviews: Don't Just Say Goodbye," *Personnel Journal,* pp. 744-750.

Tenoschok, M. (September 1988). "When Teachers Resign, Ask Why — And Then Learn From What They Tell You," *The American School Board Journal,* pp. 26-27.

Woods, R. & Macaulay, J. (November 1987). "Exit Interviews: How to Turn a File Filler Into a Management Tool," *The Cornell HRA Quarterly,* pp. 39-46.

Dr. Glenn Olsen is an assistant professor in early childhood education at the University of North Dakota. He has been an administrator at child care centers in rural and urban communities, including a campus child care center. He has conducted exit interviews for child care programs and other organizations. He is also a validator with NAEYC and conducts workshops on conflict resolution/mediation.